Personal and Social
Choices and Cha

Andy Hargreaves, Eileen Baglin,
Pamela Henderson, Patrick Leeson,
Terry Tossell

Basil Blackwell

First Published 1988

© Andy Hargreaves, Eileen Baglin, Pamela Henderson,
Patrick Leeson, Terry Tossell 1988

Published by
Basil Blackwell Ltd
108 Cowley Road
Oxford OX4 1JF
England

British Library Cataloguing in Publication Data
Personal and social education: choices
   and challenges.
   1. Life skills – Study and teaching –
Great Britain
   I. Hargreaves, Andy
   370.11′5′0941   HQ2039.G7
   ISBN 0-631-14649-0
   ISBN 0-631-14651-2 Pbk

Typeset in 10/12 pt Sabon
by Joshua Associates Limited, Oxford
Printed in Great Britain at
T. J. Press (Padstow) Ltd, Cornwall

Contents

Notes on the authors

Andy Hargreaves has been a schoolteacher and has lectured in Education at the Open University and the universities of Oxford and Warwick. He is now Associate Professor of Education at the Ontario Institute for Studies in Education, Toronto, Canada. He is the author of *Two Cultures of Schooling* (Falmer Press, 1986) and *Curriculum and Assessment Reform* (Open University Press, 1988) and has edited a number of other books on education including *Educational Policy: controversies and critiques* (Falmer Press, 1988 – with David Reynolds).

Eileen Baglin is the Leader of Oxfordshire's Lower Attaining Pupils Project. Previously, she taught at Burford School, Oxfordshire, where she worked with other staff to establish an integrated tutorial and social education programme. On secondment, she undertook an intensive case study of a Social Education department.

Pamela Henderson is a teacher of English in Oxfordshire. She has taught in comprehensive schools for over ten years and worked for one year as an advisory teacher for the Lower Attaining Pupils Project in Oxfordshire. The research she carried out on secondment examined pupils' responses to outdoor and residential education.

Patrick Leeson is Adviser for Communication and Language Development in Croydon. Previously, as well as teaching English in comprehensive schools, he was Co-ordinator for Evaluation in the Oxfordshire Lower Attaining Pupils Project.

Terry Tossell has been a Head of Department, Year Tutor and is currently Acting Deputy Head of Gosford Hill School in Oxfordshire. In addition to co-ordinating a programme of PSE in his own school, he has been associated with Pupils' Personal Records and was part of the research and development team for the Oxford Certificate of Educational Achievement.

List of acronyms

APU	Assessment of Performance Unit
ATW	Active Tutorial Work
CACE	Central Advisory Council for Education
CPVE	Certificate of Pre-Vocational Education
CGLI	City and Guilds of London Institute
FEU	Further Education Curriculum Review and Development Unit
GTW	Group Tutorial Work
LAPP	Lower Attaining Pupils Programme
MSC	Manpower Services Commission
OCEA	Oxford Certificate of Educational Achievement
ORE	Outdoor and Residential Education
PPR	Pupils' Personal Records
ROA	Records of Achievement
RPA	Records of Personal Achievement
RPE	Records of Personal Experience
PSE	Personal and Social Education
TVEI	Technical and Vocational Education Initiative

Introduction

This book is about Personal and Social Education and the different ways it can be developed in secondary schools. It has been written by teachers, advisers and a university lecturer, with teachers very much in mind. Since every teacher carries some responsibility for the personal and social development of their pupils, the book is aimed not just at specialist teachers of Personal and Social Education (PSE), but at all teachers in secondary schools.

We hope that teachers will find the book practical and relevant, but also controversial and challenging. Indeed, it is our argument that some of the most challenging and controversial aspects of PSE are also the most practical. When we discuss the kinds of values contained in PSE, for instance, we are not just engaging in abstract, philosophical debate. Such discussions have immense implications for the kinds of PSE we provide in secondary schools. If we decide that we value cooperation and want to develop it in residential education, we have to decide how to organise activities like canoeing or abseiling to ensure that this can occur. If the experience of collective group life is more important to us than the experience of adventure within a residential setting, then there is no need to present residential education in the context of outdoor pursuits. If we genuinely wish to foster attitudes of multicultural tolerance and respect among our pupils, then we must deal with moral issues concerning family life in an especially sensitive way and not assume that there is one universal standard that can be applied to all cultural groups. If we value privacy, we should consider seriously whether small-group discussion of personal feelings on emotionally sensitive topics within tutorial work should be compulsory, or whether pupils should have the right to opt out if they wish. And if we genuinely value initiative and independence among our pupils, we should provide plenty of opportunity for this in our teaching.

Value questions, then, are more than just topics for idle philosophical conjecture. They reach to the very heart of PSE practice. What we do, what we teach, what we include, what we exclude, what we consciously put in and what we unconsciously leave out – all these deeply practical matters are profoundly influenced by the values we hold, whether or not we are fully aware of them. This is most obvious in morally and politically controversial areas of the PSE curriculum. When Governments charge schools with the educational responsibility to discourage the spread of AIDS, to draw attention to child abuse, or to reduce the use of drugs, the values being promoted are clear. When legislation such as that contained within the 1986 Education Act advocates a balanced approach to the discussion and presentation of political issues and promotes sex education only in the moral context of family life, again, the value questions at stake, disputed as they may be, are quite evident. On such controversial matters as disarmament, homosexuality or race relations, the relevance of social values and their relationship to the practicalities of PSE teaching are also clear. But as we have already argued, discussions about social values are equally relevant and equally practical in less obviously controversial areas of PSE teaching, if not more so. Indeed, the more taken-for-granted our values are about the apparently small things of school life – about what we regard as good manners, polite behaviour, pupils' rights to express their opinions, relationships between boys and girls and so on – the more vital it is that we open up these assumptions to inspection; that we question, evaluate, and if necessary reconstruct the whole personal and social fabric of school life. Value issues such as these have far-reaching practical implications, and we will return to them repeatedly throughout the book.

Similar points can be made about the status of PSE within the curriculum and organisation of secondary schools. The status of PSE in relation to other aspects of secondary education is not just a subject for sociological curiosity. It has considerable consequences for the coherence and effectiveness of the PSE enterprise. Too often, teachers view failure in Personal and Social Education as their own responsibility. The failure of PSE pupils to treat the area with the seriousness and importance it deserves; the inability or unwillingness of a staff team in PSE to work together with a clear sense of common purpose; or the scepticism of parents about PSE's educational value – too often, PSE teachers regard problems and difficulties of this sort as their own fault. They must have failed to get the basic principles right. Or perhaps they did not implement them properly. These feelings of personal incompetence are often most acute when the teachers concerned have been presented with idealistic and overly optimistic interpretations of the power and potential of PSE; when difficulties have been played down, problems suppressed and limitations not explored.

Many of the problems are attributable not to individual teachers at all, but to the low status that PSE has within secondary education. The amount of resources that PSE is allocated, the practical support it receives from the head in finance and staffing, the visible standing it has in relation to academic subjects and examination work, and the priority it is accorded within Government policy compared to other favoured initiatives – all these things have powerful consequences for the fate and fortune of PSE in schools. Insufficient time to develop a meaningful dialogue with pupils in the one-to-one process of discussing their personal profiles is usually a consequence of the modest priority that is allocated to profiling in terms of staffing and resources at school and Government levels. When pupils do not see PSE courses as 'real work' and treat them with less importance than their other subjects, this is often a reflection of the school's – and especially the head's – commitment to examination results and academic success as matters of higher priority. And when pupils find it hard to adjust to the informal relationships and active methods of working in tutorial classes, this is quite often because those qualities are missing from and not counted as important within the mainstream, subject-based curriculum. If PSE is not accorded high status and priority within the whole school, its impact is likely to be very limited. It is of the highest practical importance that teachers and heads grasp this fundamental sociological principle and, if their commitment to PSE is genuine, manipulate it to their advantage wherever possible.

Values, status and other issues of this sort are clearly very practical issues indeed. Our aim in this book is to address, in an accessible way, the difficulties and controversies that they raise. We want to show how issues commonly regarded as 'theoretical' are powerfully at work in the practice of PSE. We do this by looking at the different organisational ways that PSE can be catered for in secondary school and by examining how values, status and similar issues make themselves felt in each case. *Chapter 1* reviews the range of organisational provision for PSE and spells out the sorts of choices that teachers and schools can make here. Each of the following chapters then addresses one particular type of PSE provision. *Chapter 2* deals with specialist taught courses; *Chapter 3* with tutorial work; *Chapter 4* with outdoor and residential education; and *Chapters 5* and *6* with different aspects of personal recording and records of achievement. The final chapter draws the themes of the book together and briefly discusses one or two outstanding questions concerning whole-school policy.

Having described the book's major preoccupations, it is perhaps worth saying a few words about how the idea for the book arose. Our interest in the project first began in 1984 when three of the group (Eileen Baglin, Pamela Henderson and Terry Tossell) were seconded to Oxford University for a year by Oxfordshire Education Authority to study for a Diploma in Educational Studies. Andy Hargreaves was their tutor. Patrick Leeson, then an evaluator for Oxfordshire's version of the DES's Lower Attaining Pupils Project, also joined the group at this time.

In many respects, the group operated very much like any other group of seconded teachers on a course. The three seconded teachers worked independently on extended pieces of educational research for diploma dissertations – Terry on current practices in pupil self-assessment, Pamela on programmes of residential education, and Eileen on PSE taught courses. With one or two other course members, we also met weekly to discuss issues in the academic secondary school curriculum, then later in the broader area of personal and social development.

As the year progressed, though, we felt that what was happening amounted to more than being simply 'on a course'. Andy's academic interests and the others' practical ones drew closer and closer until they became virtually indistinguishable. As we quizzed fifth-year pupils on their perceptions of their taught PSE programme, as we assessed our visits to schools making new departures in PSE, and as we took part in and critically analysed staff training exercises in Active Tutorial Work, the boundaries between theory and practice, between academic argument and professional planning, became increasingly blurred.

At the time, we did not know of any book that brought together the theoretical and practical aspects of PSE in quite the way we were experiencing. Slowly, we began to toy with the idea that we might produce our own. In our favour was the fact that the current research interests and professional experiences of the group covered much of the important territory in PSE. Most of the organisational ways in which PSE could be provided were embraced by the group's interests and experience. Between us, therefore, we seemed to have a suitable breadth of interest, a broadly shared view concerning what we regarded as the key issues in PSE teaching, and a collective commitment to bringing together theoretical and practical expertise and insight in the area.

A further factor also motivated us. Seconded teachers often do excellent research which, when completed, is ignominiously consigned to near-oblivion in the dark recesses of some university library. Such research, therefore, makes an almost miniscule contribution to public knowledge about education. This is a sad loss. In trying to counter this, we were not looking for loosely stitched together dissertation studies. But we did feel that the analytical insight and research training that had been developed within the group might be put to good effect in producing an extended, coherent statement on PSE. What, we wondered, could a group of experienced teachers and a university lecturer working in partnership produce for a professional audience? Was there some neglected potential in secondment experience that we could explore and develop?

We decided to go ahead. Over the next three years, each of us took chief responsibility for at least one chapter and we met periodically, as a group, to discuss and criticise drafts of each of those chapters in turn. Most chapters went through at least three drafts. This not only helped improve the individual chapters, but the discussions also helped clarify the purpose and major themes of the book as a whole. When all the chapters were completed, Andy then undertook the additional tasks of writing the introduction, updating material where appropriate as new policies concerning PSE surfaced, adding new sections in places to give the chapters some consistency in format, and generally tightening up stylistic and thematic continuity throughout the text. In these respects, the book is quite unlike an edited collection of individual contributions, and we have therefore not attributed separate chapters to particular authors. The effort has been very much a collective one.

This difficult, time-consuming, and at times stressful combined effort would never have been possible without the vital support, encouragement and tolerance of many people and institutions. Our partners, families and close friends are outstanding among these. The personal and social qualities they have shown in supporting our efforts in an endeavour as protracted and dis-tracting as this have been remarkable. As the research on which much of this book is loosely based was conducted we received that kind of selfless help and welcome from schools, heads, teachers and pupils that is one of the most characteristic but overlooked virtues of the British educational system. These people and their institutions are far too numerous to mention by name but we thank them all for their time and generosity. Three teachers in particular have been especially helpful. Paul Phillips and Don Amphlett kindly let us use some of their research data in Chapters 5 and 6, and through her participation in discussions, Pam Freund made helpful contributions to the development of the book when it was in its draft stage. Paul Phillips, Don Amphlett, Ike Garson, Mary Schofield, Peter Medlock and Dave Digby also made helpful comments on various draft chapters.

Our final thanks must go to Oxfordshire Education Authority. For many years it has adopted a particularly enlightened policy to teacher secondments. Its commitment to the professional development of its teachers as a force for educational renewal in schools has been outstanding, as has its partnership with the educational research and training community. Without its generous and forward-thinking approach to secondment this book would never have been written.

1 Choices and challenges in personal and social education

Background

Since the late 1970s, the development of personal and social education (PSE) in secondary schools has received wide and substantial political support in a range of official Government publications – from general reports on secondary education in England and in Scotland in 1977 (HMI, 1979) through to Her Majesty's Inspectorate's influential statement on the *Curriculum From 5 to 16* in the mid-1980s (HMI, 1983). The publication in that same Curriculum Matters series of a pamphlet on *Health Education* (HMI, 1986) and the projected publication of the Inspectorate's views on *Personal and Social Education* in 1988 has added and will add further to that national recognition. A large number of Local Education Authorities have also registered their formal support for PSE by publishing their own individual policy statements and guidelines on the area (Pring, 1984). But in many respects, this plethora of policy statements and guidelines at national and local levels simply echoes, brings together and formally acknowledges an impressively diverse array of individual initiatives in PSE made by secondary schools for a number of years.

Notwithstanding a growing measure of official political support for and recognition of PSE (at least on paper), its growth in secondary schools has in fact been largely local in origin. PSE has mainly developed in individual schools, acting largely on their own professional initiative. Indeed, in many respects, PSE is a testimony to the strength of local, school-based curriculum development as a force for innovation. But it also highlights many of the weaknesses of that pattern of change – lack of coordination, absence of support from unconvinced heads, sometimes mediocre practice resulting from teachers working in isolation, and isolated but nonetheless notorious instances of allegedly 'extreme' or controversial practice in the treatment of such areas as sex education, peace studies and anti-racism.

All this perhaps helps explain why PSE, while receiving wide public support, is at the same time often the subject of intense political controversy. Inevitably, much of what goes on in PSE will be politically and socially contentious. PSE aims to do more than add to people's intellectual understanding or improve their practical skills. It aims to develop and sometimes to change people themselves in quite fundamental respects; in their attitudes and approach to themselves, to other people and to the world around them.

The more that education tries to live up to its broad promise of being an agent of personal development and social change rather than merely a process of practical training or intellectual mastery, the more controversial and contestable it becomes. For what is at stake is not just practical or intellectual competence, but the developing attitudes, values and social commitments of young people – the shape of society in the future. Inevitably, this raises questions about our own treasured social beliefs, commitments and interests and may sometimes appear to threaten them. People disagree over what would count as 'the good society'. Some want to change society. Others want to conserve it in its present state and are fearful of attempts to develop in future generations powers of critical questioning and autonomous judgement which might threaten that order. In short, the more socially important and profound education becomes in the depth and scope of its ambitions, the more it becomes associated with personal development and social change, the more it takes seriously its business of actively contributing to the future shape and development of society – then the more controversial it becomes. The presence of such controversy in SPE is not necessarily a weakness, we shall argue, but could be one of its fundamental strengths and justifications (Stradling *et al*, 1984, Stradling 1986). However we view it, the controversial nature of PSE cannot be denied.

Controversy abounds in media-celebrated cases of individual extremism. These isolated cases are commonly presented as symbolic, 'thin-end-of-the-wedge' warnings about the shape that PSE might take throughout the school system. Teachers in Devon are prohibited from displaying badges or stickers that reveal and promote their political affiliations to causes like CND. The Secretary of State for Education and Science expresses grave concern when it is brought to his attention that some ILEA school libraries stock books which present homosexuality and the raising of children by homosexuals in a positive and supportive way. And the SDP/Liberal Alliance, in a barely-averted electioneering political broadcast, alleges censorship of children's nursery rhymes like 'Baa-baa black sheep' by racism-conscious Brent Education Authority. Incidents such as these, highlighted and dramatised by the mass media, reflect and reinforce public moral panics about homosexuality, 'extreme' forms of anti-racism, unilateral disarmament and so on, and about the ways in which schools and teachers might be promoting these things. Such moral panics about PSE culminate in and are then still further reinforced by party-political controversy over the alleged growth, according to the Conservative Party's 1986 Election Manifesto, of 'political indoctrination' and 'sexual propaganda' in secondary education.

In consequence, while offering support and encouragement for PSE in secondary schools, Government has increasingly been moved to control and limit it. Such drawing in of the political reins on developments in PSE can be seen within the 1986 Education Act. This contains provisions which in some cases have been directly precipitated by some of the cases we have just mentioned. The Act, for instance, requires that 'where sex education is given . . . it is given in such a manner as to encourage those pupils to have due regard to moral considerations and the value of family life'. It gives parents the power to ban subjects like sex education or peace studies from the curriculum if a sufficient proportion vote against them at a public meeting. Politics, too, has occasioned Government intervention through the 1986 Act. 'Where political issues are brought to the attention of pupils', it says, reasonable steps should be taken to ensure that 'they are offered a balanced presentation of opposing views'. This, then, is one source of ambivalence in Government policy in relation to PSE: general support for it in principle, but restriction of its political and moral scope in practice.

There is a further source of ambivalence in Government policy on PSE too. Government's support for PSE is essentially promotional. It is a commitment on paper to a broad educational principle. However, PSE receives no legislative support in Government policy, and unlike many other areas of the curriculum it has been given very little specific financial allocation for in-service development or experimental innovation. It is to subject learning, academic goals and public examinations that most Government policy has been committed, when it comes to hard finance and firm legislation. This is where its real priorities have been revealed. Consider a few examples.

In the guidelines for initial teacher training, first drawn up in an influential Government document in *Teaching Quality* (DES, 1983), and since reinforced and made a mandatory requirement by the Council for Accreditation of Teacher Education (CATE), students in teacher training are now required to spend at least half their time on 'subject studies'; the university level study of a major academic subject of the secondary school curriculum (Hargreaves, 1988b). No such provision of minimal time allocation is made for PSE. Indeed, *Teaching Quality* advises that teachers should only become involved in teaching PSE once they have gained substantial experience of teaching an 'ordinary' school subject.

Second, in the proposals for a national curriculum, the Secretary of State has declared that systematic attention should be given to the common teaching of a range of 'basic subjects' in which pupils will be tested for their competence at 7, 11 and 14. With the exception of technology, it appears that these 'basic' subjects are to be the academic subjects of the traditional grammar school curriculum – mathematics, English, science etc. It is conceded that attention should also be given to education in personal qualities, attitudes and values, but these are not designated 'basic', nor are they to be tested in the way that the other 'basics' are. By definition, then, within the national curriculum initiative, PSE is non-basic and therefore of lesser priority compared with mainstream academic subjects.

Third, public examinations persist in the form of GCSE, and there has been a continuing requirement since the 1980 Education Act that schools publish their own examination results as a basis for parental choice. At the time of writing the Government proposes to intensify that choice by abolishing admission limits in secondary schools and thereby allowing those schools to flourish or flounder according to the market force of parental choice. All these things virtually guarantee that secondary schools will continue to place great – possibly even greater – priority on mainstream academic subjects that are assessed by public examinations which Government legislation has effectively made the basis of those schools' reputation and survial. For these reasons, PSE is almost inevitably likely to take lower priority among teachers and schools in terms of staffing, resources and timetabling than the mainstream academic curriculum and suffer from reduced commitment from those involved. Even the Government's support for Records of Achievement for all is in danger of paling into practical insignificance in the shadow of the massive prominence being given to public examinations and the system of academic subject specialisation that it supports (Hargreaves, 1988a).

Despite Government commitment in principle to PSE, then, it is likely that other aspects of Government legislation on education will make it difficult for schools to deliver what is formally required of them in this area. Public examinations and academic subjects are likely to remain at the heart of their commitments, and PSE will continue to occupy a more peripheral and lower status position in the school curriculum. We would predict, then, that teachers and coordinators of PSE will frequently receive only tepid support for their work, and will suffer problems of status, difficulties of staffing and general lack of recognition – except perhaps, where the separate teaching and containment of troublesome, older, or 'less able' pupils is concerned.

A number of writers on PSE have attributed great importance and significance to the development of the area in recent years. McNiff (1985: 8), for instance, has claimed that 'personal and social education is a priority area in current educational thinking'. We suspect that such writers are sometimes a little over-optimistic; perhaps even slightly deceived by their own publicity. Local developments have certainly been encouraging and supportive. And there has been tentative practical support for experimentation in PSE through the development of records of achievement, and through the inauguration of TVEI and CPVE. But the overwhelming bias in recent Government legislation and financial support in relation to the secondary curriculum has been towards the academic, subject-based curriculum. This will inevitably have serious implications for the future development of PSE. It is, we believe, important to retain enthusiasm about and commitment to the educational potential and importance of PSE. But this should not lead us to overlook the political realities of current Government priorities and the backwash effects that increasing political support for the academic, subject-based curriculum will have on the place of PSE in schools, and on the problems that will be faced by those who teach it.

It is these problems and difficulties; the choices and challenges that teachers face in a still marginal area of the secondary curriculum that are at the centre of this book. How do teachers deal with value controversies, with socially and politically sensitive material, in a way that will be educationally defensible, retain teachers' professional integrity, and allay public and political criticism and anxiety? Are value biases present even in material that might not initially strike one as controversial? How can teachers of PSE improve the status of what they do in the school? What problems of resources, staffing and timetabling are they likely to face and how can they deal with these? These are our main themes.

What embattled teachers can achieve within an often marginalised area of the curriculum in their own schools is, of course, not limitless. We have already seen how many of the problems facing teachers and coordinators of PSE have their roots not in individual schools but in the priorities of Government policy which wash back to the schools, as they are intended to do, affecting the overall balance of work and commitments. But teachers do have some scope for action and influence, as the emergence of PSE on a localised basis itself indicates; the way that they deal with problems of values, status and the like will depend in part on their commitment to and definition of PSE, and on the version of it that they operate in their own schools.

It is important, therefore, to consider in general terms what we understand by Personal and Social Education and then to assess some of the organisational ways that it might be catered for and presented in schools. The remainder of this book deals with the choices that teachers can make here, and their implications – with the different organisational approaches teachers can adopt and the ways in which the problems of values, status and so on can be dealt with in each case. First, though, we must consider the broad question of what PSE actually *is*.

What is personal and social education?

Once known simply as Social Education, the area with which this book is concerned is now more usually referred to and understood as Personal and Social Education (PSE). Indeed, we have cast the title of the book in just those terms, so that potential users will recognise the areas of their practice which the book addresses. Nonetheless, we have some reservations about this label.

One of the clearest definitions of PSE has been offered by David (1983: 18).

> Personal and Social education includes the teaching and informal activities which are planned to enhance the development of knowledge, understanding, attitudes and behaviour, concerned with:
> - oneself and others;
> - social institutions, structure and organisations; and
> - social and moral issues.

We agree with most of what David has to say here, but feel he has got the emphasis slightly wrong. For David, it appears, the personal – 'oneself' – comes first (see also Pring, 1984). Hence the order – Personal and Social Education – rather than vice versa. In one sense this might seem just an academic quibble, but we feel it is rather important.

It is true that education is often viewed as an essentially individual process – how often do 'The Aims of the School' proclaim that the school is committed to 'the education of each individual to his or her full potential'! But what this approach lacks is recognition of the fundamental fact that individuals do not exist apart from the society around them. Individuals do not develop alone, in isolation. They are not Robinson Crusoes. Their selves, the kind of people they become, are formed in and through their relationships with others – with task groups and friendship groups, the school community, the neighbourhood, and society at large. Their growth and development can only be understood in the context of these other things (Durkheim, 1956; D. Hargreaves, 1982). Judgements about personal development therefore inevitably depend on judgements and decisions about social development and change, about the social good, community development or regeneration, and so on.

We are not saying that individuals are unimportant. We are not advocating that education should be the same for everyone, ignoring individual differences. Individuals have different places in their community and society, and to some extent, therefore, they have different educational needs. The focal point of the teacher's attention will indeed often be the individual rather than the small group or the class. We simply want to make the point that individuals, as human beings, are inextricably embedded within broader groups, communities and societies. Once we recognise this, we recognise also the point made by the French sociologist Emile Durkheim (1956: 78), that 'the antagonism that has too often been admitted between society and individual corresponds to nothing in the facts'.

Consequently, while we may focus our attention on the individual, what we do with him or her will depend to a great extent on our perceptions and value judgements about what is good for the class, the school or the society as a whole. Our treatment of individual pupils is therefore often heavily dependent on our own value judgements about social relationships and society. Among teachers, these value judgements about obedience, authority, fairness, hierarchy, equality, relations between the sexes, and so on, are often implicit and unacknowledged – certainly to colleagues, and often to those teachers themselves. They are private and tacit rather than public and openly discussed. Yet they have immense implications for the kind of personal and social education that teachers support and encourage – whether it will foster obedience and deference to authority of a kind that makes pupils easier to manage in school; whether it will instil vocational values that attune young people to the demands of the workplace; whether it will stick to the development of 'safe' and uncontentious personal qualities like co-operation and tolerance; or whether it will encourage more socially risky ones like independent judgement, critical questioning or assertiveness.

This is why we feel the *Social* must be emphasised in *Personal and Social Education* – because social life is the unavoidable context of human development, and because it is usually the aspect of PSE or education as a whole that teachers are least prepared to acknowledge and discuss. Because of the powerful influence of these sorts of judgements on the character of PSE, we feel it vital that they be openly and continually debated in the school community. Emphasising the *Social* in *Personal and Social Education*, we believe, will help remind teachers and schools of this vital obligation.

Developments in PSE

PSE involves general choices about values, then – whether these are made explicitly or implicitly. It also involves choices about implementation, about particular ways it should be catered for or presented within the secondary school. There are many versions of PSE within secondary schools. And indeed, this is what much of this book is about: an examination of some of these different versions, their strengths and their weaknesses, and the ways in which they cope with problems concerning values, status and so on. This book considers just some of these versions; the ones that are most commonly found and seem to carry greatest weight within the existing secondary system. But perhaps it will be helpful, at the outset, to look briefly at a more extensive range of PSE provision that can currently be found in secondary schools, so it is clear what we are selecting from.

1 Invisible, pervasive or absent

Until recently, PSE was largely neglected as a separate part of the curriculum meriting special attention. Grammar schools in particular paid little explicit attention to the personal and social needs of their pupils (ILEA, 1984:61). Yet, in a sense, PSE has always been implicit in the ethos and organisation of secondary schools. Assemblies, as well as publicly asserting the official rules and purposes of the school, also communicate messages about corporate identity and institutional loyalty. Prefect systems communicate messages about hierarchy and responsibility; sports days and examinations about competitiveness; and prize-givings about the sort of qualities and achievements that are valued or not valued by the school. At a more day-to-day level, school rules about lining up, uniform, not chewing in class and so on say things about the choices, independence and initiative that young people are deemed worthy of exercising. And routine relationships between teachers and pupils embody powerful messages about the presence or absence of mutual respect between them.

As Emile Durkheim (1956) pointed out, much of the moral learning that goes on in schools occurs not because moral principles are taught directly but because they are experienced in the life of the school. Sometimes, the implicit and organisationally pervasive features of PSE are intended; consciously planned and decided on as part of a whole school policy. We will return to this whole-school approach – the focus of *Chapter 7* – in due course. More usually though, the 'implicit' features of PSE arise by accident or linger because of historical inertia. These implicit features become a taken-for-granted, unquestioned part of school life – not open to rational discussion or appraisal. While everybody deals with PSE in some respects, no one takes responsibility for it. No one checks that the rules, ceremonies and relationships in the school do indeed embody the human qualities that members of the school claim to value. No one monitors the degree of consistency or inconsistency in all these different aspects of school life. No one, in other words, ensures that the moral learning that goes on in the daily experience of school life consistently and coherently reflects what the school itself values. The inconsistencies, omissions and unexamined biases of judgement that often arise in this 'implicit' approach have led many schools and teachers to look at more specific ways of providing for PSE.

2 Pastoral care systems

One of the first specific kinds of PSE provision came with the advent of comprehensive schools. In many areas, the end of grammar and secondary modern schools saw the end of smaller secondary schools too. Unless the secondary sector was divided up in some way by using middle schools or junior high schools, comprehensive schools became large, difficult-to-administer, and dangerously impersonal organisations. Within these burgeoning bureaucracies, it was feared, pupils' individual welfare needs would be overlooked, and the lines of staff responsibility for welfare and discipline would become unclear and break down (Reynolds and Sullivan, 1987). At the same time, comprehensive reorganisation posed major problems for the careers and status of senior secondary modern teachers. Likely to be outstripped by their better-qualified grammar school counterparts in their competition for the new Head of Department subject posts, these teachers required new posts of responsibility to match the status and salaries they had accumulated through their secondary modern experience (D. Hargreaves, 1980). It was in response to these twin problems – the career interests of secondary modern teachers, and the difficulties of making effective provision for discipline and pupil welfare in large schools – that the new comprehensive system somewhat ironically adopted and modified a system that had first gained popularity within the elite private sector: the House system of pastoral care (Lang, 1983). Later, vertical house systems gradually gave way to increasingly favoured lateral year systems of pastoral care (Corbishley and Evans, 1980). Whatever the case, pastoral care structures were here to stay as a dominant feature of comprehensive school life.

The 'conventional wisdom' of pastoral care in comprehensive schools, expressed by its leading advocates, such as Marland (1974) and Blackburn (1975) has been that it is predominantly concerned with the care, welfare and personal needs of pupils – either because such welfare is important in itself, or because it can help support the smooth running of the academic system. In practice, however, research studies of pastoral care have shown it to be overwhelmingly preoccupied with administration, paperwork, pupil referral procedures, discipline and punishment (Best *et al.*, 1983; Burgess, 1983). The way in which pastoral care structures have been organised has also often been found to be more to do with the career interests of pastoral teachers, and conflicts or tensions between teachers in the pastoral system and the academic system, than with the welfare needs of pupils (Burgess, 1987). Such failings are perhaps one reason why responsibility for pupils' personal and social development has gradually come to be seen as residing less within the province of the pastoral system, than within some specially provided experience or area of the curriculum specifically designed to foster that development.

Pastoral care structures have therefore come to be replaced or supplemented by various kinds of pastoral curriculum – curricula and educational experiences specially designed to promote pupils' personal and social development (Marland, 1980; Bulman, 1984; Button, 1983). This pastoral curriculum is less easily hijacked as a disciplinary 'back up' for teachers elsewhere in the school. How far the emergence of the pastoral curriculum and of the concept and organisation of PSE has made traditional pastoral systems redundant, is an arguable point. Watkins (1985), for instance, has argued that pastoral care and PSE serve very different needs. Indeed, he says, pastoral care structures are uniquely equipped to deal with individual casework, and are perhaps ideally placed to coordinate the overall provision for PSE and pastoral care throughout the school. In part, such arguments can be read as ideological and territorial defences of the pastoral field; of careers, reputations and identities that have been established and developed in this area and are now threatened by the claims of PSE. Some of the newly-asserted claims of PSE can also be read in this way, of course.

In our view, claims that the pastoral care system is best placed to manage and coordinate pastoral care and PSE as a whole are overstated. The task can be undertaken just as effectively, if not more so, by PSE Coordinators. Certainly, this seems a more hopeful prospect than investing coordinating responsibility in a structure rooted so firmly in the interests and processes of discipline and control. There may still be some contribution to be made by pastoral systems – in individual counselling, perhaps, as Watkins suggests. But it is our belief that the more extensive needs of pupils in terms of personal and social development, recognised in recent years, require new structures to promote and support them – structures less fixed in traditions of individual counselling, problem-solving, punishment and discipline. Pastoral care has generally been a good if sometimes overly strict parent to PSE. It has brought PSE into being and helped it find its feet. Now that PSE is moving towards maturity, it is perhaps time for pastoral care to be the supremely good parent and learn to let go!

3 Extra-curricular provision

One way that schools can make specific provision for pupils' personal and social development is outside the mainstream curriculum, in extra-curricular activity. Traditionally, this has been one of the strong points of grammar and independent school education. In such schools, clubs, teams and societies with the opportunities they offer to develop leisure interests, exercise responsibility and work with others in an informal environment, have flourished particularly well. As McBeath (1986) points out, though, where PSE is concerned, it is not *what* activities take place that is important, but how they are organised and who participates in them.

Clubs and societies can encourage co-operation, involvement in group planning, practice in organisational skills and so on. They can also encourage aggressive competitiveness, an inflated sense of importance and feelings of social exclusiveness. Sometimes, these personal and social qualities that participation in extra-curricular activity encourages are planned and intended. On other occasions, however, they may be unintended and unacknowledged, and may even run counter to the teacher's wishes. Team spirit may turn to individual competitiveness, or responsible leadership into a parody of teacher authoritarianism. If such ironic consequences are to be avoided, it is important that the personal and social elements of extra-curricular activities are carefully considered in the planning of these activities.

Even more importantly, in grammar and comprehensive schools alike, clubs and societies are commonly patronised only by a pro-school minority. It is mainly for this reason that exclusive or extensive reliance should not be placed on extra-curricular activity as the place for PSE to occur. This is especially true in an educational climate where conflicts between Government and teachers over conditions of service are leading teachers to withdraw their investment from extra-curricular work because they are being held – and are therefore choosing to stick more closely – to very specific legalistic interpretations of their professional responsibilities. Extra-curricular activity has never met the personal and social needs of all pupils, and it seems it will do so even less in the future.

4 Mainstream subject teaching

If the traditional pastoral system cannot deal effectively with the personal and social needs of secondary pupils, one obvious place to look to instead is the conventional academic curriculum. Despite its tendency to focus on intellectual-cognitive more than affective areas of experience, the conventional academic curriculum has not entirely neglected the personal and social aspects of education. History develops powers of empathy and a sense of social continuity; geography and sociology foster an appreciation of other cultures and societies, and different ways of living; the arts and English literature play an important role in the development of emotions; religious education contributes to the making of moral judgements, and so on.

Often – within a good deal of traditional history teaching, for instance – attention to these personal and social skills and qualities has arisen somewhat incidentally in the course of more narrowly intellectual treatments of the subject matter. But important national curriculum development projects within a number of these subject areas have made a much stronger, more carefully planned contribution to personal and social development. The Schools' Council *Humanities Curriculum Project*, and the widely adopted *Man: A Course of Study* are two of the best known of these, almost encyclopaedic in their coverage of social issues and processes. But other only slightly less ambitious projects like the *Schools Council History Project* and *Geography for the Young School Leaver* have, in the processes of learning they encourage, placed similar emphases on powers of empathy, independent reasoning, use of evidence, appreciation of cultural diversity and so on.

More detailed discussion of the contribution to PSE of traditional subjects and curriculum projects within them can be found in an excellent review of this particular area by Pring (1984: Ch 6). Here, four points are relevant to our broader discussion of PSE. First, it is important to recognise the contribution that mainstream school subjects do make to PSE. It is discourteous, and likely to prove a point of conflict, if this experience and expertise is overlooked in new PSE developments in any school. So, for example, PSE teachers should consult the drama department when developing role-play methods in tutorial programmes; or liaise with the social studies teachers when developing new modules on law and order. PSE is not a completely new development. It has a number of its roots in the mainstream subject curriculum. If whole-school support for PSE is to be secured, it is important that this sort of contribution is recognised and respected. We shall say more about this in the final chapter.

There are dangers in limiting the provision for PSE entirely to the existing subject-based secondary curriculum, however. This brings us to our second point. Within existing subjects, teachers and pupils (with some encouragement from Government policy) commonly place a premium on examination success. This often means that 'safer' methods of fact-gathering, regurgitation and so on predominate in subject teaching and that the personal and social aspects of these subjects become somewhat subdued.

Third, a number of aspects of PSE, particularly some of the more politically controversial or emotionally sensitive ones like child abuse or drugs education, are not easily catered for within existing subjects and therefore require extra provision. The traditional subject system alone cannot cater adequately for PSE.

Finally, the subject departmental structure of secondary schools – a complicated network of small independent states competing for territory, resources and power – insulates subjects from one another and tends to make communication, coordination and integration between them difficult. To confine PSE to the existing subject curriculum is therefore to risk fragmentation, omission and unnecessary duplication. PSE therefore merits additional provision outside the subject mainstream, as well as some overall coordinating structure across and beyond it. For these reasons, we have very serious reservations about moves currently being made within the development of the national curriculum to encourage the teaching of health education and other related areas exclusively *through* existing subjects rather than outside or across them.

5 Curriculum projects on PSE

One way of concentrating attention on PSE is through purpose-designed, packaged curriculum programmes. Two of the best known of these focus on moral education and moral reasoning.

Lifeline, a product of the Schools' Council *Project in Moral Education 13–16* (McPhail *et al.*, 1972), puts an initial emphasis on showing care for and considerateness towards others, then seeks to develop powers of reasoning in relation to broader moral issues, through the discussion of case studies. These cases become more extensive in their complexity and range of reference (up to international dimensions) as the programme progresses. Much of the *Lifeline* material is based on the project team's own research into the attitudes, feelings, beliefs, values and concerns that were most significant to a sample group of pupils in 90 secondary schools. The project therefore begins with what is already important to pupils morally, and seeks to explore and develop awareness in these areas through a wide range of teaching techniques including reflection, drama and role-play.

Values clarification has its roots more in the American than the British context (Simon, 1972). The programme and process seeks to develop moral reasoning by helping pupils make moral choices and encouraging them to commit themselves to and act upon those reasoned choices. Based on the research of Lawrence Kohlberg, *Values clarification* exposes pupils in a structured way to a series of moral dilemmas appropriate to their levels of moral development; reasoning is thereby extended to higher and higher levels of moral development over time. Pupils are encouraged to discuss what action they would take and what reasons they would give for choosing that action, with increasing awareness of the opinions of others and consequences for others. Emphasis is placed not so much on particular values as on the process of valuing itself; although commitment, on the teacher's and pupils' part, to a classroom climate of thoughtfulness and respectfulness in which moral values can be worked through is an important feature of the programme.

Criticisms have been made of both projects and they are clearly reviewed by

Pring (1984) and Strivens (1986). *Values clarification* has been criticised for its laissez-faire approach to moral choice; its apparent indifference to the inculcation of worthwhile moral values. The public nature of value discussion, especially of declared commitments to those chosen values, has also been criticised for placing undue moral pressure on young people to commit themselves to choices perhaps before they are ready. *Lifeline*, meanwhile, has been criticised less for its indifference than for its implicit endorsement of pupils' views about what are important moral issues, by taking these as the project's central themes.

Both programmes, nonetheless, usefully concentrate attention on the process of moral reasoning as something that can be learned and improved. They do this in a way that recognises both the rational, cognitive, deliberative aspects of that process, and the affective aspects of feeling, commitment and motivation. The management of these difficult processes in the classroom calls for great skills on the part of the teacher. Locating the programmes within broader tutorial schemes or PSE taught courses, dealt with by trained staff, would perhaps help meet these skill requirements, while also fitting the specific treatment of moral reasoning within a broader context of PSE. Most of all, it is important that the quality of teacher–pupil relationships throughout the rest of the school is compatible with the processes being experienced and encouraged in taught programmes of moral education. For young people do not 'learn' personal and social education only through discussion and deliberation, but through experience also. PSE is caught just as much as it is taught. Where pupils' experience of moral education lessons is incompatible with their experience of the moral codes and principles embodied in the life of the school as a whole, they will draw their own rather cynical moral conclusions.

6 Specialist taught programmes

Moral education programmes have often occurred in the context of broader taught courses of PSE. One of the earliest and most common ways of making specific provision for PSE was in the form of such taught courses, handled by small teams of specialists. Going by various titles such as *Social and Life Skills*, *Design for Living*, or, simply, *Social Education*, such courses have grown rapidly within the secondary system. Partly, this growth has arisen out of schools' own initiatives in pulling together and giving coherence to previously disconnected areas such as careers education, money matters, citizenship, religious studies, preparation for parenthood, health education and so on. Partly too, such programmes have spread due to modest Government support and encouragement through reports like the *Newsom Report* on less able secondary school pupils in 1963, and through more recent initiatives like the TVEI and CPVE which include provision for PSE within the mandatory criteria that schools must meet if they wish to opt into these initiatives.

Chapter 2 deals with this important and popular area of PSE provision. Two issues in particular are raised within this chapter which are especially pertinent to PSE when it is presented in this form. The first concerns values, fears of bias and worries about possible indoctrination. It is in taught PSE courses, more than anywhere else in school, that highly controversial moral and political issues are most likely to be encountered – nuclear defence, abortion, child abuse, racial prejudice, and so on. In the chapter we consider the arguments of the 'New Right' (eg Scruton *et al.*, 1985) who contend that these are not proper subject matter for school teaching at all (or, at least, until 16) because they embrace issues of social and political complexity well beyond the maturity and judgement of most under 16s; because many teachers are not sufficiently skilled to deal with them in an impartial way; and because they will squeeze other 'more important' subjects out of the school curriculum. In the end, we concur with Stradling and his colleagues (1984) that it is not *despite* but *because of* its controversial character that PSE merits inclusion in the school curriculum. Young people, as a matter of entitlement within the compulsory phase of education, need to develop the reasoning skills, the affective concern and the powers of independent and critical judgement to deal with and think through these contentious issues on which humanity is profoundly divided. This, of course, places an immense obligation on PSE teachers to handle such controversial issues in a fair, non-indoctrinatory manner. *Chapter 2* therefore considers various interpretations of fairness and impartiality in PSE courses along with ways in which they can be managed.

A separate PSE programme, manned by committed specialists trained in the sophisticated skills necessary for handling emotionally sensitive and politically contentious material, provides one of the best opportunities for dealing with value controversies in a professionally competent way. But it also runs the risk of developing into a low-status, marginalised enclave in the organisation of the school. *Chapter 2* examines the vulnerability of specialist taught PSE courses to such lowered status. A separate programme can be an indicator of the highest commitment on the part of the school to PSE. Or it can amount to little more than a low-cost insurance policy, reassuring the head and staff that because PSE has separate provision, it is therefore being safely dealt with already (David, 1983; Wakeman, 1984). Low status carries with it difficulties of securing appropriate space and resources – suitably comfortable rooms, flexible teaching space, handy cupboards for resources and so on. It makes it hard to get high priority in timetabling. And it can create enormous problems of staff recruitment – leaving the department to draw not so much on trained, committed enthusiasts, but on people with gaps in their timetables. The threat to PSE posed by lowered status reminds us once more of the importance of the head's commitment and indeed the commitment of the whole school to personal and social ends of education, as well as academic ones. Effective separate provision paradoxically requires widespread whole-school commitment. This is the recurring paradox of PSE.

7 Tutorial work

If lowered status tends to accompany the confinement of PSE teaching to small specialist teams, then one way to avoid this is to make PSE the responsibility of everyone. This is what tutorial schemes do. They are designed to be used by the majority of a school staff, as a routine part of its responsibility during separately timetabled tutorial periods. Tutorial schemes – originating in the developmental group work of Leslie Button (1982) in South Wales, and in the Active Tutorial Work programme of a team of developers in Lancashire (Baldwin and Wells, 1981) – place high stress on active, experiential methods of learning within PSE, both for the pupils in the class and in the training programmes of those who teach them. More than specialist PSE courses, tutorial schemes also put emphasis on the general developmental process of personal growth, increasing self-awareness and developing confidence in working with and caring for others, as well as on particular content topics like bodily hygiene or drug abuse. These developmental needs are also linked within the tutorial programme to points of crisis and choice in pupils' secondary school careers – induction, option choice, careers guidance and the like.

Group tutorial work, as we call it, is the subject of *Chapter 3*. After discussing the background to and rationale for such work, we then examine some of the key issues and problems commonly encountered within it. Again, the question of values is uppermost. Tutorial work may lack some of the more controversial subject matter of specialist courses but this does not make it altogether immune from value biases. Indeed, because the values contained in tutorial work are less obviously controversial, it is less likely that they will be acknowledged and scrutinised. Are the personal and social skills and qualities being fostered through tutorial work, we ask, skills and qualities that everyone would value; an unarguably necessary part of healthy human development? Or are they the skills and qualities, the manners and morality of particular social groups; of polite middle-class society, perhaps? We wonder whether preparation of conversation in readiness for receiving vistors, for instance, falls into this latter category. And we consider whether the developers and teachers of tutorial programmes are sometimes a little too dismissive of the skills that some children already possess. In wanting to train young people in new social skills and competences, do teachers too easily disregard the skills and competences those young people already have – particularly those pupils who come from working class backgrounds or ethnic minority groups? Is there a tendency, perhaps, for the developers and teachers of tutorial programmes to assume that different cultures are inferior cultures, or perhaps not even 'real' cultures at all?

Given the contestable nature of some skills and qualities being fostered through tutorial programmes, rational reflection on their worth would seem desirable among tutors and pupils alike. Yet in *Chapter 3* we observe that rational, intellectually rigorous appraisal is often weak or missing altogether in tutorial classes and in related programmes of staff training. The accent on active, experiential methods, on the affective aspects of learning in tutorial work may be too strong. It may bring parts of some tutorial programmes closer to emotional indoctrination than reflective education. The public and compulsory nature of group or class discussion about personally sensitive issues may also be emotionally coercive, a serious threat to personal privacy and dignity. We therefore ask whether provision should be made for pupils to withdraw from particular aspects of tutorial work where they feel their privacy, dignity or emotional integrity is under threat.

Finally, we return to the problem of status. Tutorial work might make PSE part of virtually everyone's responsibility, but for many that responsibility will be small compared to their other priorities of subject teaching and examination work. This raises questions about the commitment of form tutors, and the seriousness and skill with which they approach their work. Such matters have implications for approaches to staff training and for management strategies to introduce tutorial work successfully into schools. Inevitably, these doubts about commitment and priority return us to the perennial question of whole-school policy – the importance of methods and messages of tutorial work being consistent with those that are conveyed and experienced elsewhere in the school.

8 Direct experience

With the exception of extra-curricular provision, every approach to PSE we have discussed so far takes place in the ordinary context of school life. In a sense, few aspects of education are more 'real' and more closely connected with the needs and demands of everyday life, than PSE. Yet the environment of the school, with its timetables and classrooms, is in many ways a highly contrived, artificial one. This can make the task of bridging the gap between the personal and social learning that takes place in school and the context of life outside it extraordinarily difficult. Learning through direct experience outside the school – in the world of work, in the local community, or in the outdoors – offers one way of overcoming this difficulty; of heightening and intensifying the impact of PSE.

With the increasing vocationalisation of education, most secondary school pupils now get some direct experience of the world of work, if only for a couple of weeks or so of their secondary school life (Eggleston, 1982). The role of the school in relation to community service and community development has a much longer tradition. Indeed, historically, community education has provided one of the most important contexts for the development and expansion of personal and social education programmes (Rennie, Lunzer and Williams, 1974; Armstrong, 1986; Scrimshaw, 1981). Outdoor and residential education (ORE) provides a third source of learning by direct, intensive experience. This is the subject of *Chapter 4* – though many of the points we make about ORE apply equally well to other kinds of direct experience.

From the point of view of PSE, four issues in particular seem to us important in learning by direct experience. First, is the experience well planned? With ORE in particular, the practical experience is often presented as if the experience, the new environment, somehow teaches by iteself. In some cases, schools seem to feel that if they send pupils on work experience or residential visits, personal and social learning will take place automatically, simply by virtue of pupils having participated in the visit. Yet experiences can be highly variable in nature and they can promote very different sorts of qualities. If leadership and cooperation are to be fostered, for instance, activities need to be selected and carefully designed so that these things take place. *Chapter 4* looks at some of the principles that schools might consider when deciding what kind of residential experience they want, and when helping plan activities within it.

Second, is the experience properly reflected on? If not, the significance of the experience and its implications for personal and social development may be lost. Direct experience of work or the outdoors can sometimes be treated merely as a convenient opportunity to get pupils off the school's hands for a couple of weeks. Unfortunately, such experience is often provided at times which do not allow opportunities for meaningful follow-up; the convenience of the school timetable (as when work experience is organised after summer examinations) appearing to be more important than the effectiveness of the experiential programme.

Third, the demands of planning and follow-up raise questions about the relationship of direct experience to the remainder of the school curriculum and its programme of PSE. Without integration with the wider school curriculum, direct experience can easily degenerate into an interesting, but sporadic and ultimately irrelevant educational activity. Continuity is vital. This has implications for the overall ethos of the school. The benefits of personal and social learning through more informal and relaxed relationships between pupils and teachers on residential visits, for instance, will have little lasting value if teachers revert to the more customary authoritarian and distanced relationships of the classroom on return to school. Consistency, and commitment to direct experience as an integral part of the school's overall personal and social development programme, is the keynote to the success of direct experience.

Fourth, active reflection on the character of direct experience implies that not only should the young person's adjustment to that experience be questioned; but that the character and worth of the experience and the values contained within it should also be reviewed. This is an important issue for pupils and teachers alike. For instance, should reviews of work experience deal with young people's successful adjustment to an unquestioned work ethic (being 'good workers')? Or should they raise questions about the organisation of the workplace, and perhaps even the desirability of enterprise culture itself (Bates *et al.*, 1984)? Should community service experience be concerned just with developing the qualities and skills of individual care? Or should it also alert pupils to the importance of community, local and national politics as influences upon the structure of care in the first place? And should teachers and pupils automatically accept the validity of the notion of adventure and the principles of challenge and endurance that go with it, in outdoor education; or should they subject these things to argument and critical questioning?

At its worst, direct experience can be little more than a moralistic, puritanical lesson in adjustment to the grim and unquestioned 'realities' of life: whether these are the 'realities' of work, of human misfortune, or of nature. At its best, such experience can provide important, well planned and realistic challenges in pupils' personal and social development. If it is reflected upon critically and carefully integrated into the rest of the school curriculum, direct experience can provide pupils with an opportunity to gain not only increased awareness of themselves, their potentials and their failings; but critical and deepened awareness of the world around them, in such a way that they might ultimately want not simply to adjust to it, but to change and improve it as well.

9 Recording, reviewing and self-assessment

Reflection and reviewing, we have argued, is one of the keynotes to the educational validity and success of learning through direct, out-of-school experience. In personal recording and records of achievement, such reviewing lies at the heart of virtually all educational activity in school; outside the main subject curriculum and within it. In this sense, records of achievement and systems of personal recording that support them, provide an organising principle for personal and social education to be dealt with as an integral part of the learning process throughout the work of the school. The contribution of personal recording and records of achievement to pupils' personal and social development as something central to effective and worthwhile learning throughout the curriculum is discussed in detail in *Chapters 5* and *6*.

These chapters trace the origins of personal recording, pupil profiles and records of achievement from a few highly localised initiatives in the 1970s, through to more systematic interventions by the Scottish Council for Research in Education, the Further Education Unit, a range of LEA consortia and ultimately the DES itself, in its funded support for nine pilot schemes in the area. The chapters then go on to outline and evaluate the sophisticated and wide-ranging rationale for personal recording and records of achievement.

Records of achievement, it is said, provide a more extensive reporting and recording system for recognising and rewarding the whole range of pupils' abilities and achievements, including personal and social ones. Through the usual backwash principle of educational assessment, they therefore seek to stimulate greater emphasis on and attention to these other kinds of achievement and experience within the curriculum. They seek to motivate pupils more towards their schoolwork and towards learning in general – by giving them more experience of success (since success itself now has a wider definition); by giving them opportunities to define and declare their identities and matters of personal worth through logbooks and diaries; and by involving them more in their own assessment. Such negotiations of pupil records and statements in which pupils themselves play a central part is not only seen as motivating for the pupil, but also as an aid to the teacher's diagnosis of pupil difficulties. When it becomes routinely linked to diagnosis in this way, assessment, and the pupil's part within it, becomes an integral part of the learning process, not a terminal judgement that is made when the learning is over.

Together, all these changes are designed to alter the nature of the teacher-pupil relationship so that the pupil has a more responsible, assertive role within it – so that the personal and social skills of choice, decision-making, initiative, negotiation and self-assessment become embraced within the process of learning itself. They are designed also to stimulate curriculum change, giving pupils some stake in the design of the curriculum, and in judging and influencing the appropriateness of what is offered.

In these various ways, personal and social education ultimately becomes indistinguishable from education itself. But there are considerable difficulties and obstacles to be faced in undertaking this ambitious educational initiative of personal recording and records of achievement. These, too, are discussed in *Chapters 5* and *6*. Some of the difficulties are ones of principle. Chief among them is the fact that personal recording and records of achievement can serve purposes very different from those that many of the developers intend. Instead of being tools of pupil personal development and curriculum change, they can be used as instruments of surveillance. Records of achievement can be used as mechanisms for storing personally sensitive computerised data on the pupil population, open to retrieval by form tutors, the pastoral system or any other interested agency. They can be used as thinly disguised systems of one-sided behavioural coercion when 'agreed' goals for the future are being set and learning contracts 'negotiated'. And the inescapable process of regular one-to-one review can be used to suppress non-conformist conduct before it arises, lest it becomes a topic for 'discussion' in the future.

Perhaps schools and teachers feel it is legitimate and desirable for personal recording and records of achievement to be used in the interests of this kind of surveillance. Ethically, as a matter of human rights and dignity, we would question that choice. But there are two other points to make on the surveillance issue. First, the choice should be a conscious one, discussed and decided by the school in full knowledge of its ethical and practical implications. It should not be left to operate by default, through the continuing, unchecked and unexamined inertia of a control-centred school system. Second, where surveillance interests are allowed to remain a key feature of personal recording and records of achievement, or where they are perceived as a dominant feature of teacher–pupil relationships in the school in general, pupils are likely to withdraw the trust that is essential to an effective recording and reviewing process. *Chapter 5* includes a discussion of some powerfully critical pupil statements about the lack of trust they have for their teachers, and the way that this undermines the fundamental purposes of personal recording and records of achievement in terms of personal and social development.

Similar ethical and associated practical difficulties arise from the use of records of achievement by employers. Will this, we ask, lead the personal and social development agenda to be shaped and dominated by vocational values and the norms of enterprise culture? What implications will this have for the personal and social needs of politically or socially non-conformist pupils? The role of employers in the development and use of records of achievement is, we suggest, ripe for fundamental review.

Two of the most significant practical problems affecting the successful implementation of records of achievement are those of time and commitment. Meaningful one-to-one discussions require time and therefore staffing and resources to allow for this. Some of this time can be generated by creative administration and changes in the teaching process towards less whole-class centred methods. But extra resources will be needed too and provision of these will be a measure of the school's, the LEA's and the Government's practical commitment to the records of achievement initiative.

More important is the extent of the commitment that teachers can give to the processes of individual negotiation and curriculum change called for by records of achievement, when Government policy pulls them and their schools in opposite directions. How much commitment to these things can teachers give when Government policy is promoting a non-negotiable, national curriculum? How can teachers radically change their practice when Government policy is effectively encouraging teaching-to-the-test through the institution of new competency-based tests at 7, 11 and 14, as well as through the continuing emphasis on public examination results as a basis for parental choice? And how can teachers come to recognise and respect the importance of broader definitions of achievement and cross-curricular skills, when patterns of teacher-training and staff deployment are placing even greater stress on the importance of the subject? These, we argue, are the important challenges of principle, practice and politics that face supporters of records of achievement in years to come.

10 Whole-school policy

The problems facing records of achievement are in many respects the same problems facing most of the developments and directions in PSE that we have discussed. Initiatives designed to benefit personal and social development can very easily be hijacked for purposes of surveillance and control. While great importance might be attached to PSE at the level of rhetoric, in practice, PSE initiatives are often accorded considerably less status and importance than the subject-based, examination-dominated, academic priorities of the secondary school curriculum. The effectiveness of particular PSE initiatives, whatever their shape or form, ultimately depends on the strength of a school's practical commitment to personal and social education within its overall educational programme.

The importance of whole-school policy and commitment to the effective implementation of PSE is the subject of our concluding chapter. There are, we say, three key aspects to this whole-school policy. First, there is a need for clear mechanisms and designated positions of responsibility to draw together and give coherence to a school's provision for PSE. The pastoral and the academic, the in-school and the out-of-school, and the varying provision across all the different subject areas of the school curriculum – these are the facets of PSE provision that need to be brought together through an effective coordinating system.

Second, there is the issue of consistency. Trust, openness, initiative and responsibility are unlikely to be realised effectively within specific areas of PSE provision like tutorial work or residential experience, if these things are not a routine feature of teaching and learning elsewhere in the school. It is important, therefore, that what is valued and encouraged within particular areas of PSE teaching is consistent with what is valued and encouraged in the general ethos of the school as a whole.

This raises the third point: that the fostering of worthwhile personal and social development; the creation of autonomous, independent, caring and critically questioning young people, demands a particular kind of school ethos. It requires a particular set of teacher–pupil relationships which treat young people with dignity and respect, do not subject them to authoritarian and arbitrary treatment, give them opportunities to exercise choice and initiative, and do not call for unquestioning obedience to poorly justified institutional demands. At the end of the day, then, if PSE is not merely a device to mitigate the harshness and unkindness of life elsewhere within the school, if it is not simply a way of supporting the supposedly more important academic system, if it is more than just an institutional ruse to control and place under surveillance a potentially difficult pupil population – then it must be in evidence throughout the life and work of the school in newly built relationships of trust, respect and dignity between pupils and teachers. Meaningful change in personal and social education, then, ultimately demands extensive change in education itself. That is the scale of the innovative challenge for supporters of PSE. We will now go on to examine in more detail some of the different ways in which that challenge can be met. We begin with separate, specialist taught courses.

2 Taught courses in personal and social education

One of the most common ways in which personal and social education finds its way on to the school timetable is in the form of a taught course, hived off and separate from other subjects. While Her Majesty's Inspectorate (1977) have pleaded for a whole-school approach to personal and social development across the curriculum, they themselves observed that 'most schools responded by instituting new, separate programmes'. The titles of such courses vary a great deal: *Social Education, Personal and Social Education, Design for Living, Learning for Life* etc. The patterns whereby courses are presented also differ. Sometimes they are offered to low ability pupils only, sometimes to pupils of all abilities. In some cases they are offered only to fourth and fifth years, in others they occur right across the secondary age range.

More variable still is the actual content of these courses – each school constructing its own individual programme from an almost endless permutation of possible topic areas such as health education, careers education, moral education, parentcraft, political education, citizenship, community service, world studies, economic education and many more (ILEA, 1984: 62). Behind all the variations, though, the common distinguishing feature of PSE taught courses as opposed to, say, programmes of tutorial work, is that they are designed and presented not by teachers who simply happen to be a class's form tutor, but by teachers specially drafted in for the job – in the best cases, because they have been identified as possessing the scarce and highly valued skills and qualities needed for this exceptionally difficult and sensitive area of the curriculum.

Teachers involved in preparing and presenting taught courses of PSE have to face many problems in the course of their work – some of them quite fundamental. First, they must be able to handle controversial and sensitive subject matter in the classroom, deal with problems of bias, and avert the ever-present dangers and temptations of indoctrination.

Second, in many cases they will constantly be involved in struggles to raise the status of their course and department, to secure recognition of its importance and worth among colleagues, pupils and parents. The low status of PSE courses – a result of their non-academic image, their historical roots in secondary modern schools and the education of less able pupils, and the fact that unlike 'real subjects', they are rarely assessed by public examination – has implications for the quality and coherence of these courses and for the job satisfaction of those who teach them. Low status can bring with it low priority in staff allocations, in timetabling, in the allocation of facilities and resources – all of which will affect the capacity of PSE teachers to construct a coherent curriculum and to teach their subject effectively. Low status is the PSE teacher's burden: he or she will necessarily have to spend much of his/her time trying to elevate it.

Third, once PSE is packaged into an identifiable timetable slot where it is dealt with by a group of specialists, other staff may be relieved from feeling that they need to attend to their responsibilities in this area. Why should they need to deal with these difficult questions when they are already being safely dealt with elsewhere? In this respect, the dangers of 'ghettoisation' in PSE are even greater in special taught courses than in tutorial programmes – for in the latter case, while PSE is hived off into a specific slot on the timetable, it is at least recognised as being the responsibility of most teachers in the school.

The difficulties to be faced by teachers and managers of PSE courses in the form of charges of bias, problems of lowered status and dangers of departmental isolation are clearly considerable. But a strong, positive case for the development of such courses can also be made, even and perhaps especially where there is a coordinated policy for PSE right across the school. At the most basic level, while taught courses run the risk of isolating and 'ghettoising' PSE in the school curriculum, they do at least ensure that some kind of 'agreed' provision is made available and that certain topics and issues central to the personal and social development of pupils are addressed at some point during their school careers. It is commonly argued that PSE, like language across the curriculum and equal opportunities for the sexes, is the responsibility of *all* teachers, but once that position has been taken, it is all too easy for PSE then to fall into the cracks between the secondary school's subject departments and become the responsibility of none.

A taught course does at least guarantee some minimal coverage for PSE, then. But even where the responsibility of all teachers for pupils' personal and social education is more than a paper commitment, where there is a more coordinated approach to these matters across the curriculum, a good case can still be made for retaining a separate taught course as part of this broader policy.

The controversial and sensitive questions and issues commonly raised within taught courses – from abortion to vivisection to peace and war and politics; from the demands and responsibilities of parenthood, to the rights and wrongs of euthanasia or drugtaking – demand teachers who possess the sophisticated skills and qualities necessary for helping young people deal with matters concerning values, feelings and emotions. The treatment of PSE in the form of a discrete course staffed by suitably skilled and committed teachers has been an understandably popular option for many schools. It guarantees coverage; it can be a way of developing PSE in schools not yet ready to risk discussing and agreeing on (or disagreeing about) social and educational values as a matter of whole-school policy, or it can be a way of placing this area of the curriculum in the hands of teachers with appropriate skills, commitments and personal qualities. A taught course can be an integral part of a school's overall commitment to PSE, or an evasion of that commitment. It can be a protected, 'safe' enclave in which skilled and carefully chosen staff help young people explore emotionally sensitive and politically controversial issues, or a 'rag-bag of curricular loose-ends' that cannot be accommodated in the school's mainstream subject provision (ILEA, 1984: 64). It can, in other words, be central to the school's educational aims and practice, or peripheral to them. Where a taught course is located within such aims, the strength of a school's commitment to PSE will clearly affect the extent of the course's isolation or integration, its status and importance in the curriculum, and its overall coherence and effectiveness. It is these sorts of issues to do with status, coherence and integration, along with the ubiquitous problems of values and the dangers of bias and indoctrination, that we will explore within this chapter. Before these issues are explored in detail, though, a few notes on the historical background to the development of PSE courses and on the different forms that such courses now take might help guide that discussion.

Background

PSE courses have grown in a variety of forms and guises through developments in the curriculum, through the evolution and extension of pastoral care and through extra-curricular activity. They have done so in response to a number of needs and pressures: teachers' and schools' perceptions of necessary personal and social characteristics in a rapidly changing society; problems of motivation and purpose among young people no longer guaranteed employment after school; and, not least, teachers' own survival needs in coping with the growing disaffection and disillusionment that can result from this shrinking of hope and opportunity among their pupils.

At least four historical strands can be identified in the development of modern PSE courses in secondary schools:

1 initiatives for low attaining pupils in secondary schools following the Newsom Report (CACE, 1963) and the raising of the school leaving age in 1972;
2 the growth and changing fortunes of a more academic kind of social studies education within the secondary curriculum;
3 the emergence of a number of disparate national curriculum development projects and initiatives in the late 1960s and early 70s, in fields like political education, health education, humanities and moral education, that had clear implications for pupils' personal and social development;

4 the attempted coordination of all these piecemeal developments through the publication of curricular guidelines on PSE at local and national levels in the 1980s.

1 Initiatives for low attainers: the Newsom pattern

Forerunners of current PSE courses can, in fact, be located in a number of innovations with low ability pupils that followed the publication, in 1963, of the Newsom Report on average and below average pupils aged 13–16; the expansion of comprehensive schooling in the 1960s, and the raising of the school leaving age in 1972. As a response to these innovations and to the consequences of selection and educational failure which they signalled, special courses specifically for low-attaining and less able pupils were set up in many secondary schools in the 1960s and 1970s. As Shipman (1974: 61) has recorded, 'the decade following the publication of the Newsom Report was one of dramatic growth in large-scale innovation in the humanities/social education area'. These were the 'Newsom' and 'ROSLA' courses that became such a common feature of secondary modern schools and the lower streams of comprehensives in the 1970s.

The policy rhetoric surrounding Newsom-like initiatives in education was a powerful, persuasive and by no means insincere one. Among its major recommendations, the Newsom Report itself firmly advised that 'attention should be paid both to imaginative experience through the arts and to personal and social development' (CACE, 1963: xvi). Many 'Newsom' principles concerning the education of 'average' and 'below average' secondary pupils still carry a strong echo of familiarity and political respectability in the 1980s. Vocational orientation, practical relevance, realistic relation to work and leisure, pupil involvement in curriculum choice, personal and social development – all these things have either their exact replicas or close analogues in current government-sponsored initiatives for low attainers; in concerns with industrial awareness, relationships to 'working life', 'negotiated curriculum' and so on (Weston and Harland, 1988). Personal and social development is a central item on this recurring agenda.

Schools, too, could and did make reference to these kinds of principles in justifying their low attainer or school leaver programmes. Burgess (1983: 125), for instance, in his detailed case study of a 'Newsom' department in the 1970s, quotes the headmaster's justification of the Newsom course as being 'designed to develop and strengthen those talents in the non-academic which will be most useful to that youngster in society – job-wise, marriage-wise and recreation wise'. He also describes how Newsom teachers in his case study school accounted for and justified their work to the head in departmental meetings by claiming that the course made pupils 'more mature and responsible', and 'created the opportunity to get to know (the) group as people rather than pupils' (p. 226).

The reality of Newsom was often different from the positive-sounding professional rhetoric, though. Richard Pring (1975: 17) criticised much Newsom teaching for not providing social education at all, but only a 'limited diet of social training' with no scope for the development of a critical outlook among young people. Very often Newsom and ROSLA courses did not even achieve these limited aims. One experienced comprehensive teacher has commented that they were often little more than makeshift devices for containing 'obstreperous youths' (Wakeman, 1984). And Burgess (1983, 1984) has described in vivid detail how the Newsom lessons he studied commonly amounted to little more than sessions where pupils played table-tennis, lay across – and fell asleep on – their desks, and indulged in protracted routines for buying, preparing and drinking coffee. Developed in a hurry, staffed in a piecemeal fashion, and lowly ranked in the school's status hierarchy, this Newsom course, and others like it, found it virtually impossible to gain a secure and recognised place in the school curriculum among teachers and pupils alike, and this had serious implications for its coherence and effectiveness. No wonder some people worry that the confinement of some more recent PSE courses to low attainers, not least those operating under the rubric of the Government's Lower Attaining Pupils Project (LAPP), runs the serious risk of repeating these mistakes (Hustler and Ashman, 1985). Certainly, one lesson worth learning from the Newsom experience is the need to avoid exaggerated claims about PSE initiatives and to moderate initial enthusiasm regarding them; to inspect the fit between rhetoric and reality very closely. Eloquent rhetoric can provide grand edifices of professional justification for PSE practice – but if they are not borne out in practice, when they are eventually 'rumbled' their collapse is all the more catastrophic.

Even where PSE courses are no longer confined to the less able, the low-attainer 'Newsom' lineage still often influences the way such courses are perceived and received in schools. The way in which social education first appeared on most school timetables linked it strongly to lower ability groups, as we have seen. As a result, the low status it was consequently accorded in a system which traditionally recognised only *academic* success, has tended to fix it in an enduring image against which teachers who want to provide some kind of personal and social education for all pupils still have to battle, even today.

2 Social studies

A second strand of influence upon current PSE courses is the development of a more academic kind of social studies teaching in the post-war years. Social studies first emerged after the 1944 Education Act as a response to the curricular needs of secondary modern schools (Hemming, 1949; Cannon, 1964). As a low ability initiative, though, it was soon eclipsed by the growing aspirations of secondary modern schools to include more and more examination work and thus 'real subjects' in the curriculum (FEU, 1980). Almost killed off by the spread of examinations during that period, social studies was resuscitated by the Newsom and ROSLA initiatives. As 'new social studies' (Lawton and Dufour, 1973), it sought to retain the social relevance of earlier developments, but it also strove to avoid the previous problems of low status by infusing the subject with greater intellectual rigour. The new social studies, then, tried to improve the position of social education within the curriculum, by playing the existing rules of subject status to the full – making the work more academic, more subject based, and more examinable. Whitty (1985) has conceded that while this may, indeed, have added rigour to social education, it did so at the expense of relevance, making it just another academic subject on the curriculum. Instead of developing skills of critical thinking, in the way the developers hoped, pupils simply acquired and regurgitated academic knowledge 'about' society. The new social studies might have given social education academic respectability in the intellectual-cognitive domain, but at the same time, it took away all that was important to pupils' affective development.

This division between the intellectual-cognitive and affective aspects of PSE remains an enduring feature of teaching and learning in the area. This is perhaps best summed up by referring to an encounter one of us had with a head of humanities when we were looking at the PSE department within his school (a department in which he had no direct involvement). When asked how he distinguished his own subject, humanities, from PSE, he answered, 'Oh that's easy – they deal with the affective aspects, we deal with the cognitive ones!' This development of academic social studies has been one of the main contributors to the cognitive/affective split that can be found in relation to much current PSE provision.

3 Separate curriculum developments

Writing about developments in vocational relevance and industrial awareness in the secondary curriculum, Holmes and Jamieson (1986: 160) have remarked that 'because each school is more or less allowed to decide its own curriculum, then curriculum change comes about by what often amounts to a sales campaign mounted by various agencies'. Though they are referring to curricular initiatives in the industrial/vocational area, similar observations can be made about developments in PSE courses too. Much of the influence on current PSE courses in terms of content, materials and methods, has come from teachers' earlier experiences of a whole range of separate, independently supported curriculum projects like *The Humanities Curriculum Project*, *Man: a Course of Study* and *Schools Council Health Education Project 13–18* (Wakeman, 1984). The content, strengths and weaknesses of these different initiatives have been extensively reviewed elsewhere (eg Pring, 1984; FEU, 1980) and have already been touched on in Chapter 1. All we want to do here is point to the range of separate initiatives in different curriculum areas which have, in complicated ways, influenced the development and diversity of PSE taught courses today. Nor has this pattern of development in PSE teaching ended. Initiatives being made with increasing vigour in specific curriculum areas such as health education, peace education, world studies, political education, religious education and the like, continue to stimulate and influence the development of PSE taught programmes in schools (eg Wellington, 1986).

4 Attempts to secure coherence and coordination

In many respects, then, PSE courses, like PSE initiatives generally, have been the result of a process of 'bottom-up' innovation in schools, arising out of the separate perceptions, enthusiasms and involvement of a great number of individual schools. The pressures and need for PSE may have been national in scope – growing youth unemployment, anxieties about the examination-dominated curriculum, too much concentration on the cognitive aspects of young people's development etc – but the curriculum responses have been highly local in nature. The degree of professional latitude this pattern of development has offered may have encouraged initiative and commitment, stimulating an important sense of ownership and local relevance among the teachers involved in PSE courses. But the initiatives have been so diverse and diffuse that it may now be appropriate to try to draw together what has been achieved, and perhaps begin to discuss and eventually establish some coherent guidelines with those who are involved in this kind of work.

Nationally, the importance of pupils' personal and social development in general has long been recognised – at least since the Newsom Report. The development of the concept of an *entitlement curriculum* in *Curriculum 11–16* in 1977, where HMI argued that all areas of the curriculum (including what they called the social and political, ethical and spiritual areas of experience) should be made accessible to pupils of all abilities, moved PSE off a specifically 'low-ability' agenda and on to the agenda of educational entitlement for all young people. Yet by the time they had published their survey of secondary education in 1979, it seemed that HMI had not yet decided if provision for PSE through separate courses merited a place in the secondary curriculum. All they could advise was that

> How far this (need to provide more personal education in the curriculum of all pupils) . . . may require the development of new and separate courses and how far these needs may be better met by shifts of emphasis and content within existing subjects requires careful consideration.
>
> *(HMI, 1979: 42)*

By 1985, HMI endorsement of PSE taught courses in the secondary curriculum was less cautious. In *The Curriculum from 5 to 16*, while they recognised that the taught course was not the only way to deal with pupils' personal and social development, they nevertheless acknowledged that

> In many secondary schools, issues of personal and social morality are dealt with in specific courses for older pupils . . . These courses can be valuable when they have sufficient substance to enable pupils to engage in informed discussion of issues that bear upon the individual and society.
>
> *(HMI, 1985: 27)*

Beyond limited approval for the place of PSE taught courses, though, virtually no specific advice has been offered on the content and orientation of such courses. For this reason, HMI's proposed discussion of 'Personal and Social Education from 5 to 16' in their *Curriculum Matters* series is awaited with some interest.

After attempting to outline various ways of implementing PSE in secondary schools, Lee (FEU, 1980) concludes that 'there is no undisputed "best" approach or model'. This is not surprising, since there is no consensus about what is the most important element in PSE – the development of knowledge, of values, of understanding, of attitudes, of sensitivity or of competence. Neither is there agreement about which of these are pre-requisites for the development of others. Moreover, there are no clear research findings about how any of these are most effectively developed through teaching programmes. Clearly, in the absence of national guidelines and coordination, and without the common constraint that examination syllabuses impose on other subjects, PSE taught courses have developed in a highly diversified way. In view of this diversity, the need to 'map' the interesting but confusing territory of PSE courses, to get a better grip on just what is going on, and to evaluate the effectiveness of different kinds of provision, is obviously very great. In many respects, the 'history' and 'geography' of PSE programmes is only just being written in terms of school and LEA case studies. Most of the important work has yet to be done.

Types of provision

If PSE courses are highly varied, they are not so diverse and disconnected as to be absolutely unique to each individual school in which they operate. There *are* certain forms of orientation and modes of implementation which enable one to group PSE courses into broad categories of approach and presentation. In the absence of detailed research these categories are somewhat 'rough and ready' in character at the moment, but they are presented in the hope that they might help schools identify their own approach or consider alternative ways of implementing new programmes.

Forms of orientation

Some PSE courses are primarily content-based, others can be seen as predominantly skills-based. Some teachers perceive a need to provide their pupils with certain information, eg about government and the law, or health and finance. This leads them to devise courses which are predominantly content-based. Courses of this kind tend to focus on topics like law and order, careers, nuclear defence, animal welfare or drug abuse.

Certain kinds of information, such as knowledge of first aid, are probably essential to almost any PSE programme. Their inclusion arouses little controversy. The relevance of many other kinds of information to young people's immediate life needs, however, is much more debatable. It is strange, for instance, that many courses deal with the more distant financial issues of mortgages or income tax, but neglect what is for many young people the most immediately pressing financial concern: claiming benefit. Other kinds of topics, such as law and order, nuclear defence or AIDS are more controversial, and here attitudes and social skills are demonstrably just as important as the acquisition of information – if not more so; though even the most uncontroversial areas, it should be said, contain elements of skills as well – the skills of resuscitation in first aid, for instance.

A second type of PSE course focuses on pupils' development as people and provides opportunities for exploration of how they feel and behave. These sorts of courses are more skills-based in nature. Courses that centre on skills and activities which help pupils develop and cope with social interaction often put great emphasis on the kinds of social activities in which we all engage, such as making decisions, presenting an opinion, arguing, sympathising, encouraging, making friends, or organising. Useful checklists of such skills and activities have been compiled by the Assessment of Performance Unit (1981) and by Pring (1984) as aids for helping PSE teachers plan their courses. Skills-based courses may include problem-solving exercises or opportunities for pupils to develop skills through practical experience such as receiving visitors, giving talks or demonstrations, working in groups or making real decisions. For this reason, they usually put great emphasis on 'active' teaching and learning methods which offer opportunities for experiential learning, creative activity, the practice of skills, exploration of attitudes and feelings, and so on (FEU, 1980).

In practice, the distinction between these two kinds of courses – content and skills-based – is far from clear, and there is considerable overlap. For example, a consideration of legal rights and responsibilities necessarily draws on understanding, appreciation and criticism of the concepts of 'rule' and 'law', and the ways in which rules and laws vary between groups and societies. Similarly, skills and attitudes cannot be developed in the absence of content. Empathy, for instance, can initially be developed only in relation to particular groups or persons – the physically handicapped, the aged, people in authority, ethnic minorities etc – and one needs to have some knowledge of these groups and their problems and purposes before one can develop empathy with them. In short, although the prevailing emphasis of particular courses may be skills- or content-based, the guiding principles are likely to be very closely interlocked. The mistake is to believe that as a teacher one is *only* passing on information or *only* developing skills and attitudes. In practice, teachers are almost always doing both.

Modes of implementation

Whatever their orientation in terms of teaching style and methods of learning, PSE courses can be organised or 'packaged' in a number of different ways, each with its own advantages and disadvantages. The main ones are:

1   *The PSE course*   Such a course is introduced in years four and five as public examination courses begin. This is possibly the most usual manifestation of personal and social education courses. Courses of this kind may be:

a   part of the students' compulsory core of subjects, although personal and social education may have less time allocated to it than other subjects.
b   a compulsory subject appearing on the options grid, perhaps in three or four columns. Pupils must choose PSE in one column. This can be seen as a constraint on other option choices or provide a useful device for 'mopping-up' pupils who find it difficult to make a choice.
c   an examined option subject which pupils may choose in the same way as they choose other options. The one culminating in the Associated Examining Board examination in *Lifeskills* is an example of this.

The taught course for pupils aged 14 plus has the advantage of broaching difficult and delicate personal and social issues close to the time when young people are going to need to deal with these (in mid to late adolescence and in life after school). The tightly-packaged programme also requires only a limited number of staff to teach it – and this can make recruitment less of a problem. On the debit side, though, if schools confine their PSE provision to a course for the 14 to 16-year-olds, this creates a misleading impression that the personal and social development of younger pupils is less important. Links with a tutorial programme for younger pupils, however, can help counter that impression and create stronger continuity in PSE teaching throughout the school. More intractable is the problem of the low status that attaches to a non-academic course which is confined to particular years, and thus to a small group of staff who may have difficulty meeting and planning at the same time as other departments. This can seriously threaten the coherence of PSE in the school.

2 *A PSE department*   Such a department will have the same status as others in the school, with staff appointed specifically to it. In this case, PSE appears on the timetables of pupils throughout the school. Such departments may be called Social Studies or General Studies or Social Education.

The organisation of PSE in a special department extends PSE provision across the school and makes coordination of this area much easier. As a sizeable department able to meet at the same time as others, it also strengthens the status of PSE in a school. In order to achieve a viable department, however, especially when it reaches Faculty proportions, membership may sometimes need to be somewhat contrived (by including PE in the PSE Faculty, for instance). Also while separate PSE faculties and departments are relatively easy to establish in new schools, their development can be more difficult in schools of longer standing, for the emergence of a new department will be seen as threatening the existing interests of others in the school.

3 *Special low attainer programmes*   These are the modern equivalents of Newsom and ROSLA. These may appear on the options grid as a non-examination option, or form part of a core programme for a designated 'Low attaining' group as in the DES-sponsored Lower Attaining Pupils Project (Weston and Harland, 1988).

Personal and social education elements in special low attainer programmes do inject a useful dose of social relevance into the work of pupils who have been 'turned off' school and academic learning – and they do this at a major crisis point in their educational careers. But if confined to such groups, personal and social education will also be prone to the problems of lowered status that afflicted Newsom courses and will undermine the principles of comprehensiveness and common curricular entitlement in which personal and social education should be the educational right of all.

4 *A rotation module*   Whether SPE courses are offered to all pupils or to older and less able ones only, they can be 'packaged' in different ways. Two such kinds of course presentation have been usefully described by the Devon Education Department. These they call the 'rotation module' method and the 'team approach'. In the rotation module method, 'the teacher takes a group of pupils for all the personal, social and moral education periods in a given number of weeks and covers one component in that time' (Devon Education Department, 1982: 9). The advantage of this method is that teachers become very familiar with the material they teach and can capitalise on their expertise in the area. Moreover, they can give the particular component they teach – health, careers, etc – a high degree of coordination. On the other hand, coordination between the major parts of the module can be less strong, giving PSE the appearance of a kind of circus made up of different, interesting, but uncoordinated acts. The relationships on which sound PSE teaching rests are

also difficult to build up in short modules of six weeks or so in length. This contrasts sharply with the team approach.

5 *The team approach*   Here 'each member of the team keeps the same group of pupils throughout the year and is responsible for covering an integrated personal, social and moral education course' (Devon Education Department, 1982: 19). This pattern is much more conducive to the kinds of teacher–pupil relationships that PSE requires; and it strongly assists the process of systematic team planning and course review as well. The range of material to be covered by each individual, though, does mean that teachers need to work exceptionally hard in keeping themselves knowledgeable and up-to-date right across the area.

Summary

In this section, we have examined the historical background and types of provision in PSE courses. These historical factors help us understand some of the current issues affecting PSE courses – their low status, their association with low ability pupils, the affective/cognitive split betweeen social education and social studies, and so on. Knowledge of the types of courses available also enables us to see different ways in which problems of status, staffing, coherence, relationships etc, can be tackled in different schools – and to assess how effective each of these different curriculum strategies might be. It is time to turn, then, to some of these major issues affecting PSE courses – to questions concerning values and bias, status and staffing, assessment and evaluation. We begin with the difficult problems of values and bias.

Issue and problems
Values and biases: indoctrination or education?

All kinds of PSE provision, without exception, are prone to political and social bias, to the (often unintentional) promotion of particular social values. 'Macho' versions of challenge and adventure in outdoor education, middle-class norms of polite conversation in group tutorial discussion, manipulations of personal statements in the process of pupil profiling – these just are some of the dangers that confront teachers in various aspects of PSE. But PSE taught programmes, with their agenda of controversial social issues, present especially strong threats to fairness and impartiality. It is in the taught course, more than anywhere else, that PSE is most vulnerable to charges of bias and indoctrination.

Few would argue against all pupils understanding the rudiments of First Aid, but topics like alcoholism, law and order, drug use, sex education and so on, form a veritable minefield of controversy and contention in taught programmes. Charges of political bias or social indoctrination are easily levelled at teachers who deal with socially difficult questions such as these – and they can just as easily come from the right or left of the political spectrum. It is worth devoting a little space to examination of these critiques, to look at the validity of the points they raise, and to explore ways of dealing with the questions they throw up.

We will focus on two areas that have aroused a series of biting right-wing critiques: peace education and world studies. But many of the points we raise here will apply equally well to other areas, like sex education. Critiques of peace studies and world studies have been published by individuals associated with groups and organisations such as the Social Affairs Unit, the Centre for Policy Studies, the National Council of Women and Families for Defence and the Institute for European Defence and Strategic Studies (Scruton, Ellis-Jones and O'Keefe, 1985; Scruton, 1985; Cox and Scruton, 1984; Marks, 1985; O'Keefe, 1986).

Identifying some of the political and organisational affiliations of these individuals should not be read as an attempt to undermine the worth or rationality of the views they are presenting (though *they* have been much less generous than this in their treatment of those they see as their political opponents). As we shall see, their critiques do, at points, raise issues of great importance to those concerned with personal and social education. But a recognition of these people's affiliations and loyalties does give some sense of the overall, internally unified position from which they are arguing, no matter what aspect of education they are discussing.

The critique these writers make of the most politically controversial aspects of PSE consists of eight basic points. Politically controversial aspects of PSE, they say, are:

- powerful examples of the unwarranted intrusion of politics into the education of the young;
- too complicated to be understood properly by most, if not all, young people;
- prone to be based on biased selection and presentation of materials that affirm a set of foregone conclusions;
- commonly based on teaching styles which use emotional manipulation instead of rational discussion;
- promoted and supported by political interest groups of a left-wing nature;
- camouflaged in a seductively broad, all-encompassing and unexceptionable rhetoric of aims which encourage peaceable conduct, the appreciation of cultural diversity etc, and into which highly controversial political aims such as sympathy towards or responsibility for disarmament are then smuggled;
- not a real discipline or subject and therefore have no justification for inclusion in the secondary curriculum;

- a threat to the place of proper subjects, 'real' education, and traditional standards because they clutter up the secondary curriculum with unnecessary additional elements.

The last two points really concern the status of PSE as a 'real' subject, not so much the political and social values that it allegedly promulgates, and will therefore be discussed later. It is the first six that are of major concern to the question of values, and four of those have immediate and direct implications for the teacher in school. We will deal with these four points in turn.

1 Does much PSE coursework bring about an unwarranted intrusion of politics into the curriculum?

In response to this, it is important to recognise at the outset that all organised education is unavoidably political. First, it is political insofar as it awards credentials that affect the distribution of life chances, opportunities and the chance to exercise power in adult life. Certificated education confers power – and power is political. Second, and more importantly for the present discussion, education contributes to the developing consciousness of the young. It helps form values and shape judgements. Teaching and schooling are, in this sense, closely intertwined with social values and assumptions. As we have emphasised already, schools are continually 'teaching' personal and social education to their pupils, through the kinds of behaviour, conduct and attitudes they support and encourage on a day-to-day basis. This point, Scruton and his colleagues acknowledge. Good manners, they call it; an approved and necessary part of the overall ethos of the school.

But there is good reason to believe that social and political consciousness is influenced through the teaching of the official curriculum of school subjects as well. The way that history is taught, for example, has a bearing on people's political consciousness. The treatment of kingship, despotism and dictatorship has implications for pupils' developing attitudes towards authority. The treatment of conquest, 'discovery' and colonialism has implications for attitudes towards the First and Third Worlds in particular, and towards cultural differences in general. The treatment of the Peasants' Revolt, slavery and the suffragettes has implications for attitudes towards the rule of law and towards the conditions under which it might be breached for the furtherance of higher moral ends, and so forth. In subjects like geography, history and English, then, it is clear that the treatment of these sorts of issues, their inclusion in or exclusion from the syllabus, will frequently have implications for young people's developing political awareness.

Scruton and his fellow critics concede this possibility, but regard it as a non-essential by-product of subject teaching; not its major aim. In sidestepping the issue in this way ('It often happens, but we don't intend it') these critics are in our view effectively encouraging subject teachers to abrogate one of their central professional responsibilities. Once it is acknowledged that teaching does affect consciousness in ways that might be socially, morally or politically significant, it is surely better that this process be carefully guided according to conscious professional judgement, rather than determined by the teacher's unchecked value assumptions or those implicit in the course. This necessity to acknowledge the place of moral, social and political judgements and guide the way they are handled is as central to mainstream subject teaching as it is to PSE courses. PSE courses cannot therefore be dismissed on the grounds that they introduce political concerns into the curriculum. They are demonstrably already there. All that PSE courses have done is to heighten awareness of this overall process of personal and social education in schools, of the judgements contained within it, of the appropriateness of these social and political judgements, and of the ways in which they might best be handled.

2 Do politically controversial elements of PSE courses demand a level of intellect and maturity of judgement beyond the reach of most young people?

Commenting on the place of peace education in the school curriculum, Sir Keith Joseph, when Secretary of State for Education and Science, stated that the principles of discussion and judgement necessary for the skilled teaching of peace issues were difficult to apply to young, immature or less-able pupils (Joseph 1984, quoted in Marks 1985: 3). Cox and Scruton (1984: 24) express the more general worry that teaching 'burning issues' as a whole, simply results in the child spending 'much of his time in the classroom attending to matters which lie beyond his comprehension, and which are in any case the subject of continual dispute and incomprehension even among adults'. 'Not every subject', they say, 'can be taught to pupils of every age and attainment', and peace education, like law and philosophy, is one example of this (*ibid.*, p. 8). As a result, right-wing critics of peace education and of other politically controversial aspects of the curriculum, recommend that 'politically contentious subjects should normally form no part of the curriculum for those below the age of 16' (Marks, 1985: 46).

Three responses can be made to this argument. First, there is evidence from Britain and the United States that many young people in early and mid-adolescence already think and worry about nuclear issues a great deal. Many consider it quite likely that there will be a nuclear war in their lifetime, and the shadow of the nuclear threat causes appreciable misery and anxiety among a fair proportion of young people unbeknown to their parents (summarised in Tizard, 1984). Nuclear issues may not be the foremost source of worry among adolescents, but they are certainly an important one. If that is the case, it is clearly preferable that the worries and anxieties that are at the heart of young people's personal and emerging social awareness and development – whether these are to do with nuclear issues, their developing sexuality, the availability and effects of drugs or the problems of famine in the Third World – are dealt with seriously, in a carefully guided and professionally controlled way, rather than being left to the moral lottery of family life (White, 1984). Peace education, development education and the like are often accused of arousing unnecessary anxiety among young people – and where this kind of education is mismanaged, such dangers are clearly very great. But it is evident that a diffuse sense of anxiety and helplessness amongst the young in relation to these issues is already widespread. In this respect, PSE courses, by improving knowledge and increasing awareness of alternatives and of ways in which influence can be exercised (if only through the ballot box), can do much to alleviate the fear by helping the young channel their responses into purposeful directions.

Second, it is claimed that peace education, world studies and the like, raise issues that are emotionally and conceptually too difficult or controversial to be discussed by most young people under 16. While the handling of difficult material is always a problem for secondary teachers, we find it strange that elements of PSE have been picked out for special criticism here. The discussion of complicated adult emotions like romantic love, jealousy and self-sacrifice in English (especially Shakespearean) literature; the treatment of concepts like omnipresence, resurrection and transubstantiation (however they are paraphrased) in religious education, or getting an adequate empathic grasp in history of the intensity of the emotions that would make Henry VIII want to break with Rome – are these elements in the mainstream subject curriculum not equally difficult things for young people to understand? If difficulty is a criterion for curricular exclusion, why are these things not to be found in Scruton and his colleagues' hit-list? In the light of such intellectual inconsistency, one can only suspect that Scruton and his colleagues might have other than intellectual motivations for wanting to remove controversial political issues from the curriculum up to 16.

Third, contrary to the protestations of Cox and Scruton, it is our belief, in common with the distinguished psychologist Jerome Bruner, that almost any subject or topic can be taught in an intellectually respectable way to a child of almost any age. Appreciation of this fundamental point has fostered excellent developments in primary science, for instance, going far beyond the study of autumn leaves, frog spawn or animal hibernation. The level of treatment needs to be adjusted to age and ability, of course, as history and geography teachers, say, do all the time. But just because 14 or 15-year-olds cannot grasp the international politics of strategic defence or world trade at a level of sophistication appropriate to undergraduate or postgraduate study, should we exclude peace studies or development education from their curriculum? To set this requirement for the study of controversial issues is to apply a counsel of perfection that can be found nowhere else in the curriculum. If controversial issues are sensitively handled, whatever is done, and at however elementary a level, is almost bound to offer pupils a more sophisticated, informed and professionally-guided awareness and understanding of the issues in place of the diffuse and distressing anxieties they may otherwise experience (Stradling *et al.*, 1984; Stradling 1986). Difficulty therefore provides no grounds for deletion.

3 Is PSE coursework presented and taught in a biased way?

From within and outside the PSE department, anxieties about bias are always likely to be felt and will need to be faced. Whose values and standards is PSE promoting? What is the position of the department on contentious subjects like peace education and homosexuality? Can the pitfalls of indoctrination be avoided? Critics of PSE courses – both right and left wing – are sceptical. Cox and Scruton (1984: 7) claim that peace studies, for instance, 'is taught in such a way as to discourage critical reflection, and encourage prejudice, about the matters of peace, war and disarmament' and rests on 'the assumption of foregone political conclusions . . . (which) are immensely damaging to our national interests' (though that, in itself, seems something of a foregone conclusion!). In other publications, they argue that the teaching of controversial issues like this often rests on false premises of feminism, anti-racism, or the belief that 'man' is basically good, which are not themselves subjected to question (eg Scruton, 1985).

The examples used in materials on controversial issues are said to be ideologically selective. Conflict is discussed as it arises in Northern Ireland, South Africa and the Middle East, but not in Afghanistan, Poland or Cambodia. The relationships between the *First* and Third Worlds are discussed, but not those between the *Second* and Third Worlds (Marks, 1985: 12; Scruton, 1985). Lists of source materials recommended to teachers and pupils for further information are said to represent overwhelmingly only one ideological position – broadly left-wing in nature. There are claimed to be ideologically significant omissions from materials and courses – eg the case *for* a police force and an army. Even the titles of courses or elements within them are accused of being ideologically loaded, not least the term 'peace education' (rather than 'conflict studies') itself.

Nor are these criticisms confined to the political right wing. Titles of course elements like drug abuse (rather than drug use and abuse) might be a source of concern to the left. Geoff Whitty (1985: Ch. 7), writing from a self-avowed left-wing stance, has taken issue with current developments in political education (Crick and Porter, 1978; Porter, 1979) on the grounds that they endorse the acceptance of parliamentary democracy, understress the availability and legitimacy of other more direct forms of political action and therefore seem to be 'more concerned to preserve rather than improve upon the basic form of society in which we live' (p 157).

Sir Keith Joseph himself, it is worth noting, has actively encouraged 'slanted' treatment of certain social and political issues (a prime example, one would have thought, of the kind of one-sidedness of which Scruton and his colleagues complain so bitterly).

> We are surely right to expect our schools not to encourage pupils to take a favourable view of notions which are wholly alien to our society – for example that government should be other than parliamentary or that the rule of law should be abrogated.
>
> (Joseph, 1984, quoted in Cox, 1985: 5)

It must be said that there is some substance in these allegations. It is often not the intention of advocates of peace studies and the study of other controversial issues to indoctrinate pupils. Indeed, David Hicks (1983: 19), one of the *bêtes noires* of the peace studies movement to right-wing critics, has proclaimed that peace studies explicitly seeks to avoid indoctrination and is 'about offering alternative viewpoints and procedures in an often violent world'. Even so, inspection of existing source materials on areas like peace studies and world studies does indicate over-representation of one particular set of (albeit broadly spread) views and too heavy a reliance on materials and organisations on one side of the political spectrum only – for example in the Appendices of the National Union of Teachers' (1984) discussion document on peace education. The Conservative Government's own interventions in relation to peace education have indeed been made in an effort to counter such imbalances (*Times Educational Supplement*, 5.3.84).

In areas other than peace education – in political education, for instance – materials have been more sensitively produced (but then the latter has a longer, more sustained tradition of development). Clearly, until more sophisticated learning materials are available which enable pupils to engage actively with a wide range of contrasting positions and opinions and which therefore match up to the non-partisan ends proclaimed by Hicks (1983), the responsibility for balance and open-endedness will rest heavily (as in some measures it always will) on the shoulders of the teacher. This has serious implications for teachers' approaches to and handling of social and political values, both in formulating course policy with colleagues, and in teaching the material that arises from it in the classroom.

For both the school and department, the inclusion or exclusion of programmes of anti-racism or anti-sexism, for example, entails social and political judgements, choices and biases which may be difficult to defend against those who subscribe to different social and political values. Nor can these difficult matters of judgement and choice be justifiably avoided by dealing only with uncontroversial and apparently value-free topics: with First Aid rather than 'Band Aid', for example. For this would only result in a bland, *lowest-common-denominator* course: one which would misrepresent the central purpose of personal and social education as a 'planned educational development related to self, others and society' (Elliott and Pring, 1975). Consequently, PSE taught courses call for teachers (and pupils) to engage in a continuous process of self-evaluation, of analysing their biases and their representations of a range of views and opinions.

Much the same applies in the classroom. Where controversy abounds, a position of absolute neutrality, as adopted in the *Humanities Curriculum Project* (Rudduck, 1986), might initially be an attractive option for teachers. But the failure to state or reveal views under any circumstances can dehumanise teachers, make their position look false or contrived, give them the awesome appearance of a 'praying mantis', as one teacher described the neutrality stance (Gleeson, 1979), and undermine the closeness of the teacher–pupil relationship on which effective PSE depends. Pupils are quick to detect false statements from staff; to detect pretension, insincerity or anxiety in their teacher.

Perhaps the wisest advice here is that, in general, all staff and pupils should have the freedom to state their own views if they wish, but not be compelled to do so, and that no one should coerce or browbeat anyone else into accepting a particular point of view. In this respect, we agree with Sir Keith Joseph's statement that the teacher

> ... cannot afford to allow his political issues to influence his presentation of other people's ideas. He has to be more careful in his choice of words and in his whole presentation than he would be in dealing with his fellow adults. If asked by his pupils for his own views, he should as appropriate, declare where he himself stands but explain at the same time that others ... may disagree with him. He should explain that such disagreements are legitimate given the complexity and value-laden nature of the issues and that pupils need to weigh the evidence and considerations for themselves and try to reach their own opinions, respecting as they do so, the contrary opinions of others.
>
> (Joseph 1984, quoted in Marks, 1985: 3)

Even so, it is dangerous and impractical to be too doctrinaire and inflexible when making recommendations about balance, fairness and impartiality. There is no single practice, no unarguably consistent way of teaching controversial issues, that these broad principles necessarily entail. Procedural neutrality of the *Humanities Curriculum Project* sort, where the teacher holds back from supporting or criticising any of the views being put forward by pupils in the classroom, may not be advisable as a general teaching strategy, but might be useful in the early stages of discussion in order to 'flush out' the widest possible range of opinions from a class. At other times, a more active kind of neutrality – what Bridges (1986) calls affirmative neutrality – might be a more appropriate stance to adopt. Here, different sides of a question can be presented by the teacher with an equal enthusiasm and commitment. Although this approach can run the risk of overloading students with too much information, it can be valuable where some views have not occurred spontaneously to class members and where the more passive stance of teacher neutrality might lead to bias by omission. On yet other occasions, the initial presentation by the teacher of a singular committed stance (be it genuine or contrived) on some controversial issue might be justified either as a way of counter-balancing views that are dominant and perhaps even over-represented in the mass media and other areas of pupils' experience outside school, or simply as a way of generating interest on a topic about which students might initially be somewhat apathetic (Stradling *et al.*, 1984).

We therefore agree with Stradling and his colleagues (1984: 11), when they state that:

> It is simply not possible to lay down hard-and-fast rules about teaching controversial subject matter to be applied at all times. The teacher has to take account of the knowledge, values and experiences which the students bring with them into the classroom; the teaching methods which predominate in other lessons; the classroom climate . . . and the age and ability of the students . . . These different circumstances in the classroom require different methods and strategies.

Nonetheless, the guiding principle still holds that whatever methods are adopted, staff have a duty to encourage pupils to be aware that there are several standpoints, and to ensure that the manner in which these are put is disciplined and fair. This will also require that they are as objective and clear-headed as possible about the underlying assumptions on which they build and present their course. Biased practice is clearly bad practice – and in any area of teaching bad practice is not hard to find. But the identification of bad practice suggests the need for improvement. It does not constitute a case for removal of controversial subject matter from the curriculum.

4 Are controversial issues in PSE unnecessarily and dangerously presented in an emotional rather than a rational way?

Sir Keith Joseph, in his statement on peace education in schools, advised that 'the approach in the classroom should be rational and not emotional.' (Joseph 1984, in Marks, 1985: 3). In many respects this is sound advice; views should certainly not be influenced by an excessive degree of 'playing upon' children's guilt about Third World famine (Scruton, 1985: 33–34), or by the stimulation of excessive horror and fear of nuclear holocaust (Cox and Scruton, 1984: 26).

One of our arguments throughout this book is that where PSE is seen to have an exclusively affective rather than cognitive focus, it opens young people to the dangers of political manipulation by emotional means. Extensive opportunities for rational discussion in which a wide range of alternatives is made available is essential to the protection of intellectual independence and autonomy of judgement. But there are dangers of excess in the opposite direction too – of concentrating on rational discussion alone. Discussion and consideration of controversial issues without attention to feeling, to empathy and the like – and to all the teaching methods such as simulation, drama and group work that help develop these fundamental personal skills and qualities – simply becomes reduced to a rather arid, information-centred kind of social studies. Where rational discussion prevails to that extent, all that is personal and social about PSE disappears, and what we are left with is something that contributes no more to young people's political awareness and social development than the teaching of British Constitution. If children cannot be helped to 'feel' and develop concern about issues of great social importance, it is doubtful whether PSE is worth teaching at all.

PSE teaching should not, then, be emotional in the sense of manipulating social judgements by scaremongering, arousing excessive guilt, and so on. But it should contribute to the development of emotional awareness and social concern (in whatever political direction). Any dangers of one-sidedness that might follow from this should be adequately tempered by rational appraisal of alternative viewpoints, including ones of which the Secretary of State himself might personally disapprove (regarding morally justifiable breaches in the rule of law, for instance). It is the striking of such a balance between the rational and emotional aspects of PSE teaching that is most essential to the development of educationally sound classroom work.

Summary

To sum up: the difficulties encountered in teaching controversial issues highlight the centrality of values and the dangers of bias in PSE courses in general. Politics cannot be kept out of PSE courses, just as they cannot be kept out of most other areas of the curriculum. What matters is that they are handled in a sensitive and open way, in a context where teachers continuously discuss and reflect on their values with their colleagues, and guard against the *unwarranted* intrusion of such values into their treatment of and discussion with pupils. If PSE courses did not arouse political and social controversy they would not be worth doing – for choices, alternatives, personal decision-making and the discussion of desirable social futures are at the heart of this kind of work. This is the importance of PSE coursework and it demands the highest levels of teacher skill and sensitivity.

Teachers' skill and qualities

High quality pupil–teacher relationships are, of course, central to all successful teaching, but they are particularly crucial in PSE teaching. The PSE team therefore needs to be comprised of staff of the highest calibre in terms of classroom management, of being open, balanced and flexible, and of possessing authority without being authoritarian. The stance of a PSE teacher is not that of a conventional subject specialist who is often prone to see teaching as the transmission of knowledge and passing on of information. Rather, it is that of a partner who is in some measure sharing in the learning while continuing to hold ultimate responsibility for it.

We have already considered the kinds of skills required in handling politically controversial material, in avoiding bias while retaining a proper sense of human concern and involvement with the issues at hand. This, as we have seen, demands teachers who can recognise, reflect upon and discuss their own value commitments and guard against these exercising undue influence on their teaching. Equally, teachers of PSE will have to deal with and confront a whole range of difficult human emotions (Wakeman, 1984) and will therefore need to have faced and begun to come to terms with these themselves – with their own feelings about love, sexuality, birth, death, loss and prejudice, for instance (Wakeman, 1984; Prendergast and Prout, 1985). This calls for teachers of emotional maturity. Lastly, in addition to possession of political balance and emotional maturity, PSE teachers need to have a high degree of flexibility in the classroom – an ability to use methods such as role play, simulations, group discussion and a generally 'open' approach to their pupils. This is no mean job specification; it has powerful implications for initial and in-service training and for staff recruitment.

In *Teaching Quality*, the DES (1983) remark that

> Secondary teaching is not all subject based, and initial training and qualifications cannot provide an adequate preparation for the whole range of secondary school work. For example, teachers engaged in careers or remedial work . . . need to undertake these tasks not only on the basis of initial qualifications but after experience of teaching a specialist subject and preferably after post experience training. Work of this kind . . . (is) normally best shared among teachers with varied and appropriate specialist qualifications and experience.

We disagree with certain aspects of this view. While sharing the DES's apparent reservations that young teachers should not be thrust into emotionally difficult and politically sensitive areas in their first years of teaching, we also recognise that in-service training in this area is often not readily available and that staffing of PSE courses, as we shall see, is frequently done at short notice for pragmatic reasons more than anything else. Consequently, many teachers come to PSE coursework ill-prepared for the job. Indeed, it seems to us that there is a certain conflict in government policy which is urging the strengthening of subject-oriented teacher training while also encouraging the development of personal and social education. This means that schools have to find staff to teach PSE courses who have been trained as subject specialists, and who, along with their subject knowledge, may have picked up particular attitudes to teaching style, relationships with pupils etc, which are often associated with that subject (Barnes and Shemilt, 1974; A. Hargreaves, 1986, 1988b) and which may not be compatible with the kinds of approaches required in PSE.

This means, firstly, that some preparatory attention *should* be paid to this area of the teacher's work and the skills it requires in initial training (David, 1983: 37). Second, in-service provision should be more widely available to teachers of PSE courses. The local authority should have details of what is available, though Wakeman (1984: 61) lists voluntary organisations that also provide relevant training, and David (1983) presents some practical ideas for school-based in-service work. Third, given the shortcomings in both these kinds of support for teachers, much of the responsibility for staff development in this area will inevitably fall upon the school itself – on self-evaluation and review of the course as it runs, on regular team meetings to give support and deal with problems. In the short term, schools should ask themselves whether they have enough staff expertise and commitment to enable them to embark on a PSE course. If they do, they must be prepared to have to discuss, share and learn from the inevitable mistakes.

Staffing and recruitment

Given the rare personal qualities and skills that are evidently required of PSE teachers, clear staffing policies, and well-thought-out approaches to recruitment and selection are vital.

In PSE courses, as in most things, volunteers are normally to be preferred to conscripts. Yet staff often find their way on to PSE courses for reasons that have little to do with any special qualities they might have to offer to the area. Especially in schools where it is not a high priority, some recruits can be diverted to PSE simply because they are 'supernumaries' within the mainstream curriculum: redeployed teachers, teachers with 'gaps' on their timetable, 'Careers' teachers overtaken by broader PSE developments and so on (Baglin, 1984). This rather casual and random method of staffing is ill-suited to the creation of departmental coherence and should be avoided and resisted wherever possible.

Other teachers can find themselves co-opted into PSE coursework and sometimes into PSE coordination, as part of the job specification for another post – as deputy head or senior teacher, say (Rose, 1986). Again, such a policy usually reflects a weak commitment to PSE on the school's part and is not likely to assist the effectiveness of this area, since there is no guarantee that teachers interested in the 'main job' will also be committed to this part of the package. Again, the inclusion of coordination within much wider job specifications should be avoided if at all possible.

The recruitment of senior staff to PSE can be a mixed blessing. On the one hand, senior staff can bring to the PSE course those qualities of maturity and experience that are essential to good teaching in this area, and can, by their involvement, also enhance the course's status in the school. But the classroom atmosphere set by deputy heads in particular may not always be so benignly avuncular. Many deputy heads (pastoral) hold positions with ultimate responsibility for discipline and punishment. A reputation as the school's 'Mr Agit' among pupils (as one PSE Coordinator confessed to us) is hardly conducive to the development of open classroom relationships. The involvement of senior staff can also be resented by colleagues who may see their position of authority as inhibiting collective planning and discussion (Ribbins and Ribbins, 1986: 28). Moreover, senior teachers and deputies may be so involved with responsibilities in other areas of the school that they do not have the time to prepare fully, attend team meetings or take proper part in planning and review of the course. The attractions of involving senior staff in PSE course-work are clearly very powerful – they have experience, are often more than willing to give some of their time to this area, and, not least, have the necessary gaps in their timetable. But for the reasons we have mentioned, the possible costs of their involvement should be weighed carefully before a commitment is finally made.

Some staff move into PSE departments because of the area's perceived advantages for their own career development. Sometimes such teachers may be ones who have found their conventional career routes blocked or interrupted. They may be teachers with poor qualifications in mainstream subjects, for instance, who need to search for opportunities elsewhere. Or they may be prepared to give time to PSE in order to gain the head's favour and therefore a chance of promotion elsewhere in the school later on. At worst, movement into PSE can be an act of desperation by teachers who, like one or two of the teachers in the 'Newsom' department studied by Burgess (1983), have 'failed' in conventional career terms.

There are, then, real dangers in recruiting out-and-out careerists to PSE courses. This is not to frown upon career aspiration as such; only where teaching is exploited for career ends only. Career advancement is perfectly compatible with a more idealistic commitment to PSE. Indeed, the absence of a proper career structure and formal recognition of responsibility in PSE can weaken staff motivation, undermine the status of the area and deprive it of effective leadership.

Be it as co-ordinators or as ordinary classroom teachers, people who are willing to give their energy and loyalty to this area are a great asset to departments (Baglin, 1984). This is not to say that one should wait for such 'idealists' to volunteer. Senior staff can play a very useful part in 'spotting' colleagues who appear to have the appropriate skills, qualities and commitments, and in persuading them to join the course. Such idealism brings in with it all the advantages of innovatory enthusiasm and is therefore usually to be welcomed. But beware! If the course depends almost exclusively on a strong but solitary individual, it may go under if ever that particular member of staff leaves (and the more successful they are, the more likely it is they will do so). A broader basis of support in addition to the zeal of individual missionaries is therefore very much worth having.

To sum up: in some schools, the tendency has been to use the PSE course as little more than a device to fill up people's timetables, resulting sometimes in ill-assorted and unenthusiastic teachers, few of whom see the area as a major priority. Fortunately, this is by no means always the case and many schools do actively recruit people with the appropriate skills, qualities and experience, and give them sufficient support, reward and a clear departmental structure to get the job done effectively. The difference between these sorts of schools in staffing policy with all its implications for departmental effectiveness, usually reflects differences in the status and priority accorded to PSE within the curriculum. It is this issue of status we want to examine next.

Status

If PSE courses are to have any significant effect or usefulness, they must have status within the curriculum and be recognised by staff and pupils alike as a worthwhile part of school life. This is not easy when most of the activity in schools is directed towards conventional academic goals and when subjects derive their status from the scholastic success that their pupils achieve.

For historical, economic and political reasons, high status attaches to areas of learning and knowledge in schools that are academic, intellectual-cognitive, theoretical, easily examined and that lead to extensive quantities of written work or enumerated results on paper (Young, 1971; Apple, 1979; D. Hargreaves, 1982). New subjects seeking to establish themselves in the curriculum, it has been observed, must usually meet these criteria or perish (Goodson, 1983).

Right-wing critics of aspects of PSE like peace studies and world studies have argued for their exclusion from the curriculum on the grounds that they are not 'real subjects' and do not have a coherent intellectual discipline at their base (Cox and Scruton, 1984: 8, 27; Marks, 1985: 1; Scruton, 1985: 30). This seems to us a misplaced criticism for several reasons:

- few advocates of PSE themselves credit it with a 'subject' label;
- there is a legitimate place in the curriculum (as HMI (1977) recognise) for many aspects of learning that do not take the form of subjects as such;
- there are many other 'non-subjects' in the curriculum, such as information technology and, arguably, home economics, which have not been 'specially' picked out for exclusion in the way that PSE has;
- what comes to be accepted as a real subject is often more a matter of social judgement than philosophical purity – indeed the emergence of 'subjects' like geography and environmental studies was initially resisted on the grounds that they were not 'real' subjects and would take precious time in the curriculum away from those that were (Goodson, 1983).

The broad political charges levelled against the status and importance of PSE are, however, perhaps less significant than perceptions at school level by teachers and pupils alike that PSE, like Newsom studies before it, is 'not a real subject' (Burgess, 1984). It is at this level that PSE encounters its most serious difficulties in relation to other subjects. First, it does not meet the criteria of high status knowledge – of being academic, theoretical, written down or able to be assessed. Second, it intrudes upon and therefore threatens the identities of other subjects like social studies, humanities and biology. Third, by taking up curriculum space, it poses a potential threat to vested curriculum interests which may have to lose space or numbers as a result (Cooper, 1985). Last, it challenges existing styles of teaching and learning within high status subjects and may meet with suspicion and resistance as a result.

For these reasons, the establishment of a strong, coherent and widely recognised PSE course within a school is unlikely to be successful without the most powerful backing and leadership from the head – a vital point in the success of most departments (Ball and Lacey, 1980) – and without a measure of whole-school agreement on or recognition of the importance of personal and social development in the school's overall policies. If status is not achieved for the PSE course within the school, a number of undesirable consequences will follow that will impair its overall coherence and effectiveness. Even where there is such status, the following difficulties can still easily arise and should be headed off where possible.

Time and timetabling

Without full commitment from head and staff, PSE courses are likely to receive low priority in timetabling. This will have implications for the work that can be attempted in lesson time. Inconsiderate timetabling, especially where PSE is filled in last, can certainly undermine the hopes about what personal and social education could achieve. It is not easy to achieve tolerant group discussion with 28 fourth years – who are taught together in social and personal education because they are the bottom Maths set – during last period on a Friday after a double Maths lesson, especially if the lesson has to take place in one of the art rooms with scarcely enough chairs and certainly not enough working spaces! PSE calls for small groups in decent surroundings. Without such conditions it is arguable whether it is worth doing at all. Can these conditions be achieved? At what expense?

When the timetable is constructed, will PSE form part of the compulsory 'core' or will it appear on the options grid? If it is the latter, then it might be seen as a device for accommodating pupils who have made effectively no choice at all. This may be administratively convenient, but is it an effective way to introduce a new course? In other words, are pupils being offered a real choice or are they being allocated to the course by default? The designation of PSE as a 'low attainers'' option in this way, or even the provision of permission for 'able' pupils to 'drop' personal and social education in favour of taking an extra academic subject like a second language, only confirms the low status of the area. In these circumstances, lack of status is soon detected by pupils and staff alike and quickly undermines any positive work that is being done.

Apart from the arrangements for timetabling there is the more general question of how much time should be given to PSE. Too little can negate its whole purpose and make effective work almost impossible. Too much can lead to overkill. How much time is allocated will in part be affected by judgements about where it is to come from. If it is to be taken away from other departments this can cause bad feeling; their power and interests will be being threatened. Perhaps the whole timetable will have to be restructured, though this is clearly easier to achieve in a new school than a well-established one.

Space

The availability of suitable space and territory is as important to effective PSE work as it is to mainstream school subjects. 'New' subjects find trouble in establishing their own territory. This applies not only to rooms and furnishings but to cupboards, noticeboards etc. We know of one school, for instance, where the PSE department conducted a long and heated dispute with the mathematics department over the 'ownership' of a cupboard. Be prepared for resistance over these things.

Securing of space and territory brings with it a measure of identity and freedom to operate away from the eyes of suspicious colleagues. But it can also bring with it a set of rather less obvious difficulties in terms of isolation. Even where a PSE course has been established in a school after extensive staff discussions, the teachers involved may still not have the total support of their colleagues. They may have to work in an atmosphere of isolation and struggle; to meet challenges and criticisms about what they are doing. If this defensive position has to be taken, it can all too easily result in the creation of a 'charmed circle' of staff responsible for PSE who communicate only with each other within the protected confines of a separate department. Of course, many established departments also operate in this way – science teachers with their own coffee and kettle in the labs, for instance. But with a new department, isolation of this kind, be it chosen or imposed, can be a serious mistake. Informal communication with and acceptance by colleagues in the staffroom is vital to the PSE department's success in the school. In addition, involvement of other subjects wherever possible in the PSE department's own work will help reduce its isolation and also enhance its status and credibility in the school (ILEA, 1984: 62).

Resources

In addition to rooms and furnishings, a PSE course needs money for books, videos, speakers and other expenses. For these reasons, if PSE is to have the status of other departments it requires its own capitation. It should certainly not be funded on an *ad hoc* basis through the headteacher's patronage. Once resources have been allocated, relevant agencies will need to be contacted for materials. Useful lists of these are available in FEU (1980), Wakeman (1984) and Pring (1984).

Assessment

The British secondary school system is strongly geared towards maximising attainment in public examinations. This has been even more true since the 1980 Education Act required schools to publish their examination results, and it does not look as if the GCSE will immediately do anything to alleviate the pressure. In this kind of context, and especially in schools which prize achievements in examinations particularly highly, subjects and courses which do not culminate in an examination find it difficult to acquire status in the eyes of pupils, teachers, parents or the world at large. Any learning which does not easily fit into the examination mode tends to be seen as second rate and of lesser importance; it can be difficult for teachers faced with presenting PSE courses which are not examined to raise enthusiasm and commitment from staff and pupils alike.

If you want to get it recognised, get it assessed – this appears to be the general rule to follow within the secondary curriculum. Some have therefore recommended this route, albeit reluctantly, as the appropriate one for PSE, given the existing rules of subject status (eg ILEA, 1984). We can understand why some teachers feel pressed into adopting this strategy, but assessment by public examination seems to us entirely inappropriate to the whole character and purpose of PSE. Assessing PSE might confer more status upon it, but in doing so, it would, in the kind of work, attitudes and relationships it encouraged, take away much that was at the heart of work in this area. It would be a denial of PSE's identity and purpose. SOCIAL EDUCATION – FAILED is a kind of stigma no one should inflict upon a pupil. Other, more open-ended patterns of assessment (especially self-assessment) and recording seem to us to be better suited to the purpose and rationale of PSE (see Chapter 6).

Methods of working

Where schools are especially dominated by the pressures of examinations and therefore by examination-type work, PSE teachers might feel pressed to set similar kinds of work in their own classes – not least by the pupils themselves. Teachers here will have to face dilemmas concerning the use of folders, exercise books and written work. If no written work is set, will pupils take PSE seriously? Will they feel that they are really learning anything? If too much written work is set, is the subject fulfilling its aims any more?

Leadership and responsibility

The use of examinations and reliance upon extensive written work are strategies to which teachers resort in examination-dominated, academically-oriented schools where the status of PSE is depressed and needs to be raised. They are clearly strategies of desperation and ones which can threaten the whole character and purpose of PSE. Such strategies are no substitute for effective school leadership which is able to establish and gain acceptance for other educational goals and purposes alongside examination-centred, academic ones. Only where a clear, whole-school commitment to personal and social development is among the school's major aims, and where this is supported at the top, is recognition of – and effectiveness in – PSE courses possible. All other status-raising strategies are 'make-do'. Indeed, if a PSE course does not slot easily into the framework of the school or match its ethos, it will be potentially confusing to the pupils and may be a worthless or even counterproductive exercise. Effective and committed leadership is needed at departmental level, and this will require appropriate formal recognition in terms of incentive allowances.

Planning, involvement and review

It should now be clear that the status and effectiveness of PSE courses depends very much on how well they are integrated with the overall aims and purposes of the school and how far they are seen as being a central part of these. This has important implications for how and how well the PSE course is planned and developed. Full staff discussion is probably essential to the establishment of an effective course. It may be helpful to appoint a working party to consider detail, but unless the staff feel *au fait* with developments and informed about them, lack of communication can cause damaging breaches of understanding and trust. When a wide range of staff are involved in discussing the aims and purposes of the PSE course there will be a tendency to search for a lowest common denominator consensus in order to conceal differences, but, as we have already indicated, in avoiding controversy, these solutions will at the same time also avoid most that is central to personal and social development. Although it will understandably generate some tension and disagreements, the question of values must be faced and thrashed out if clear decisions and effective policies are to be made. This is a necessary part of successful implementation, but undoubtedly a stressful one. The most careful and sensitive management will be needed to handle and deal with the controversial value questions, the basic questions of educational purpose, without skirting around them. Rushing in with unwarranted haste or brushing past difficulties will only cause all manner of problems later.

Talking through course aims and objectives will lead to writing the syllabus – and clearly this should be done before the course begins! Of course there will be constant adjustment and modification to any PSE syllabus once it is underway, but thoughtful early planning will provide a full foundation for later changes. At this stage it is also worthwhile considering whether any pupils can be encouraged to participate in the planning.

With difficult questions of organisation and purpose to resolve, it is clearly important that there should, as far as possible, be *whole-school agreement* or involvement in deciding upon the answers. Is the course to be part of the core or should there be an element of choice? Are the groups to be tutor groups, mixed ability groups, groupings determined by another subject that PSE is set against, or what? How are the staff to be recruited? Should the department meet at the same time as other departments? How can this be arranged? Where will PSE appear on the timetable and how much time should it be given? Should PSE be examined? How much written work should be required? If these questions are thrashed out with the whole staff *before* the course begins, four vital purposes are served: a wide range of issues is fed into the planning process; the place of PSE within the curriculum as a whole is clearly identified; staff are educated about PSE by the very fact of their assisting in planning it; and commitment to PSE across the school is improved.

Once the course has been agreed, relevant people need to be informed about developments. Pupils need to be told very clearly what the PSE course entails; why they are taking it and what staff hope they may get out of it. So too do parents – a clear letter outlining the course's purpose and some of its content will forestall damaging gossip and rumour, as will opportunity for discussion on parents' evenings or on a more informal basis. Inclusion of some comment about work in PSE will also assist the process of communicating with parents and do no damage to the reputation and status of the PSE course either.

Evaluation

Broad involvement in the planning and development of the PSE course enhances its standing in the school. So too can evaluation of its effectiveness, but this is by no means guaranteed. Evaluation of the course can present serious dilemmas. If it is evaluated (by whom? for what purpose?), this may only highlight the difference between PSE and other departments, and attract criticism. If there is no evaluation, this may hinder the course's success.

Evaluation of personal development, in any respect, raises huge technical difficulties. The task of untangling the influence of a PSE course from all the other influences on young people, perhaps at some distance from the experience, is a daunting one. Having said that, however, teachers have always made informal judgements about the success (or otherwise) of their efforts to influence and develop pupils' attitudes and values. A more systematic process of evaluation, however imperfect, will almost certainly improve on this; provide a wider range of evidence to assist the process of course adjustment; and signal to colleagues that this new 'curricular experiment' is at least being subject to some measure of objective public scrutiny.

Even so, just *how* public any such scrutiny should be is a moot point. How much information about its work should the department share with other departments? If too little or too much, subject staff might well become overly critical and feel threatened. The 'hidden curriculum' messages passed on to pupils about PSE courses by sceptical staff can be very unhelpful; a balance has to be struck between over-exposing the PSE department so that every painful detail of its conception and birth is known to all, and not telling other staff enough so that they become intrigued about and suspicious of the mysteries!

Conclusion

This chapter has drawn attention to some of the issues which arise when a school is considering the introduction of a PSE course. One of the central themes of our argument has been that a course which is 'bolted on' to the school's existing curriculum is not the most appropriate way to provide pupils with PSE. Rather, the inclusion of PSE in the form of a taught, discrete course requires the most serious review of the school's policy and curriculum intentions as a whole. Pupils are inescapably exposed to values and attitudes in school in a concentrated and sustained way. Many schools have come to the conclusion that by establishing a course as part of a wider programme of personal and social development, proper attention can be paid to these responsibilities. By introducing topics and themes in a clear and organised way to pupils who understand fully the purpose of their PSE course, teachers can present lessons on controversial and delicate subjects with overall impartiality, declaring their own point of view, perhaps, but without imposing those opinions on others. Running a PSE course is obviously not a task for the timid. It requires teachers with determination and forethought and with the skills of persuasion and negotiation which they hope to replicate in their pupils. With high quality staffing, sound leadership, and a clear and recognised place in the overall aims and ethos of the school, such a course can be a most beneficial element of a pupil's secondary education.

3 Group tutorial work

Introduction

Few forms of PSE provision in schools are more contentious among teachers themselves than Group Tutorial Work (GTW). Public critics have attacked GTW as a rather insidious kind of social control – a way of keeping pupils in order by teaching them how to look after their school uniform properly, how to organise their homework and get it in on time, or how to relate civilly to people in authority, for instance. Others have regarded GTW as a damaging distraction from 'real learning', as a threat to academic standards posed by 'trendy' liberal preoccupations with 'personal growth'. In school staffrooms, though, the major concern among sceptical teachers is not so much with these sorts of issues, but with GTW's apparently bewildering nature. 'What are all these party games really about?' teachers sometimes wonder. Hand greeting, trust walks, making squares from bits of card – what possible educational purpose could be served by exercises like these?

Controversy is, of course, to be expected within any part of schooling that explicitly concerns itself with young people's personal and social development. For the desired nature of that development and of the society in which it is to take place is unavoidably and properly a matter of value judgement, and therefore of doubt and disagreement too. This is a point we stress throughout this book. In this respect, the contentious nature of GTW is no different from taught programmes of PSE of the kind we discussed in the previous chapter, for instance. But three further, more distinctive features of GTW give it a special note of added controversy: its unusual and demanding pedagogy; the scope of its impact across the school; and its openness to public inspection.

First, GTW involves not only the discussion of topics of personal and social relevance in form-tutor time, but the exploration of such themes in a particular way. GTW, that is to say, has its own pedagogy – extensive use of small group work and role play, maximum use of active pupil participation, involvement of visitors, and open-ended pursuit of small-scale 'action research' by pupils – a pedagogy which is much less common within a good deal of mainstream subject teaching. Where subject teachers become involved in GTW, this kind of pedagogy and all the changes it requires in their role, in their way of relating to pupils, can often generate feelings of suspicion, anxiety and hostility, much more so than any unfamiliar elements in GTW content. Moreover, the existence of an elaborate national training programme to develop teachers' expertise in GTW methods, and the fact that the training is itself broadly experiential in nature, serve only to highlight the strangeness and therefore the contentiousness of GTW.

A second factor contributing to the controversial status of GTW is the scope of its reach across the school staff. Neither confined to one subject department, nor to any one age group, GTW can often encompass almost an entire school staff, with or without their consent, as a matter of school policy. To be fair, GTW is not always as extensive as this, and is just as commonly adopted within one or two year groups broadly sympathetic to its approach. But where the involvement is much wider, where personal and social education is brought in from the sidelines and made part of almost every teacher's overall responsibility, few remain untouched by it. In these circumstances the probability of, and potential for, disagreement is significantly increased.

Third, there is the public nature of GTW. Its packaging in a set of carefully designed, lesson-by-lesson, year-by-year guides makes it open to comment and criticism even by those who scarcely do more than glance at the published schemes; by casual observers and staffroom cynics alike. As in Open University courses, once schemes are published and made widely available in this way, even mildly controversial elements are greatly magnified under the lens of public scrutiny. This places GTW practitioners under continuing pressure to explain and account for their practice, even to those with but a passing curiosity. Again, that kind of demand and routine pressure is much less common in the well-bounded confines of conventional subject teaching.

Yet if GTW arouses controversy among secondary school teachers, it also generates a quite remarkable degree of enthusiasm and support. In a recent evaluation of GTW, for instance, it was found that of 57 LEAs who felt 'able to estimate the use of GTW in schools', 33 reported that it was used in over a quarter of their secondary schools, and a dozen of those said it was used in more than half. Several LEAs, like Staffordshire and Berkshire, have indeed invested heavily in the development of tutorial work. Moreover, the national training courses were immensely popular among most of those who participated, not least because of their impact on the participants' own personal development (Bolam and Medlock, 1985).

GTW, then, creates loyal converts and supporters, yet also doubtful heretics and dissenters. It inspires, yet it also divides. Widespread in its impact, contentious in its implementation, GTW clearly constitutes a serious and substantial, but not uncontroversial, option for dealing with and developing PSE in schools. In this chapter, therefore, we want to examine the background to and purpose of this important development, along with some of the problems and pitfalls that might be encountered in its adoption.

Background and purpose

In his book *The Tutor*, Keith Blackburn (1975: 5) notes how, in some schools, the role of the tutor has for a long time amounted to little more than that of a register clerk – checking attendance, issuing timetables, collecting money for dinners and trips, handing out notes to parents and so on. Britain's most infamous adolescent diarist, Adrian Mole (age 13¾) would doubtless agree with him (and with more than a hint of resentment too).

Friday September 11th

> Had a long talk with Mr. Dock (new form tutor). I explained that I was a one-parent-family child with an unemployed bad-tempered father. Mr. Dock said he wouldn't care if I was the offspring of a black, lesbian, one-legged mother and an Arab, leprous, humpbacked-dwarf father so long as my essays were lucid, intelligent and unpretentious. So much for pastoral care!
>
> (Townsend, 1982: 110)

So much indeed! Mole's picture of pastoral care in the form tutor context is, of course, a fictitious caricature. But it is true that until relatively recently – the last decade or so – form tutoring has often been confined to discharging administrative and disciplinary duties with, perhaps, the dispensation of occasional 'emotional first aid' as circumstances demand. As the concept of tutors' broader pastoral responsibilities for pupils' all-round personal and social development has emerged and strengthened, however, and as more time has been allocated for these tutorial responsibilities to be carried out in many secondary schoools, this has in turn created a need for some kind of tutorial curriculum, a programme of work, something worthwhile to 'fill up the time' (Baldwin and Wells, 1981).

Blackburn (1975) was one of the first to outline such a programme, to be covered with the tutor group as a whole during form time. This programme, Blackburn suggested, should revolve around five main themes.

1   Orientation to the learning that pupils do in school
2   Issues that have arisen in pupils' experience in school
3   Issues that relate to the personal growth of pupils
4   Questions that will help the pupils towards choices of study in school and beyond, and of work
5   Ideas towards an understanding of their place in society.

(Blackburn, 1975: 60–61)

These themes, Blackburn continued, are not meant to be sequential, but are seen as 'aspects of pupils' experience that need to be covered each year in a way appropriate to their age' (p 61). Through this kind of programme, Blackburn claimed, not only would the personal and social development needs of the pupils be met, but the relationship between tutor and pupil, their mutual understanding, would also be improved.

Unlike some of his successors, who have produced quite specific and detailed materials for a sequence of tutorial sessions, Blackburn stuck to general guidelines and illustrative examples of the kinds of issues that might be raised in tutorial time, and the ways in which they might be introduced. But while there was guidance about suitable content for tutorial work, very little advice was given about pedagogy, save that discussion should be open, with 'pupils' opinions being listened to and treated seriously.' (p 79).

Prescriptions about pedagogy are not for the fainthearted. Whatever curriculum developers might say about content, pedagogical issues, discussions about how pupils should be taught and how teachers should relate to them, have traditionally been regarded as matters for the individual teacher's professional judgement. To intrude here has been to risk treading on the very foundations of teacher professionalism. There have, of course, been notable exceptions to this pedagogical taboo – most notably in the *Humanities Curriculum Project* with its advocacy of neutral chairmanship when dealing with controversial issues (see Chapter 1). The Schools Council *Integrated Science Project, Schools Council History, Geography for the Young School Leaver* – these and other innovations have also contained powerful recommendations about changes in teaching methodology to allow for more discovery-based learning. Interestingly, though, research evidence has consistently shown the capacity of teachers to resist the changes in pedagogy called for by these projects. They have embraced the new content, but not the new teaching method. In the Schools Council *Integrated Science Project*, teachers were not supposed to encourage revision or to teach from the board, but they did (Weston, 1979; Olson, 1982). In Schools Council History too, many teachers under pressure of time to get pupils through large quantities of material, have fallen back on more traditional didactic methods not recommended by the project (Scarth, 1987). And the first evaluation of the new GCSE again confirms the persisting ingenuity of teachers in adapting new curriculum projects to their existing pattern of teaching (Radnor, 1987).

In subject-based innovations of this kind, teachers can resist changes in teaching method and still achieve a good measure of classroom success. They have their content, their subject knowledge to fall back on. In tutorial programmes, however, the content is itself much less familiar. Indeed, we have heard teachers claim that there is scarcely any content at all. With no clear content to fall back on, the changes demanded in teaching method become all the more threatening, that much more difficult to avoid. The recommendations advanced for changes in teaching method in tutorial programmes, therefore, are more potent and more threatening than those that have been embodied in more subject-based innovations. Let us now look at some of these changes.

Douglas Hamblin (1978) proposed that tutorial work should be focused on a number of 'critical points' in a pupil's secondary school career, times of decision and change which are surrounded by uncertainty and anxiety such as induction into secondary school, subject option choice, preparation for exams, and so on. Hamblin recommended a structured developmental programme of activities and offered examples of the form it might take to help pupils cope with these crisis points.

It is, however, in the widely adopted work of Leslie Button and of the Lancashire-based Active Tutorial Work Project, that tutorial programmes have been developed in the most detail, and advice on pedagogy, on the teaching skills required is most specific. Moreover, in each case, the required changes in teaching skill and approach have been backed up with the force of intensive, experientially-based training programmes. Nothing could be a greater intrusion on teachers' pedagogical choices than this.

Leslie Button's approach to tutorial work is outlined most coherently and most systematically in his two published programmes on *Group Tutoring for the Form Teacher* (Button 1981, 1982). Here, Button sums up the central principles of what he calls *developmental group work* in schools.

> To be human is to be in relationship with other people. And in order to learn how to develop and maintain those relationships, a group of people must be available as an arena in which they can be learnt and practised. Developmental group work is a way of offering people opportunities for vital *experiences* with other people, through the membership of *supportive groups* who are learning to help one another in *personal* ways. It is *developmental and educative* as distinct from problem or crisis-based (note the difference here from Hamblin – eds). Our ambition is to help young people *build up their personal resources* so that they can *cope more adequately* with life – and its problems – as it comes along.
>
> (Button 1982 – our italics)

The essentials of developmental group work, then, are threefold. First, there is its long-term developmental character. Rather than being focused on particular crisis points, the content of Button's tutorial curriculum consists of a number of main themes – the pupil's place in school; the pastoral group as a small caring community; relationships, the self and social skills; communication skills; school work and study skills; academic guidance and careers education; health and hygiene and personal interests (Button, 1982: 3). These are repeatedly returned to, in a spiral curriculum of increasing sophistication, at various points in the pupil's school career. This is not to say that particular 'crisis points' like induction and option choice are not dealt with in Button's programme, but the emphasis is always at least as much on the developing nature of pupils' personal and social skills, competencies and awareness, as it is on resolving the particular problem in hand.

Second, there is the importance of small group support in which learning and development is to take place. With its roots in small group psychotherapy, developmental group work lays great store on the trust, security and support of the small group setting in which difficult emotions can be explored and discussed. In this sense, as Button (1982: 1) himself puts it, 'the methodologies upon which these programmes are based, are as important as the topics and materials included within them.'

This connects with a third principle of developmental group work – its 'active', experiential character. 'It is not enough', Button says, 'to offer a series of topics, since relationships and responsible attitudes need to be experienced and practised *rather than* to be talked about' (Button, 1982: 1). Through active involvement in a range of tutorial activities on a mainly small-group basis, developmental group work claims to encourage pupils to become more aware of and responsible for their own personal and social development. These active, experiential methods encompass a wide range of suggested techniques which include a particular form of hand-shaking or hand-greeting; various support and trust activities – including trust walks; rocking and catching in pairs; Socratic group discussions; brainstorming; role-play; receiving visitors; and undertaking action research.

Following a statement of these general principles of developmental group work, Button's two booklets – one for a first- and second-year programme; the other for years three, four and five – then set out a series of programmed activities (around 35–45 per year) in clear diagrammatic form to be undertaken with the tutor group. A large number of working papers for teachers to use and draw upon in relation to the tutorial programme are also provided in appendices to each book, made available for duplicating purposes.

The Lancashire-based Active Tutorial Work (ATW) Project bears many similarities to Button's developmental group work: not surprisingly, since Button was himself involved with the first major proponents of ATW, Jill Baldwin and Harry Wells, when tutorial programmes were first being developed and piloted in the county. This possibly explains the existence of certain striking similarities between the two schemes. There are, however, important points of difference between them. While Button's programme is bound within two volumes, the ATW programme is packaged in five booklets – one for each 11–16 year group – and a sixth, published in 1983, for the 16–19 age range. Like Button's booklets, the ATW consists of lesson-by-lesson teacher guides with linked worksheets in the appendices (also available for duplication). There is a slight difference in format though; Button's lesson guides being divided into two columns (one describing the programmes, one listing objectives and other comments) and the ATW ones being laid out in three rather more easily scanned boxes (pupil objectives, organisation and method).

In overall approach, again there are broad similarities. Baldwin and Wells (1981: xvii–xviii) explicitly endorse Button's belief in the importance of small groups in the tutorial setting. Equally, they place a good deal of emphasis on the active, experiential nature of the programme – not least in its title – with a similarly wide use of role play, trust exercises, action research and receiving of visitors. Like Button's programme, ATW also deals with a number of recurrent themes. However, while some of these relationships and social skills are much the same as Button's, others, particularly the focus on pupil self-assessment, are more distinctive to ATW.

While the National Directors of the ATW project feel, like Button, that the overall process of pupils' personal and social development and the developmental group work approach that underpins it lies at the heart of their work, the ATW books themselves are rather more topic-focused, with more of an emphasis on the daily life, events and problems faced in school. Certainly, this is how teachers perceive them (Bolam and Medlock, 1985: 50). In Button's scheme, there is more emphasis on the continuous development, growth and support of the caring group – making it somewhat less individualistic than its ATW counterpart. We shall pick up some of the implications of these differences later.

Notwithstanding these differences, though, the overall impact of tutorial programmes with an explicitly active and experiential thrust has, in recent years, been very substantial. Exactly *how* substantial is not known. However, although the national evaluation of the Lancashire-based ATW project indicated a wide take-up in many LEAs (even if this was often confined to the first and second years of secondary school), the exact extent of provision of other tutorial schemes like Hamblin's or Button's or, just as importantly, of the numerous home-grown tutorial schemes which schools have developed and adapted themselves, is, as Marland (1985) tells us with some regret, not yet known. Research evidence is lacking.

What then, are the major issues facing those who develop and implement group tutorial programmes in schools; the choices of purpose and direction, the obstacles to successful implementation that they must face? It is to these issues that we turn next.

Questions of purpose and direction

A damaging distraction?

One criticism of GTW is that it lowers educational standards and brings about 'progressive', perhaps even permissive, tinkering with young people's emotions in school. Though this view is held by a not inconsiderable number of subject teachers who regard education as being centrally and almost exclusively concerned with the transmission of subject knowledge, it has also been committed to print in the pages of the *Sunday Telegraph* colour supplement. And how colourful GTW can be when subjected to sarcastic caricature!

Writing in the supplement, Berwick Coates (1983), described as a history teacher and writer, accepts the need for 'caring' form tutors in large and impersonal comprehensives, but warns about the expansion of the welfare network – of counselling sessions, case conferences, social education, community service etc. – within the school system. 'All this,' he complains 'takes time out of a child's working week' when the child (particularly if able and well integrated) 'feels he could be better employed working for his O-levels.' 'No wonder,' Coates jibes, 'our standards of examination performance are going down'.

Coates' *bête noir* among these meddling distractions is the Active Tutorial Work Programme. 'I have seen these books', he writes, 'I am a teacher of 25 years' experience and they made my flesh creep.' He goes on to present a lurid caricature of ATW.

> This will take another hour a week out of the timetable, absorbing the child's mind with such topics as 'decision making' and 'whispered rumours'. Tutors are advised to get the children to pin labels on each other (literally), play soft music in the background 'to break the ice' and discuss terms used in sex education films (I leave the examples to your imagination). All this in 'groups' of course.

It is not difficult to undermine the credibility of something as unfamiliar to parents' own experience as ATW. Some well chosen stylised phrases ('whispered rumours'), a few examples of fragmented activity ripped out of context and juxtaposed as if they all occurred together, strategic deployment of sneer quotes, and appeals to a commonsense which the writer presumes his readers share ('I leave the examples to your imagination', 'all this in "groups", of course'); all these clever literary devices create just the right note of emotive repugnance. Who needs careful, rational appraisal, when parents' and teachers' emotions can be manipulated and mobilised with this kind of effectiveness?

Even if the judgement were expressed in more measured tones, however, it seems to us that it would still be an unfair one. For one thing, time taken up by ATW is usually very little – around an hour a week or less – and is often gained not by trimming back on the rest of the curriculum, but by reorganising lunch hours, assembly arrangements or other parts of the school day. Secondly, as the authors of the ATW books themselves point out, this kind of programme, like GTW generally, is not an intrusion on academic learning but a necessary prerequisite for it. Troubled, unhappy or emotionally preoccupied children do not make effective learners. Many of the activities pilloried by Coates have, on closer inspection, a perfectly rational justification: labels help with identification (as headteachers on large conferences know); games like 'whispered rumours' enhance the ability and willingness to listen, and so on. More than this, though Coates neglects to mention it, much of the ATW programme is in fact quite explicitly geared to the business of academic improvement, to the development of study skills and the like. There *are* controversial features of ATW, as we shall see, but a threat to academic standards it is not!

Politically conservative?

In contrast, a second criticism sometimes made of Group Tutorial Work is that it is shot through with elements of political conservatism. This does not mean that Group Tutorial Work peddles particular views about the nature of wealth creation, the virtues of free enterprise, or the importance of Victorian moral values, for instance. GTW certainly does not engage in that kind of blatant indoctrination.

The charges of political conservatism, rather, arise not from worries about any one view that GTW might be presenting, but from worries about its more subtle emphases on the kinds of behaviour and actions that are appropriate and (not least by their omission) inappropriate for people to adopt. This sort of criticism has been presented most clearly in an exploratory appraisal of the Lancashire-based ATW texts and lessons by Peter Foster (1985). After examining the texts and their objectives, Foster noted that there was

> an emphasis on individualism by objectives to develop individual self-knowledge, self-esteem, autonomy, *personal* values and beliefs, a *personal* philosophy, to maintain *individual* physical, emotional and mental well-being; to foster a belief in the individual's capacity to frame his/her own future, and influence social change. There was also an emphasis on realising *one's own* potential, on *individual achievement* through motivation, commitment, making appropriate *personal* decisions and developing appropriate academic and social skills. A second major emphasis was on the values of tolerance, empathy and mutual understanding, so it was thought important to encourage pupils to explore (uncritically) the values and beliefs of others, to empathise, to take on the perspectives of others, to withold hasty judgements, allow for differences of opinion and feelings, and to help others to cope with problems. Finally an emphasis on co-operation and responsibility was evident indicated by objectives to encourage co-operation with others in and responsibility to the tutorial group, ·care and responsibility in personal relationships, concern and care for the local community, and participation and responsibility for a future society.

The emphasis of the ATW texts and perhaps even more of Button's scheme is therefore very much upon coping and caring; listening and sharing. They centre on personal, individual issues or ones concerning the immediate small group, more than on social issues of a broader nature. They are concerned much more with adaptation than with change (especially where school matters are at issue), more with listening and tolerance than with assertiveness and challenge, more with reason and fairness than with those strategies – direct action, sanctions and the like – that are sometimes needed when powerful interests have to be confronted.

Our quarrel is not with the undoubted virtues of caring, reason, empathy etc, as such. Nor do we wish to suggest that the other kinds of skills and competencies we have raised – assertiveness, criticism and so on – are entirely neglected within tutorial programmes. The Lancashire Project's *Book Five*, for instance, makes use of a highly stimulating and provocative worksheet on the nature of work which makes reference to capital and labour, to questions about profits, who gets them and the consequence of that process, and so forth. It would be misleading to suggest, then, as some critics of similarly organised social and life skills programmes have done (eg Atkinson *et al*., 1982), that they amount to *nothing more* than an exercise in social control (Bates, 1984: 214).

Nevertheless, the socially more comfortable, less politically contentious emphases on personal and small group behaviour, on adjustment and self awareness, and on tolerance and empathy within GTW, are certainly the overridingly dominant ones. Since these programmes have their origins in small group psychology and psychotheraphy, and since they have been supported for an important period of their development by the Health Education Council, the presence of these kinds of emphases is very understandable. And where the rather more controversial kinds of skills, attitudes and understandings we have discussed are systematically provided for elsewhere in the curriculum, in taught Social Education Courses, for instance, then these emphases are, perhaps, justifiable.

But it is important to check first of all that these other complementary kinds of provision do indeed exist – hence the importance of integrating tutorial work into a whole-school policy for PSE. More than that, it is important to check that they exist for *all* pupils and not just for low attainers, or those involved in the TVEI programmes, for instance. If these more socially active, challenging and assertive competencies and skills are not provided for elsewhere, then individual tutors or groups of tutors in a year team or a school should ask whether their programme really ought to be adjusted and developed to take account of them. If the range and diversity of skills and understandings is not expanded in this way, then those programmes, by emphasising only skills and understandings of a 'safer' nature, might well be open to charges of implicit political bias by omission.

Middle-class bias?

There is a second possible source of bias in some aspects of GTW, about which teachers need to be especially vigilant. The question underpinning this worry is this: are the skills, attitudes and ways of relating to people in GTW ones that everyone might agree are a vital part of *all* peoples' development, or are they characteristics which belong to or are typical of only *certain* groups – be these social class groups, ethnic groups or whatever? In other words, do GTW activities help produce better people? Do they foster more mature attitudes, better behaviour and more highly developed social skills? Or do they help create *particular types* of people, casting them in preferred human moulds?

Some aspects of Group Tutorial Work, it seems to us, can certainly be criticised in this way. As with many social and lifeskills programmes, some of the activities and methods seem designed less to develop generally agreed worthwhile human qualities, than to train pupils in the niceties and etiquette of polite middle-class society (Cohen, 1984). Take 'receiving visitors' as an example. Here, before visitors are invited, pupils are asked to prepare questions and to decide in advance the order in which they will be presented. All this, it is claimed, will 'offer them the opportunity for practising their social and conversational skills and developing these further' (Baldwin and Wells, 1981: xx).

The problem here is that this method of receiving visitors treats relationships as objects, to be reflected on, prepared for, manipulated. It drains them of any spontaneity or direct emotional engagement of the kind that is common in many working-class and ethnic minority communities. This might, of course, be appropriate for some occasions, when the circumstances are formal, when business agreements are to be transacted, when there may be a strategic need to be diplomatic or to manipulate the relationship to advantage. And indeed, in recent years, teachers of English have increasingly recognised the importance of adjusting the form of language, speech and overall communication to the context – formal, informal, informational, expressive etc – in which it is being used. But to elevate these principles of conversational preparation, rehearsal and personal distancing to some kind of general rule of overall conversational skill suitable for all occasions, is to try and squeeze young people into the manners and style of the middle-class drawing room or the Oxbridge College! It is to encourage a peculiar and worrying kind of duplicity; to bring about not self-realisation but self-suppression, to urge young people to publicise what in private they are not (Cohen, 1984).

All this, of course, implies a denial or rejection of the cultural inheritance of many working-class and ethnic minority children; of the kinds of speech and personal relationships, with all their spontaneity, that are central to their home and community life. In this respect, the difficulties arising from tutorial work return us to some of the age-old problems that have dogged the schooling of the working class and ethnic minorities for many years. We are now familiar with the experience of working-class children who, when confronted by the alien culture of the grammar school, either kicked against that culture or became estranged from the values and lifestyle of their family or community (Jackson and Marsden, 1962). We know that many ethnic minority and working-class pupils found the (often unnecessarily) elaborated styles of speech used in secondary school classrooms intimidatingly unfamiliar (Bernstein, 1967). Once profound research insights, these things are now scarcely more than educational clichés – and we perhaps like to think we have overcome the problems they highlight through comprehensive reorganisation, language policies across the curriculum or similar initiatives. But are we, in some of the new tutorial programmes, in danger of repeating some of these mistakes of recent educational history?

In an evaluation of a tutorial programme in an urban comprehensive school, John Quicke (1986) has found that, in some respects, it seemed to have been mounted to offset or compensate for perceived cultural or social deficiencies in the neighbourhood. Teachers had few positive comments to make about the neighbourhood. They believed that most of their pupils came from back-grounds which made them 'narrow' and restricted socially. They spoke of inward-looking cliques, family feuds, violence and conflict. It was against this background of alleged cultural deficit that the tutorial programme, with its apparently neutral focus on 'kids and their relationships' was launched (Quicke, 1986: 226).

Now, we do not want to romanticise the life of working-class or ethnic minority communities. We recognise that people in such communities often face serious social and economic difficulties – in employment, in housing, in the family budget, and so on. And this takes its toll on family life and child-rearing. But to view such cultures and communities only in terms of their problems, in terms of the things they lack, is to undermine the dignity, the humanity, and the integrity of the people who live within them. It is to adopt the standards of the colonial missionary, wanting to bring culture and civilisation to the 'primitive' tribes for whom he has been given pastoral responsibility. In the tutorial classroom, such a view can lead the teacher to neglect and thereby deny the considerable social skills and qualities that young people in such communities already possess.

Among these skills and qualities, within working-class communities, are open, direct, spontaneous and emotionally honest ways of communicating with and relating to one another. Practice in the skills of polite and considerate conversation, or introspective explorations of personal feelings in small groups, may be intended as ways of improving self awareness, and tolerance of and interest in others, that are valid for all young people, whatever their background. But education in such communicative arts – ones that would perhaps fit nicely into the *Guardian*-reading world of Posy Simmonds – can be experienced as alien and threatening to many children whose cultural backgrounds are different from their teachers. It is not as if such children do not already possess any skills of relating to and communicating with others. Rather, they possess different *styles* of communication and relationship which the tutorial programme is failing to recognise. To deny such skills and qualities is to deny the dignity of young people, to treat them as if they have nothing of social or cultural worth to bring to the classroom. What is asked of them in tutorial classes therefore also runs powerfully against the existing cultural grain. This, in fact, may be one of the explanations for much of the pupil resistance to tutorial activities that teachers often encounter.

We are not, of course, suggesting that all or even most of GTW is beset by these difficulties. But important parts of the published programmes – such as hand-greeting, techniques for receiving visitors, particularly notions of friend-ship, or even attitudes to personal grooming – do strike us as vulnerable to these tendencies. We would suggest, therefore, that tutors become more sensitive towards the cultures from which their pupils come, and more aware of some of the positive strengths of those cultures. Such multicultural understand-ing should, of course, apply to class cultures and ethnic minority cultures alike. Information and insight of this kind is more likely to come to light when teachers have timetabled individual discussions with their pupils, when the pupils themselves are given considerable opportunity to take the initiative and talk about things of value and importance to them. Records of achievement, which we shall discuss in Chapter 6, provide for this kind of opportunity and can, along with their many other advantages, be helpful in raising teachers' cultural awareness about the backgrounds and communities of their pupils which goes beyond stereotyped notions of deficiency and disorganisation. Once teachers have developed a more appreciative stance towards the cultural background of their pupils, and towards the patterns of relationship and communication with which their pupils are already familiar, then the existence of middle-class cultural bias in tutorial programmes will be easier to detect, and those programmes can then be reviewed and perhaps amended accordingly.

An invasion of privacy?

Another fundamental question that those using tutorial programmes need to consider is how far all individual pupils shall be expected or compelled to participate. One difficulty with GTW is that it often treads on areas of great personal and emotional sensitivity and as a result can sometimes be experienced by pupils as threatening, intimidating or embarrassing. Of course, risks of this kind are inevitable in any programme that wishes to deal meaningfully and effectively (ie through experience) with the whole area of personal and social relationships and the development of self-awareness in young people. But this principle, important as it is, provides no ultimate warrant for intruding upon personal feelings or exposing private emotions regardless of how preciously the child may wish to protect them. Here, Berwick Coates (1983), in his critique of ATW, has a sound point to make, even if it is somewhat overstated.

> The reformers seem to have forgotten that a child has a sense of privacy. With all this 'frank' discussions in groups . . . they have taken the therapist's couch out of the consulting room and dumped it in the classroom.

Elsewhere in society this kind of 'therapy', with its exposure and appraisal of feelings and emotions, is normally entered into voluntarily by the person undergoing it. Only among people committed to psychiatric institutions is the process compulsory. When such matters as friendship, isolation, bodily hygiene and so on, are being discussed, teachers need to give serious consideration to children's rights to withdraw from the discussion.

To be fair, the ATW authors do offer constructive guidance on this matter at various points. In a section on friendship, for instance, Baldwin and Wells (1981: 73) note that 'many teachers feel that to highlight a pupil's isolation by discussing friendship in the manner suggested here, is unkind and counterproductive.' They mention the need to attend to matters of confidentiality and to the supportive atmosphere of the group. But, at the end of the day, they firmly advise that 'it is necessary to look for ways in which an "isolated" pupil can be helped to become less "isolated".' In our view, while this advice is well meant and put forward for the best possible reasons – the improvement of children's personal happiness and well-being by stressing ways of engineering pupil involvement – it does underemphasise children's rights to be protected against unwanted emotional exposure and intrusion. It draws attention away from the need to respect pupils' personal privacy; a fundamental human right.

In our view, then, in the most sensitive parts of their tutorial schemes, teachers would do well to consider whether there are indeed dangers of infringing pupils' rights of personal privacy and whether, if this is the case, individual pupils ought at these points to be informed and reminded of their rights to withdraw and be allowed to get on with something else, if they wish.

Above appraisal and beyond reproach?

Given all these uncertainties and differences of opinion about the direction and purpose of tutorial work, it is clearly essential that programmes should be subjected to the most careful and scrupulous rational appraisal at all levels of their development and implementation – in the individual classroom, the year group, and the school as a whole; in the training courses and in the booklets themselves. Yet according to Bolam and Medlock's (1985) evaluation of ATW, that kind of rational appraisal has, to date, been in rather short supply.

The training courses for ATW are, perhaps rightly, strongly experiential in focus. The course participants engage in ATW activities, receive visitors and so on, to get a 'feel' for the method and its potential and, not least, to appreciate the opportunities it provides for their own personal development and growing self-awareness. Where a very different and unfamiliar approach to teaching has to be grasped, new skills have to be acquired, and changed perceptions of the kind of teacher one is, perhaps confronted for the first time; then all this is surely better than merely lecturing to teachers about the purported benefits of tutorial work. Emotional shifts are rarely secured by mere instruction.

Notwithstanding the undeniable advantages of this method, has the emotional, experiential approach perhaps been emphasised too much? In some respects, the training methods of GTW are perhaps more akin to a process of emotionally charged religious conversion than one of rational persuasion. Many religious conversion movements geared to engineering a shift in people's fundamental beliefs, provide a programme of intensive experience in a socially isolated environment, cut off from the rest of the community. Here, through activities and social processes which generate a good deal of self-doubt and personal insecurity, and weakened by the exhausting and demanding nature of the whole programme, people become unhooked from their present beliefs and emotional commitments. Then, in an environment of small-group support and interpersonal trust, they are slowly nurtured into the new beliefs and social certainties which they now seek. Many of these characteristics of religious conversion would apply equally well to GTW training. With these sorts of semi-religious overtones, it is little wonder that GTW can often be a divisive force in staffrooms (Bolam and Medlock, 1985: 63) – creating passionate communities of believers and non-believers.

In raising these doubts, we are not arguing for the abandonment of experiential methods in the training process – it *is* important to grasp directly the special nature of GTW and to be able to do this in a constructive environment of trust and support. We do worry, though, that without equal credence being given to processes of rational discussion and appraisal, the training process can amount to an irrational manipulation of teachers' emotions, dividing them into warring factions of believers and non-believers, and placing GTW in the somewhat arrogant position of being above appraisal and beyond reproach.

At present, while some space is given to open discussion in GTW training programmes, the time for this is usually severely compressed and (in ironic contrast to the rest of the training), the discussion itself is often rather unstructured. As a result, Bolam and Medlock (1985: 21) found that in an introductory school course, 'the least successful activity was the question session at the very end of the course . . . owing to lack of time, the questions were limited in number and several course members did not get the opportunity to raise matters of significance to them'. Similarly after observing an LEA course, they concluded that 'some teachers would welcome a clear and coherent statement of the ATW approach, including its theoretical and curriculum underpinning, both for themselves and to explain to colleagues' (p 25). And even in the advanced national course, which dealt with trainers whose commitment to ATW was already very high, a minority still 'requested a coherent statement of ATW's rationale, less activity based methods in the advanced course and more written handouts' (p 32).

Where fundamental questions of values, purpose and direction of the kind we have discussed so far are at issue, it seems to us essential that the process of rational appraisal and discussion should be given much stronger loading within the GTW training process at all levels; that substantially more time should be allocated to it, and that it should be as tightly structured as the other experiential work, not just *permitting* questions and disagreements but, through well planned small group and plenary work, positively encouraging it. A better balance between the experiential (affective) and rational (cognitive) components of GTW training would lead to a more rationally defensible format, would deal effectively with any accusations of emotional brainwashing and would encourage teachers to consider thoroughly the values underpinning personal and social education in general. In-service work in tutorial methods has tended to adopt a *training* focus – transmission of information and practical experience in using a particular approach. We believe that in tutorial work, as elsewhere, such *training* should be supplemented by a broader process of in-service *education*, by which we mean the involvement of teachers in critically questioning and making autonomous judgements about the programmes to which they are being exposed. In an area of such high educational controversy, this seems a vital necessity if the dignity of the teacher's independent judgement is to be protected, and if unvocalised resistance and resentment are to be averted.

Problems of implementation

Following our discussion of overall purpose and direction, we now want to raise, rather more briefly, a number of problems that surround the actual implementation of GTW in schools.

Tutorial work, like many other kinds of PSE provision, is always susceptible to a certain kind of *'ghettoisation'* in secondary schools. By offering an identifiable space and time slot in which PSE can be delivered, tutorial time can all too easily come to be seen as the place where PSE has been 'covered'. Equally, even if PSE is consciously provided elsewhere too, it is important to make sure that GTW is carefully integrated with it, to ensure that there are no yawning gaps or large overlaps between them. In this sense it is important to relate GTW to the broader pastoral curriculum (Marland, 1985) and to whole-school policy on PSE.

This raises a second problem: that of *inconsistencies* between the kinds of relationships and patterns of learning to be found in GTW and those that pupils experience elsewhere in school. It is little use emphasising the virtues of care and respect for others in tutorial time, if the school's punishment system is draconian, if teachers are frequently sarcastic or unnecessarily abusive to children in class and so on (Pring, 1984). Similarly, as Bolam and Medlock (1985) found, pupils will very quickly become wise to any inconsistencies between tutorial work and ordinary subject teaching in your approach to them: hence the need, as the ATW National Directors themselves indicate, for 'active learning' methods to be fostered and applied throughout the whole curriculum and not just confined to tutorial time. Active learning across the curriculum has tended to supplant active methods in tutorial time alone as a focus for innovation and in-service training in recent years (FEU, 1982). This development has certainly been stimulated by the inauguration of the TVEI and the GCSE, but it is also a testimony to the influence and success of the active tutorial innovation itself. Whatever the reasons, the spread of active tutorial work into active learning as a whole, points yet again to the importance of establishing agreed whole-school policies for PSE of which tutorial work is but one part.

Whole-school discussion, or at least thorough consultation within the relevant year group, is also essential when ATW is being implemented. Its strangeness, compared to much conventional subject teaching, and its unusual openness to public appraisal because of the texts used, mean that GTW can easily arouse anxiety, suspicion and hostility among sceptical or unsympathetic colleagues. Widespread consultation and forewarning may head off possible conflict and other difficulties before they arise.

A related point here is that in order to gain maximum support, it may sometimes be best to implement GTW gradually, on a year team basis perhaps, and expand it slowly from there. This helps to ensure that maximum support is gained from a high number of sympathetic teachers at the outset – and that the likelihood of demonstrable success can then be proven early on.

Equally, it is both considerate and politic not to exclude staff who might have relevant expertise to offer – not to 'tread on their toes'. Many of the skills used in GTW are not unlike those that have been employed by English and drama teachers for many years. To take no account of this expertise would be not only to miss a valuable source of help, but to sow seeds for hostility later.

Not all teachers, however, already possess the very special skills that GTW demands of them. The comment overheard in one staffroom conversation that 'Oh, Active Tutorial Work's easy. I just put it up on the board then get on with marking their work', is perhaps unusual but it does point to the dangers of misinterpretation and misunderstanding of the scheme's intentions that may arise when teachers have not had access to relevant training. As the ATW project directors stress most emphatically, the texts themselves provide only a set of resources for ATW: it is the training, the development of new pedagogical skills that stands at the heart of their work. Many LEAs do offer relevant training and it might be worthwhile consulting the appropriate LEA Adviser about this before embarking on a new programme.

That the texts are not 'gospel', to be followed slavishly from beginning to end, is an important principle to remember. Schools should consider adapting the schemes to their own particular needs – as many schools currently do. They may feel, for instance, that the very sensitive and difficult-to-organise trust walks appear too early in Leslie Button's programme, and prefer to leave them until later. Schools should, however, be aware of the dangers of being overly selective – in particular of choosing only the safest activities (study skills, looking after uniforms etc) and omitting all those that make a substantial contribution to personal and social development.

All these new skills and unfamiliar activities together with the unusually tightly structured textbook format can give GTW an appearance of being contrived, 'forced' or artificial. This is of course true, but only if the base-line assumption is made that the remainder of classroom life is somehow 'natural' – and this, with its element of compulsion, of teacher domination, of a pattern of questioning where the answers are usually already known, it clearly is *not*! In that sense, perhaps, it takes one contrivance to neutralise the effects of another. Even so, whatever the merits of the justification, GTW can still seem odd or unusual not only to other staff but also to pupils too – not 'real work' at all. Tutors must therefore be prepared to encounter a certain amount of resistance (small group work provides a good 'cover' for unofficial activity) and to consider the necessity of explaining the purpose and rationale of the work to their tutor group.

Unusual as they are, though, the innovatory methods of tutorial work can wear thin after a while. Many good things in education are effective because they are exceptions; a bit different from the mainstream. Use them too much and they lose their special value. They suffer from overkill and become as ordinary and routine as the systems they were intended to replace. 'Oh no! Not *more* worksheets/group discussions/roleplay!' Teachers, then, need to beware of tutorial fatigue among their group. Continual variations in teaching and learning methods are important if this is to be avoided. More than this, if schools find that pupils really are finding tutorial work something of a dreary routine by Year 3, say, then a change of format, to a specialist taught programme, perhaps, might well be worthwhile.

Conclusion

Group Tutorial Work has the considerable advantage of getting almost all teachers in a secondary school to recognise and take some responsibility for the personal and social development of their pupils. Organisationally, it can also be spread more easily across the age range than can the specialist taught programme. Most importantly of all, the development of Group Tutorial Work has been accompanied by an impressive, elaborate, and, in many ways, effective training structure, giving teachers valuable practical experience and much-needed professional support as they take on and develop the difficult skills that this unfamiliar area demands of them.

When so many teachers are brought in to teach an area as new and unfamiliar as this, anxiety, scepticism, lowered commitment and resistance are all to be expected. Intensive programmes of training and support of the kind we have described can alleviate some of these difficulties, but only if these programmes recognise the existing professional competence and judgement of the teachers who are to be trained. Not all teachers who object to or are diffident about Group Tutorial Work are entrenched diehards. Many of their doubts and objections are highly rational and should be taken seriously.

This means, first, that proponents of GTW should not exaggerate its novelty. The experience and expertise that many teachers already have in some of the allegedly new teaching and learning methods like simulation, role play, or drama games, within their own subjects, should be recognised and built upon. Second, it means that opportunities should be created for teachers to voice rational objections to aspects of GTW, or even to the rationale of GTW as a whole. The dignity of their independent professional judgement should be recognised. In part, this can certainly help teachers concerned by creating opportunities for misconceptions to be corrected and doubts to be shared. It can also help the scheme itself, exposing major and minor areas of difficulty, and encouraging constant review and renewal from the bottom up.

The encouragement of rational appraisal is especially important given the susceptibility of some of the processes within GTW to cultural bias. That bias makes GTW vulnerable to charges of indoctrination. It can also be a source of resistance among pupils attached to different values and cultures than those being implicitly promoted by the GTW programme. Vigilance about such bias will be more likely if there is a more general climate of acceptance of rational appraisal of GTW among the teachers involved. This reinforces our recurring point about the importance of staff continually discussing their own values in relation to PSE.

As long as the sorts of bias we have described are continuially monitored within a general climate of rigorous and rational appraisal and review, GTW can make a highly valuable contribution to pupils' personal and social development– especially where that programme is effectively integrated into the PSE provision for the school as a whole.

4 Outdoor and residential education

Outdoor and residential education (ORE), school journeys and camps, youth hostel visits and the like are not new to the secondary school. From the beginning of the century, the value of activities, camps and courses at Outdoor Education Centres has long been recognised as an important recreational addition to (or diversion from) the main curriculum. But it is only now, with the growth of personal and social education in secondary schools, that the distinctive contribution of some kind of outdoor and residential experience to a young person's development is coming to be fully appreciated. It is this aspect of ORE – its contribution to personal and social development – that we shall be considering in this chapter. Before we examine these personal and social aspects in detail, though, a few words about the general context and character of ORE might be helpful, especially for those teachers who have so far had little direct contact with this type of educational experience.

The term *Outdoor and Residential Education* is an imprecise and all-encompassing one. It covers not one, but many kinds of educational activity and experience. It can refer to subject specialist field studies of the kind already offered in many courses of history, geography, biology and the like; to rugged, demanding programmes of outdoor pursuits; or simply to 'holidays', 'trips' and 'visits' (activity-based or otherwise) thought to be good in themselves. The National Association for Outdoor Education draws together all these different possibilities when it defines outdoor education as:

> . . . a means of approaching educational objectives through guided experience in the outdoors, using as learning material the resources of the countryside and coastline
>
> (NAOE, 1984: 17)

Equally generally, in a supplement to their discussion document *Curriculum 11–16*, Her Majesty's Inspectorate (1977) argue that oudoor education covers most educational activities concerned with living, moving and learning out of doors.

These official definitions of ORE are indeed very broad – too much so, perhaps. Even so, they do effectively make the point that ORE is not just another subject, but rather a medium for an approach to learning and personal development that can be applied to virtually every subject or area of educational experience (aesthetic, scientific, social, physical and so on) right across the secondary school curriculum (NAOE, 1984; HMI, 1983; Mortlock, 1973).

Working within these broad aims, the Schools Council Geography Committee attempted to specify more precisely what it took to be four main objectives for outdoor education. These, it stressed, may either be pursued separately or in combination: they are not a package but a range of possibilities.

1   Physical involvement in a journey by land, sea or underground for leisure or adventure. This may foster the particular skills that are necessary for the journey, the discovery of personal attributes such as courage and determination, the development of social attitudes and of the ability to be self-sufficient or to cooperate with other people.
2   The development of social relationships through pupils' living and working together in small groups in new or unusual situations. The exploration of relationships is most significant when the group is involved in an expedition requiring an overnight stay and is responsible for determining its own progress.
3   Investigative studies or fieldwork. Such studies are almost bound to be closely linked to the curriculum (often . . . to examination requirements) . . .
4   The development of an appreciation of the environment and a care and concern for its proper maintenance.

(Schools Council, 1980: 3–4)

These four aspects – which appeal to notions of adventure, community living, concrete investigation and environmental awareness respectively – usefully clarify the *range* of work that can be embraced by ORE. At the same time, their very diversity raises important questions about the whole identity and focus of the area. Is ORE at best a device for giving some experiential support to conventional school subjects (fieldwork), at worst, perhaps, a rest or diversion from them (school 'trips')? Or does it, over and above these things, have a definite and distinctive contribution to make to pupils' personal and social development? And if it can do this, how can it be organised to ensure that these important educational aims are indeed met? Are the experiences of community living the most vital aspects of ORE, for instance? Or is it the adventure component, with its elements of intense personal challenge, that is most likely to foster personal and social development? Does it *matter*, in other words, *what kind* of outdoor and residential experience pupils get?

Whatever the purpose of any particular programme of ORE, be it explicitly directed to personal and social ends or not, most teachers who have been involved with it appear to agree that personal and social benefits rank among the most significant gains of this kind of work (Schools Council, 1980, 1983). On the face of it, there are indeed many good arguments in favour of extended visits and residential experiences. Such experiences provide opportunities for teachers and students to work together in a more 'natural' and sustained way than the conventional school day normally allows. Unpunctuated by school bells, by the arbitrary stops and starts of the school timetable, and the fragmented and somewhat artificial forms of contact this creates between teachers and pupils, residential experience makes it possible to build closer relationships, to relax those patterns of distance and impersonal authority that characterise many secondary school classrooms, to allow teachers and pupils to glimpse hitherto unrecognised aspects of each others' personalities. In short, in the residential setting, teachers and pupils can each become that little bit more 'human' to one another.

> 'I like (my teacher) now, I feel I've got to know her more.'[1]

> 'I didn't think my teacher would have joined in like she did.'

Add to this residential experience an outdoor setting and you have a relatively insulated environment, far from school, almost custom-designed to provide an extended period of sustained human contact, along with a sense of real physical and social (rather than contrived, academic) challenge. At its best, this combination of outdoor and residential education can inspire pupils with a renewed or newly found sense of their own worth and capabilities.

> 'Before I went, I was pretty shy. Now I ain't. I can stand up to people.'

> 'I believe in myself more. I feel more confident.'

> 'I feel more confident. I know I can get along without being surrounded by friends.'

> 'I feel I have less to prove. I'm more confident and I can take the teasing.'

Pupils can also learn to support and cooperate with their peers more by sharing real tasks and challenges.

> 'Instead of shouting at each other, we worked it out together and got it right in the end.'

> 'You can't divide people into "O" level and "CSE" when you're climbing. You just have to ask for help.'

> 'I feel some barriers have broken down. There was bad feeling before. The boys used to call us snobs and creeps but now we talk much more and get along better'.

The sense of achievement, personal awareness and group belonging can often carry through into school, helping pupils to see their school experience in a more positive, constructive light.

> 'I'm trying to stick at school.'
>
> (Malcolm – a persistent truant)

There are, of course, pitfalls in organising and presenting ORE in an educationally worthwhile way, as we shall see in due course; but there are also strong and frequently cited arguments in support of ORE as an important contributor to pupils' personal and social development. The rest of this chapter is therefore devoted to an evaluation of ORE. Following a brief account of its origins and of the kinds of outdoor and residential provision that are currently available, we look closely not just at some of the practical problems to be overcome in planning and presenting ORE (problems of implementation, so to speak), but also at some of those central values like 'challenge' and 'adventure' that underpin the whole area. Though the worth and success of ORE often seems obvious to those who have been involved with it, it is as well to remember that here, just as in any other area of personal and social education, major choices and decisions about desirable personal and social qualities are being made – and these should not be regarded as self-evidently 'good' but be subjected to careful appraisal. Before that task is undertaken, though, we need to sketch in some of the background to the development and range of ORE, so that we will then know just what kinds of experiences are in fact being appraised.

Background

For many experienced secondary teachers, ORE will have associations not so much with modern comprehensive education but with older traditions of secondary modern schooling. In 1963, the Newsom Report, *Half Our Future*, dealing with pupils of average and less than average ability, drew attention to the particular value that camps, expeditions and residential courses might have. The report confirmed the conviction of many teachers that these activities provided opportunities for general educational stimulus, personal and social development and closer teacher–pupil relationships, and were of special significance for the disadvantaged. It suggested that such experiences should be extended to a much larger number of pupils, especially adolescents.

Given this post-war development of ORE as part of the secondary modern experience, it is interesting that ORE has even more long-standing associations with a very different and much more socially exclusive group of young people: fee-paying public school boys; the children of the wealthy. Many of the existing principles of ORE have their origins in, and can be traced back to, the Outward Bound movement, a movement which was created mainly as a result of the efforts of the exiled German educationalist, Kurt Hahn, the founder of Gordonstoun Public School in 1934.[2]

Like Reddie, the founder and headmaster of Abbotsholm Public School, Hahn aimed to provide an all-round education which valued the moral, physical and social development of his pupils, as well as the intellectual aspects. He considered that the boarding school environment provided the ideal situation in which this would take place. Such aims are still recognised in many public schools today.

Hahn was impressed by the principle of education being a training of character rather than intellect. He was also interested in the prefect system which emphasised the older pupils' responsibility for the welfare of younger ones. The idea of the school as a community in which each contributed to the wellbeing of the whole was to become the basis of Hahn's educational philosophy. In these matters, Hahn was not unlike his other public school colleagues. Where he differed from them was in his views on adolescence. For Hahn, the problems of adolescence were not an inescapable part of a young person's development. Many of them, he felt, could be avoided if only pupils could be correctly motivated. An integral part of this motivational strategy was adventure, physical challenge and outdoor experience.

With these principles in mind, Hahn founded Salem school in Germany in 1919, placing physical exercise and practical work in the community at the centre of the school's life. Through adventure and challenge, Hahn hoped the pupils would gain 'the experience of defeating their own defeatism' (James, 1957: 1). Training programmes included athletics, expeditions, projects and rescue services. Hahn felt strongly that the opportunities enjoyed by a fortunate few at Gordonstoun should be available to all young people, and in cooperation with Laurence Holt, he opened the first Outward Bound school in 1940.

By 1949, the 'Outward Bound idea' was crystallising and the following principles were published:

> the schools must be residential and the courses must last for a minimum of four weeks. They must be open to all, based on a spiritual foundation, and must contain a diversity of occupations and nationalities, without political and sectional bias. They must present each boy (sic) with a set of conditions and give him, possibly for the first time, the opportunity to discover himself. They must endeavour to develop character through training with a vocation or other practical interest.
>
> (James, 1957: 25)

Many of the current aims of ORE, then, to do with adventure, challenge, the development of 'character' and so on, have their roots very much in the public school tradition.

In some ways, this might strike people as a curious development. Yet there is a common thread running through the growth of ORE, first in public schools, then later among low attainers in the state system. ORE in the private sector was indeed targeted at socially-privileged groups, but in Hahn's day, while academic credentials and university entrance were certainly important for many of these young people, they were by no means always essential. Jobs in finance or family business, established through personal connections and 'the old school tie' were always available to many, and private schools could therefore afford to place the personal and social virtues of 'character' and 'leadership' high among their aims and achievements. In important respects, therefore, many public school pupils were able to 'stand above' the race for educational qualifications in which their bright, state-educated counterparts had to compete. Character, leadership and other personal qualities were educational luxuries the private system could well afford.

By contrast, if the privately educated stood above the scramble for educational qualifications, those low-attaining pupils who were the subject of the Newsom Report in many respects lay below it. These were the pupils on whom much of the débris of the academically-dominated state secondary system fell. They got less well-qualified teachers, inferior resources and lower expectations (Banks, 1955). Many responded in predictable ways: lower motivation, behavioural disruption, resistance and resentment. Such was the atmosphere in many of the lower streams of secondary modern schools in the 1960s (D. Hargreaves, 1967; Willis, 1977; Woods, 1979). Newsom aimed to combat this and the Report's suggestion for providing residential experience was just one way of making available other kinds of achievement to low-attaining pupils, and thus making them more motivated (and more manageable!) too (CACE, 1963: para 156).

Public school pupils are now being drawn more into the academic mainstream; they are having to compete more and more with their state-educated counterparts for the qualifications that will give them access to the new prestigious posts in high technology business and commerce, and less and less emphasis is placed on character and leadership (Salter and Tapper, 1983; Walford, 1985). It is ironic that it is at just this time that the 'character-forming' experience of ORE is expanding most rapidly among special groups of pupils which tend to exclude the highest attainers: TVEI pupils, pupils in the Government Lower Attaining Pupils Project, young offenders and young people on Youth Training Programmes. These separate forms of provision, often for socially 'at risk' groups, are certainly far removed from that comprehensive vision of universality or common entitlement outlined by Hahn. In our view, these current emphases are regrettable. The enhancement of personal and social development is surely a right of all pupils, even and perhaps especially the most academic, not least because of the power and influence they are likely to gain and exercise in adulthood. That entitlement, we believe, is as essential to ORE as it is to any other area of personal and social education.

The precise influence of the Outward Bound Movement, or of major education reports like Newsom, on the growth of ORE over the past 25 years or so is difficult to trace without further research – but growth there has certainly been. According to Her Majesty's Inspectorate (1983: 3), in 1960 (before the publication of the Newsom Report) there were only two or three LEA residential centres for outdoor activities. Yet a report by the Countryside Commission (1980) indicated that by the late 1970s there were 364 such centres. If the number of field study and outdoor pursuits centres used (but not owned) by LEAs is added to this figure, there were well over a thousand centres in operation by this time (and this excludes the facilities provided by independent, voluntary organisations such as the Youth Hostels Association). Expansion seems to have been very rapid indeed. Yet even these large numbers exclude all the huts, cottages and the like acquired by many individual schools over the years.

Looking across the whole range of current provision, it is hard not to feel that while provision is widespread, it is also patchy and fragmented – confusing to the consumer and difficult to monitor and control to ensure that adequate standards are being maintained. Without such coordination and control, there are real dangers that the broad market economy of ORE provision will, just like the uncontrolled market economy of Victorian times, have damaging and despoiling effects on the environment. The Countryside Commission (1980) recognises this and is becoming increasingly concerned about the proper use of the National Parks; the overuse of certain areas and the pressure placed on rural communities (see also Sandford, 1974). Concern has also been expressed about standards of instruction and safety being maintained when very large numbers are involved. The ideal of ORE being a part of every child's educational experience clearly poses considerable problems of access and conservation if it is to be achieved. For environmental and safety reasons alone, careful planning, preparation, coordination and monitoring of outdoor and residential provision should clearly be given high priority by all those involved.

If schools are to secure an effective match between the type of provision and their own needs, some classification of the diversity of ORE provision is needed. This is our next task. We would like to stress, though, that what follows is *not* a comparative evaluation of these different types, *nor* a *Which* guide to the quality of goods on offer, but a consumer atlas, to help customers find their way around complicated territory.

Types of provision

1 Outdoor Education Centres

Outdoor Education Centres vary widely in atmosphere, rationale and resources. For teachers, this range of choice can be bewildering, but careful consideration of the exact purpose of the planned residential visit can help guide the selection of an appropriate centre. In any case, it is always advisable to make a preliminary visit to any centre being used for the first time, before confirming a booking. The importance of advanced planning for pupil safety cannot be stressed enough and we will examine this later when we look at planning and preparation in more detail.

Courses offered by outdoor education centres are usually offered as packages. These packages differ according to the resources available and the location of the centres – wild mountain areas, coastal settings, small rural villages etc. Packages have their obvious attractions, especially where outdoor pursuits are involved. The programmes are usually varied and carefully prepared and arc led by specialist staff who are skilled and experienced in the area. This can be especially attractive to schools becoming involved with the outdoor pursuits side of residential experience for the first time. On the other hand, packages can sometimes lack flexibility. To be fair, many centres are good at adapting programmes to schools' individual needs, but this needs checking and negotiating beforehand. How well, for instance, can the centre cater for younger pupils, physically-handicapped pupils, or pupils involved in a school amalgamation? Or, to take another example, if the school places a high premium on environmental awareness, on contributing something to the community in which the residential experience is based, is the centre willing or able to make the necessary adjustments to allow or encourage this? Indeed, does it have a suitable community location in the first place, or is it too isolated for these purposes?

Packaged courses can also sometimes generate tensions or misunderstandings between centre and school staff. Accompanying teachers often have valuable skills and abilities to contribute to residential courses, but these can be over-looked in pre-set, packaged programmes. Moreover, while such teachers will usually gladly defer to the centre staff's greater technical expertise, the boundaries of responsibility for who organises and disciplines the pupils can sometimes become blurred, and approaches to this task may differ. The style of centre staff might often seem much more relaxed and informal than some teachers are used to in school. We do not wish to exaggerate these difficulties – outdoor centres are normally very experienced in coping with them – but they do need some discussion and thought in advance.

Staff qualifications might be another factor guiding choice of centres. Centres owned by LEAs are staffed by qualified teachers and the cost of the courses may be subsidised. In centres run on a commercial basis, it is possible that not all the staff will be appropriately qualified and it may be necessary to check the standard of instruction, equipment and safety before booking. Even so, while there is no financial subsidy for such courses, the cost is often very competitive and usually offers good value for money; and because they are commerically orientated, some of these centres offer a very attractive range of activities.

2 Youth hostels

Many teachers will already be aware of the advantages of youth hostels and the Youth Hostels Association has now published booklets aimed at teachers accompanying school parties. The YHA gives details of those hostels most suitable for use by schools and provides information on activities possible in the vicinity of the hostels. The cost of using hostel accommodation is low in comparison with established centres. On the other hand, accompanying teachers carry even greater responsibility for supervision than in package-type centres and a good staff-pupil ratio is therefore vitally important. One further reservation that some schools have about using youth hostels is that other residents can restrict and inhibit the response of the pupils. A good counter argument to this, though, is that shared residential visits, while initially threatening to teachers and pupils, can help pupils develop socially by encouraging them to get to know entirely new groups of people.

3 School-owned centres

Many schools have acquired their own residential facilities. These are usually converted buildings which have been donated to the school or acquired by fund-raising. They may be used for field studies, induction courses and staff in-service training as well as for the more conventional outdoor activities. Schools often prefer to use and acquire their own centres not just for obvious reasons of cost-saving, but also because they encourage more extensive use of residential experience in the school curriculum, helping staff acquire a more thorough knowledge of the centre's environment and its educational potential; and enable each residential experience to be specially adapted to the needs of those undergoing it.

On the debit side, however, while recurrent costs may be low, initial outlay on equipment can be expensive. Similarly, each programme will need to be staffed entirely from within the school's own resources (leaving additional problems of 'cover' for those left behind), and where outdoor pursuits are involved, thought will need to be given to training a sufficient number of staff in the appropriate skills. Last, but not least, the demands of constant supervision are more onerous here even than in other kinds of provision. There are no wardens here to take the strain – it's just you and the kids, 24 hours a day, and no let up!

4 School holidays abroad and exchange visits

To parents, skiing holidays, educational cruises, visits to France and the like are perhaps the kinds of residential experience with which they are most familiar. Such activities are well established in many schools and usually take place durng the school holidays. Indeed, they are commonly viewed as 'holidays' by the pupils. In the main, though, it is probably fair to say that while the skills gained and knowledge acquired on such 'holidays' are often extensive (due in no small part to the planning and preparation of the teachers who lead them), less thought is usually given to the personal and social aspects of the experience, to the personal and social qualities teachers are keen to promote, and to the activities and experiences that might best realise them. The personal and social pay-offs are too often regarded as incidental and left to chance. If they *are* considered important, perhaps they should be planned for too.

These, then, are the major forms that ORE provision can take. They are not the only ones of course. Many schools use camping, canal barges, or many other facilities as well. We have simply tried to illustrate some of the implications of choosing different sorts of residential experience. Many schools will be tied to one of these types by experience and tradition, but in our view, they would still do well to consider other options, for, as we have seen, they each have very different implications for planning, follow-up staffing and flexibility.

The course context of ORE

If the nature of ORE can vary according to where it is located and who controls the facilities, it can also vary according to the way it is offered in the school curriculum. As we saw at the outset, ORE, in the form of field study, is already an accepted part of examination courses in many subjects. It is also sometimes offered as an examination option in its own right.[3] Equally, outdoor education is in some cases available as a non-examination course, and increasingly, it is coming to form a small but important part of the curriculum in Government-sponsored schemes such as the Technical and Vocational Education Initiative and the Lower-Attaining Pupils' Project, where costs are usually heavily subsidised.

In all these cases, there are major questions to be asked about whether ORE should be available only to restricted groups of pupils. Might not its confinement to the option choice system limit take-up to those who already see themselves as physically adventurous – who make their choices, perhaps, on physical rather than personal and social criteria? Similarly, might not its restriction to lower attainers confer on it a kind of remedial status – something fit only for those not capable of 'real learning'? It seems to us that if the place of ORE is not to be marginalised and its importance under-valued, then its availability to *all* pupils as a matter of common entitlement must be encouraged wherever possible.

Issues and problems

As soon as we begin to consider what might be the most appropriate kind of centre for a residential visit and how pupils should be selected for it, attention is immediately and almost inevitably drawn to some of the major and controversial issues surrounding ORE. What is its purpose and value? Can other, less enthusiastic members of staff be persuaded of this? What particular *kinds* of personal and social qualities is it meant to realise? How can we be sure that these are achieved, that ORE justifies the expenditure laid out on it? What is the relationship of ORE to the rest of the curriculum and how might that relationship be strengthened? These are difficult but vital questions and our discussion turns to them now.

1 Purpose and values

ORE can be intensely satisfying to those who experience and teach it. This is one of its obvious strengths. But it is also a source of weakness. Most of the books and pamphlets on outdoor education in particular are written by people deeply enthused by and committed to it. The cursory evaluations of the area that have been undertaken to date also tend to be based on interviews with those who already have a strong involvement (Schools Council, 1980, 1983). Such descriptions of ORE are therefore unsurprisingly favourable, often glowingly so. Many of us involved in writing this book, it should be said, share these enthusiasms. Between us, we have descended potholes, abseiled down viaducts, walked long-distance footpaths and ridden surf in cold winter seas – and (sometimes to our surprise) we have found these experiences exhilarating. But there is a world of difference between finding activities and experiences personally enjoyable, and establishing a sound educational justification for those same activities and experiences as appropriate for all young people. That kind of task requires us to put our enthusiasms aside and inspect the purpose and rationale of ORE very closely. We recommend this for two reasons.

First, like many other areas of personal and social education, the distinctive character of ORE – its unusual content, strange setting and unfamiliar pattern of teacher–pupil relations – can easily surround it with a kind of mystique, dividing insiders from outsiders, converts from cynics. It is not enough simply to say to sceptical colleagues – as advocates of personal and social education are sometimes inclined to do – 'Oh, when you've experienced it yourself, when you've felt what it's like, you'll know it's worthwhile'. Colleagues will often be much too dubious to take that important first step, and even should they do so, there is no guarantee they would view the experience positively. For this reason, reliance on conversion by experience and emotional involvement alone is a risky staff development exercise, uneven and unpredictable in its impact. A rational, carefully thought out approach to clarifying the aims and demonstrating the effects of ORE is therefore needed.

A clear statement of aims and objectives, along with details of how they might best be fulfilled, is certainly one way of scotching the common but infuriating greeting teachers often get from their colleagues on returning from an exhausting outdoor education course – 'Did you enjoy your little holiday, then?'. More helpful still is a careful programme of evaluation which can point to ORE's positive benefits – short and long term – for pupils' personal and social development.

But if clear statements of purpose and demonstration of effects help persuade colleagues of the benefits of ORE, they are even more vital to those who are centrally involved in promoting and developing the area – as a check on what otherwise might become excessive enthusiasm. Statements of aims and thorough evaluation are not just good for public relations, they are an essential ingredient of self-evaluation too. And that kind of self-evaluation must be rigorous; getting to grips with the central values as well as the technical details of ORE. There is not space to discuss all of these values here – though some of them, like persistence and endurance, or leadership and teamwork, do seem to us contentious and worthy of debate. We take one example only to illustrate the kind of questioning we feel needs to be undertaken: the concept of challenge and adventure.

The concept of adventure and challenge is central to the outdoor pursuits side of ORE. Drasdo (1972) sees adventure as a way of encouraging 'character building' (p 6), that is, 'the strengthening of the individual through contact with the forces of nature' (p 10). For Mortlock (1973: 4), a key writer in this area,

> Adventure is a state of mind that begins with feelings of uncertainty about the outcome of a journey and always ends with feelings of enjoyment, satisfaction or elation about the successful completion of that journey . . . The initial feeling of uncertainty of outcome is fear; fear of physical or psychological harm. There can be no adventure in outdoor pursuits without this fear in the mind of the pupil. Without the fear there would be no challenge.

Citing the turn-of-the-century psychologist, William James, Mortlock goes on to justify adventure education as a 'moral substitute for war', a means of satisfying the human being's need for challenge in a way that is not destructive of fellow human beings (p 10). Indeed, he argues, there is an instinct for adventure in everyone. Consequently, 'virtually all young people can find satisfaction from adventure, regardless of their physical, mental or emotional limitations.' (pp 6–7).

In part at least, then, the justification for adventure education seems to rest on two interrelated principles: the satisfaction of allegedly natural instincts for adventure, challenge and even aggression; coupled with the displacement of these things, of excitement, tension and so on, into a non-damaging setting. Much about these claims might strike people as appealing, but our worry is whether some of the characteristics mentioned are, in fact, desirable, whether they might at some points come into conflict with other aims of ORE, and whether their allegedly instinctual base has any secure foundation.

The instinctual basis of adventure is a particularly precarious claim. The argument that everyone possesses this 'instinctual' need is greatly exaggerated – certainly it is difficult to apply it when facing the lukewarm and cynical response of some colleagues to the alleged attractions of outdoor pursuits. Where has *their* instinct gone?

There is also a 'macho' toughness about some of the personal qualities being encouraged, qualities which could arguably be fostered just as effectively by peacetime National Service as outdoor pursuits! Indeed, given the interests in the deliberate stimulation of fear or creation of physical discomfort, one wonders how far outdoor pursuits has been infiltrated by the 'cold shower', 'if-it's-unpleasant-it-must-be-good-for-you' brigade of PE teaching. In this respect, perhaps it is no coincidence that for all its personal and social aspirations, many of the teachers involved in outdoor pursuits are PE trained and experienced (HMI, 1985).

One side effect of this kind of 'macho' emphasis might be a measure of discouragement to and discomfort for girls. To be fair, most existing evaluations of ORE comment positively on how well outdoor centres make their courses available to *both* sexes – and the Schools Council (1983) favourably reviews the development of an outdoor pursuits course in an all-girls school which has the intention of demonstrating to girls that this area is for them just as much as it is for boys. Such discussions of equal opportunities, however, are usually narrowly restricted to questions of course access only. Much more important perhaps, is the style and tone of the course's presentation – its *hidden curriculum*.

In some respects, the hidden curriculum of ORE is perhaps less discriminatory, in gender terms, than the hidden curriculum of ordinary schooling. Humberstone (1986) for instance, in a case study of gender differentiation in outdoor education, reports that, if anything, instructors spend more time with the girls than the boys – the exact reverse of the usual situation in school classrooms. To a large extent, though, patterns of interaction that appear to favour the girls arise not because of the instructors' concern about equal opportunities, but because they tend to concentrate their attention on the less confident youngsters who need more encouragement – and these are more often the girls. In gender terms, then, the important point is not how much time is devoted to boys and girls respectively, but what is done with that time. If the tone of the interaction between instructors and pupils is overly 'macho' – right down to the 'matey' barrack-room atmosphere of the warden's jokes ('Oh, you're like a virgin's drawers – always on!')[4] – then it is likely that many girls will come to feel they are being forced to compete in a men's world on men's terms, and will consequently feel excluded. Certainly, the tendencies towards feeling excluded are already there in many girls' perceptions of outdoor activities as 'male' activities. As one of the girls observed by Humberstone (1986: 203) put it, 'Why don't we do any girls' activities?'

The staffing of outdoor education centres does not do a great deal to alleviate these problems. In a survey of outdoor centres, Ball (1986: 29) found that of the dozen who replied, out of a sample 32, men made up 100% of the centre heads, 92% of the chief instructors, 74% of the other full-time instructors and 81% of the part-time instructors. Such staffing leads to a shortage of positive female role models in the area of outdoor pursuits, and gives women little opportunity to place their own distinctive stamp and interests on the ethos and organisation of outdoor centres. We do not wish to exaggerate the extent of gender bias in outdoor pursuits. In terms of equal access, the distribution of instructors' time, and even the similarity of dress between boys and girls, outdoor pursuits is one of the least discriminatory areas of schooling. As many of the girls interviewed and observed by Humberstone (1986), for instance, commented positively on how ORE improved the relationships between boys and girls, made them more appreciative of each others' strengths and weaknesses, and generally broke down stereotypes. Even so, in patterns of staffing and styles of leadership, we have seen marked elements of male bias in outdoor pursuits education that would certainly merit further discussion and investigation.

We are not saying that the components of adventure education we have outlined are universal or unavoidable. But some of the qualities being encouraged here seem to us questionable, their possible sexist implications strike us as worrying, and their tensions with some of the more caring, cooperative, group-based objectives of ORE appear to us to be a potential point of difficulty (though many centres do seem to resolve such tensions exceedingly well). We do not wish to undermine the whole concept of adventure. But neither do we want to encourage bland acceptance. Careful discussion and questioning among those taking part is what is most urgently needed.

This is most vital when the needs of individual pupils are at stake. Failure to help a pupil with a maths problem in class will at worst result in disappointment or frustration. Failure to offer appropriate support to a pupil in physical difficulties in outdoor education may transform anxiety or mild fear into unmitigated terror. Mortlock (1973) draws a useful distinction here between adventure and misadventure. *Adventure*, he says, involves a degree of fear of physical harm, of uncertainty and danger (though this danger should always be apparent, not real). The experience of adventure is that of success in overcoming these difficulties. *Misadventure*, meanwhile, occurs when the challenge is beyond the control of the person and either physical injury or psychological trauma results (pp 4–6). As an example of misadventure, he cites this pupil's log-book entry:

> Then we had to do abseiling at a hundred foot drop. I was really petrified at first, when I had to step off the edge onto a tiny ledge. I was trembling and fumbling with the ropes. As I was going down, it seemed as if it would never end . . . When I got to the bottom, my arms felt horrible. I was really shaking. I don't think I am the sort for that and I don't think I will do climbing again.
>
> (p 24)

A major problem here is that the boundaries between adventure and misadventure will be set differently for different individuals. Activities therefore need to be carefully matched with the needs and experience of the group. Strenuous hillwalks in bad weather can build up qualities of endurance, but as HMI (1983) have observed, they can also lead to exhaustion and demoralisation. The difficulty for the ORE teacher or leader in these matters is knowing just when or how to intervene. Obviously, shrewd judgement and effective intervention (or non-intervention) depend on deep prior knowledge of the pupils concerned (Schools Council, 1980: 4). This suggests that wherever possible teachers who already know the pupils well should be included in the party, and, of course, that there should be a climate back in school where that kind of personal understanding is encouraged and developed. Where these things are lacking, the boundaries between adventure and misadventure will be easily transgressed.

Matching objectives and activities

Once you have established what kind of personal and social qualities you wish to develop, the next obvious set of decisions concerns how far a Centre's programme and balance of activities is likely, or even specifically designed, to foster those qualities. If you have your own centre or want to negotiate your programme with an independent or LEA one, you will need to decide for yourself what activities are to be selected and how these are to be structured.

Choosing a centre   If qualities like group cooperation and decision-making are much higher on your list of priorities than, say, notions of adventure and challenge, does your residential visit require a specific 'outdoor pursuits' focus? Many of the benefits claimed for *outdoor* and residential education, particularly those concerning close community living over a period of several days, would apply to virtually *any* kind of residential experience, even one in an urban setting. This is one reason why objectives should be clarified: to guide the choice of centre. As one HMI has succinctly put it: 'Do we have to travel all the way to Anglesey to do something that can be accomplished here?' (Belshaw, 1985).

Selecting and structuring activities   The inclusion of 'The Normans' on a history syllabus provides no guarantee that pupils will learn anything significant about these people, still less that they will grasp the concept of invasion, develop their sense of chronology, or increase their ability to evaluate evidence. Whether these learning outcomes are achieved depends on how this item on the syllabus is organised and taught. The same applies to ORE. There is nothing inherent in any physical activity that will automatically realise particular personal and social outcomes. By themselves, activities like caving, canoeing or horse-riding can have all manner of personal and social consequences. It all depends on how they are structured and taught.

Among examples of practice we have observed here where personal and social objectives and the presentation of activities have been closely matched are the following: an instructor timing stages of a mountain walk so that the carrying of rucksacks is shared equally; pupils being deputed to accompany stragglers so as to make them feel part of the group; leadership roles being rotated to allow everyone to participate in that experience; lights being switched off when progressing through a cave in the dark in order to encourage pupils to support and communicate with each other; and pupils being asked to stand up and support each other in canoes, to build trust and cooperation in the group.

Much of this kind of experience is and ought to be planned in advance, not just allowed to happen. But like all good teaching, a great deal is also improvised according to the opportunities of the moment. HMI (1983) for instance, describe how one instructor increased environmental awareness among his group by pointing to examples of plant and bird life around a cave entrance and asking for care before caving began. In sharp contrast, they describe elsewhere an activity of boulder-scrambling along a coastline where the physical skills were emphasised to the exclusion of environmental factors (HMI, 1985). In these small ways personal and social qualities, environmental awareness and the like are either fostered or frustrated.

Living in the centre   When the day's outdoor activities have ended and everyone returns to the centre, it is tempting to think that the curriculum has stopped. Yet it is here that some of the most important social learning of all will be taking place – and that too can be structured. One way in which many teachers already do this is by having pupils record in diaries or log-books what they have done or achieved during the day. HMI (1985) have expressed reservations about the use of these log-books. In one centre, they observed that

> the structured log-books which children completed after supper after an intense day on the hills and the water did not inspire them as much as reliving the events through discussion. (p 9)

An evening of writing up notes can indeed be dreary work for all but the most highly motivated pupils. Undoubtedly, some do feel the effort is worthwhile – 'I'm glad I wrote it now. I've read mine through quite a lot, but it was a pain at the time'.[5] In general, though, it is interesting that it is here, in an environment that most closely resembles that of the secondary school classroom – where tasks are written and the achievements are intellectual-cognitive in nature – that misbehaviour and disruption is most likely to occur. Other forms of recording with more desirable personal and social consequences therefore need to be considered. In particular, collective discussions of what has been achieved, what difficulties have been faced, and so on, can both remind pupils about and heighten their awareness of the personal and social elements of the experience. Photographs, tapes, films and models can provide equally valid records of the residential experience, as written ones too.

Careful attention to grouping arrangements can also add further to the achievement of personal and social ends in a course. Pupils will normally want to be with their friends. Teachers are often tempted to keep their own groups separate from those of other schools, or to keep particular pupils apart in separate dormitories so as to avoid trouble. But whereas for many secondary teachers, trouble is an interruption to the main curriculum and something to be avoided, for centre staff, as a personal and social issue, its place in the curriculum is absolutely central. Working through trouble, in fact, is an integral part of the ORE curriculum – a key, if difficult, aspect of personal and social development. This is often why centre staff prefer random allocation to groups and dormitories – not out of caprice or for reasons of administrative convenience, but in order to meet the personal and social ends of the course. It is helpful if accompanying teachers appreciate this point – otherwise some awkward staff tensions can ensue.

Planning and preparation

Clearly, then, given the need to clarify aims and objectives, and to match these carefully with activities, any outdoor and residential experience should be thoroughly discussed and planned in advance. The support and expertise of a wide range of people, such as teachers, parents or senior management, will not only make the planning more thorough, it will also help establish the importance of ORE among a broader group and help secure for it a meaningful and recognised place in the wider school curriculum.

A rather more controversial proposal is that pupils themselves be involved in the planning and preparation. One obvious benefit here is that pupils are likely to feel more commitment to the residential experience if they are genuinely and extensively involved in the planning and preparation. More important still is the learning, the problem solving and decision making involved in a significant piece of real-life planning. Just how extensive the involvement in planning should be will depend on the pupils concerned – though part of the purpose of pupil involvement in planning is to develop the very qualities and capacities it presupposes. Many TVEI schemes argue that pupil involvement should be very extensive indeed (eg Dudley Education Authority, 1985), though HMI (1983: 16) have noted that this aspect of pupils' personal and social development is too often overlooked. One can understand why this happens. There are risks of mistakes and errors, perhaps substantial ones, and teachers may not want to carry these. A group purchasing food for an expedition may all too easily acquire triple quantities of dessert and only a quarter of the necessary vegetables! But a shrewd teacher will recognise that such decisions, and their rectification, are themselves a vital part of pupils' personal and social education – not necessarily something to be avoided.

Clearly, effective planning and preparation for any residential visit is important for the personal and social development of the pupils who will be involved. It is also essential for their physical safety. In May, 1985, when four boys from Stoke Poges Middle School were tragically swept into the sea and drowned at Land's End, what were once matters of technical procedure for those directly concerned with ORE became matters of major public concern. Among the many criticisms that were made of the staff, and indeed of the LEA, for their part in that particular tragedy, one of the chief ones concerned poor planning and preparation. In his report on the Land's End incident and the implications arising from it, Buckinghamshire's Chief Education Officer concluded that 'the preparation and planning for the visit by (the head) was inadequate and in a number of ways seriously unsatisfactory'. He went on:

> Because the supervisors and (the head) in particular, did not know Land's End at first hand, because no detailed information had been obtained beforehand and no reconnaissance was carried out immediately on arrival . . . children reached a part of Land's End which they were never intended to reach. Some children scrambled down the cliff to rocks very close to the sea, without any supervisor at first being aware of this . . .
>
> (Buckinghamshire County Council, 1986: Para 5.79)

The report recommended that notes of guidance on planning and preparation should be issued by LEAs in the future, and many have now done this. It also advised that the expenses of the preliminary visits should, as part of the essential planning and preparation procedure, be included in the overall costs of the school visit, and passed on to those who have undertaken to pay for it. As more rigorous attention is paid to such preparatory work, this will, of course, have serious implications for the financing and staffing of residential visits, to which we shall return later. All we want to stress at the moment is the immense importance of effective advanced planning from the point of view of physical safety, as well as social and personal development.

Follow-up and integration

If careful planning and preparation is vital to the construction of an effective residential programme, so too is close attention to follow-up. Nothing is more likely to undermine the personal and social benefits of a residential visit than failure to follow it up and demonstrate its links and continuity with the rest of a pupil's school experience. More than anything, it is that kind of neglect which will confirm the popular view of ORE as merely a 'holiday' or 'break'. Of course, the form that follow-up takes will depend on the aims and purpose of the visit: a certain amount of follow-up work can be included in the planning of the residential visit but there will also be new materials and ideas arising from the experience for the pupils to develop on return to school. Debriefing can take place during the residential visit and afterwards in school. Discussions in groups or informal interviews with other members of staff can help to reinforce the value of the experience for the pupils, while displays of drawings, photographs, written work or video films can all be used to consolidate and explore the pupils' responses to the experience. This is obviously easier with whole-class groups, than with pupils drawn from several classes: a point to be borne in mind at the planning stage.

This is the most specific kind of follow-up that can be provided. Residential work can also be followed up in mainstream subject areas like humanities or biology – and where fieldwork has been undertaken, this will be quite explicit. Clearly, though, for residential experience to be integrated effectively with the mainstream curriculum, the involvement of subject departments at the planning, implementation and follow-up stages is essential.

The most difficult kind of follow-up of all to secure runs across the entire range of pupils' classroom experience and their relationships with their teachers. Sadly, ORE can too often be an isolated, 'one-off' experience for a limited number of pupils. It is not just failure to fit an outdoor or residential experience into traditional subjects that is the point at issue here. There is a need for teaching styles and patterns of classroom learning to be considered also. The teaching of outdoor education in particular is based on the principles of 'active learning', small group work and short term goals which capitalise on pupils' successes. If teaching approaches of this kind are not then evident in the rest of the school curriculum, pupils may well feel bitter and resentful about the contrast. There are few things more infuriating for young people in school than to return from an intensive experience which has confronted them with significant challenges, conferred on them real responsibility and encouraged them to work cooperatively and informally with adults and fellow pupils alike; to a school environment which systematically denies these things, where classroom tasks may seem mediocre or contrived, where a return to the conventional, passive and individualised pupil role is demanded, and where teachers may once again retreat behind those masks they call authority.

Evidently, then, there is little point in offering a short, dynamic burst of residential activity if it is to be nothing but an entertaining intermission in the otherwise humdrum routine of ordinary school life; and if this is the kind of 'normal service' that will be resumed as soon as pupils return to school. It is likely that the personal and social benefits of ORE will be lasting only if the pupils' experience and relationships are broadly compatible with the ones they already have in school; if ORE is seen not just as some way of salvaging sagging pupil motivation and morale, but as a reinforcement and development of whole-school policy and practice in relation to personal and social development. Of course, as part of a staff development exercise, involvement in residential experience might be a valuable interim strategy for heightening the teacher's awareness of the need for and benefits of changes in relationship and teaching style elsewhere in the curriculum. But in the long term, sustained benefits for pupils are unlikely to be maintained unless ORE sits comfortably in the surrounding ethos of the school. Once more, a very specific aspect of personal and social education has quickly taken us into much broader issues of whole-school policy and practice.

When the place of ORE within the school curriculum more generally has been widely recognised and agreed, then it will be possible to identify at what points in a pupil's career it might most usefully be offered. It may be possible, for instance, to offer some kind of outdoor and residential experience as an induction for new pupils, either at first year or sixth form level. Similarly, teachers introducing new courses in the fourth year, or bringing together groups of TVEI pupils, for example, may also wish to introduce a residential experience in order to establish supportive group relationships. Moreover, if there is a whole-school commitment to ORE, the experiences and learning can be organised progressively, becoming more intensive and challenging, perhaps, as the pupil moves through school.[6]

The teacher's role

One of the most consistent claims made for ORE is the positive effect it can have on teacher–pupil relationships. Teachers involved in residential education often gain a new understanding of their pupils, particularly if they are prepared to join in the activities with them. Getting wet and cold together, showing unexpected daring when 'polybagging' down a steep slope, revealing equally unexpected diffidence and vulnerability when descending a pothole, or simply chatting with pupils over cocoa in the evening – all these things can help break down those rather stylised authority barriers that often exist in school, and open up opportunities for improved relationships. On the other hand, there can occasionally be stressful clashes, particularly if pupils do not feel a sense of responsibility for or commitment to the residential visit (though this is much less likely if they have been involved at the planning stage).

Some teachers will, of course, feel reluctant to take on these new roles – they may feel they would 'lose face' and that their authority would be undermined. Teachers who have been widely involved in ORE do not normally complain of these consequences – quite the contrary. But the reluctance of some members of staff to enter into the spirit of ORE must be anticipated. Support and persuasion from colleagues might help here, but some teachers, like some pupils, will always resist full-scale involvement. In that case, the advantages and disadvantages of their accompanying a residential visit must be weighed very carefully. One reason for this is that not only does reluctance to relax conventional patterns of classroom authority do little to unfreeze teacher–pupil relationships, it can sometimes be a source of friction between school and centre staff as well. As we have seen, centre staff frequently take a much more relaxed (though no less firm) approach to pupil discipline and where teachers feel the need to keep things tight on conventional school lines, this can, predictably, create conflict, for centre wardens will see such interventions as running against the ethos of ORE. Perhaps the inclusion of such teachers in a residential programme may be justified by their own staff development needs. But given the potential conflicts and tensions we have outlined, it is obviously a decision that needs to be considered very carefully.

Evaluation and assessment

Teachers involved in ORE work in schools need to evaluate the visits to determine how far the aims and objectives are being achieved and to establish what can be improved in the future. The opinions of the pupils themselves will provide useful insights here. These can be collected through informal interviews, discussions and even questionnaires.

Failure to evaluate the effects and effectiveness of ORE is a constantly acknowledged weakness of the field (Schools Council, 1980, 1983; HMI, 1983; MSC, 1979). There are, of course, serious problems involved in evaluating the personal and social benefits of ORE, as there are in the rest of the affective domain. Benefits may be long term, they may be indirect, they may be mistaken for changes caused by other factors, and so on. Too much should not be expected of evaluation, therefore, especially at school level. But some evaluation is better than none. Certainly, some indication of pupil response, of the impact of the experience on leisure patterns and on personal and social development in the short and medium term is needed if sceptical colleagues are to be persuaded and programmes are to be successfully reviewed. Nor need all the evaluative work be left until return to school. As members of Her Majesty's Inspectorate (1985: 10) recommend, visiting teachers can contribute a good deal to reviews of the work of outdoor centres by recording the nature and success of activities and young people's response to them on the spot.

Just as the worth and effectiveness of ORE programmes need to be evaluated, so too do pupil responses and achievements need to be recorded and assessed. Assessment of qualities and skills by numbers or grades is probably not to be encouraged. Such systems, though occasionally used as part of outdoor education examination courses (examples are in Schools Council, 1980), may be demotivating for pupils whose grades are low – and this may be extremely worrying where the judgements being made are unavoidably subjective. More open systems of recording and profiling of the kind being developed in Records of Achievement, in which pupils play a strong role in assessing their own progress and discussing this with tutors (as a way of reflecting on their own development and achievements) would seem a course worth pursuing (see Chapter 6). This is likely to give more meaning and purpose to diary and log-book writing as a basis for discussion. Moreover, as HMI (1985: 16) have observed, these patterns of recording might effectively 'contribute towards assessment procedures and pupil profiles more generally'. In this respect, it is interesting that many TVEI pupils' summative statements now include a section on Residential Experience. This seems to us an excellent way to begin integrating residential experience with the curriculum and assessment structure of the school more generally.

Summary

In summary, these are the sorts of major questions that seem to us to be at the centre of planning and structuring a programme of residential experience. Teachers, we would urge, need to think carefully about the kinds of qualities they wish to foster through ORE and they need to ask themselves just how desirable those qualities are. They need to make judgements about how far the programmes of different centres or their own school-generated ones are in tune with these desired qualities, then make their course selections and programme adjustments accordingly. They need to plan programmes meticulously to ensure the closest possible match between objectives and activities, and they need to involve colleagues and the pupils themselves in that process wherever possible. Thought needs to be given to how the residential experience can be followed up and built upon within the school curriculum (which will have implications for subject teaching, teacher–pupil relationships and the ethos of the school as a whole). And the entire experience and its effects on pupils needs to be evaluated carefully and periodically. In this way, a pattern of residential experience that has a justifiable and widely recognised place within the wider curriculum and assessment structure of the school will have some chance of being established successfully.

In addition to all these major questions of values, purpose and effectiveness, there are, in ORE, a large number of technical and managerial problems that can create serious headaches for those embarking on planning this kind of venture for the first time. We therefore close this chapter with some advice and suggestions on these more immediately practical concerns; though we will see that many of these apparently small scale issues ultimately return to the first-base ones of values, purpose and planning.

Implementation and organisation

1 Staffing

Although it makes sense for teachers accompanying pupils on residential visits to have had regular contact with them beforehand, by no means all teachers will be willing or able to commit themselves to this kind of work. They may have domestic reasons for not wishing to take part, they may have responsibilities in school which they feel they cannot neglect or they may, as we have seen, feel alarmed at the prospect of the activities and of what will be demanded of them. These matters clearly need to be discussed at the planning stage.

As well as certain teachers being unavailable, there will also be restrictions on staffing due to the need for 'cover' back in school, but if possible more than one teacher should accompany a party, not least for moral support and help with responsibilities. Certainly, a mixed-sex group of pupils should be accompanied by a male and a female teacher. Because of this need for as generous a staff ratio as possible and because of the distinct advantages of groups being accompanied by teachers who know them well, schools need to try and create a substantial pool of teachers committed to and experienced in the area, from which any particular visit can then be staffed. This also avoids the problems that can occur in some schools when undue reliance is placed on one or two people, and then those people become unavailable or leave.

Most LEAs will have policy statements on staff–pupil ratios, especially in the wake of the Land's End incident. LEAs may also need to be contacted about supply cover for the actual visit itself and for 'reconnaissance' visits in advance of it. Policy on this is likely to be variable, though, and schools will sometimes have to fall back on their own resources in arranging cover. Where LEA support is most wanting, this can place the whole commitment to residential education in serious jeopardy. There is clearly a policy issue at stake here that stretches far beyond the individual school itself.

Special difficulties can arise where staff do not just accompany pupils to other centres, but lead specialist activities of the outdoor variety in their own. These sorts of activities will need to be supervised by staff with special qualifications such as the Mountain Leadership Certificate. Many LEAs run training courses leading to this certificate and other qualifications and there are obvious advantages in these being acquired by several staff. In any event, it is essential to obtain some experience of ORE before running your own visits. Visits to other schools to observe practice, or a week's voluntary help at a centre, might provide useful experience here.

Unfortunately, there is sometimes a tendency to think that staff INSET needs end with the acquisition of a Mountain Leadership Certificate or other specialist qualification. As we have indicated, though, ORE provides staff challenges well beyond those of mere physical skill and technical expertise, and the wider aspects of personal and social development, structuring of programmes, evaluation and assessment, and integration with whole-school policy are also important topics for inservice discussion at school and LEA level.

2 Finance

The financing of ORE is often a particular worry for schools and needs to be considered carefully. Is the LEA prepared to make an additional contribution to support these courses, and how far will the pupils be expected to contribute towards costs? Is help available from a government-supported project in school such as TVEI? If the programme is part of the school curriculum, should funding come out the school's capitation allowance, as it does for books and scientific equipment? The question of who pays has to be discussed well in advance. Equally, the costs of different centres and the quality of service they offer also needs to be compared. If staff are clear about objectives, this will enable better judgements to be made about securing cost-effective provision.

At the time of writing, the prospects concerning more general financial support for ORE look uncertain. On the one hand, a ruling of the Ombudsman in 1986 that Wiltshire County Council should refund £95 to a parent for the costs of sending her son on a field trip, has, for a while at least, shifted towards LEAs the burden of responsibility for providing financial support for essential residential visits (*Times Education Supplement* 21.2.86). Although the Ombudsman added that it would be 'unfortunate' if the ruling led to the abandonment of residential field courses, it was a judgement that nevertheless cast substantial doubt on the future of ORE, by effectively setting conditions that would require LEAs to give it extra financial support.

On the other hand, the Conservative Government's proposed programme of educational reform (commencing in 1987) includes provisions for some of the costs of state education currently born by the LEA to be passed directly on to parents instead. Alongside such things as swimming classes and aspects of music instruction, field trips are included within these provisions. This, too, could prejudice the future existence and status of ORE – making it even more dependent on direct parental support, placing its basic financial viability in question, and putting it on to the margins of a secondary curriculum otherwise deemed worthy of full state support.

3 Length of stay

A short overnight stay might be the most appropriate way of introducing residential work to pupils. Younger pupils in particular may not be ready for a week away together and teachers too need to have the confidence to know they can cope with a longer stay. On the other hand, many primary and middle schools have a strong commitment to residential education, and consultation with feeder schools to determine what residential experience pupils have already had and how this might be built upon, is advisable.

4 Travelling

The kind of transport available and the time spent travelling during the stay need to be considered when planning a visit, not least because of the cost implications. It is easy to regard journeys as separate from the main residential experience, simply a means of getting there and coming back. We are not suggesting that teachers take on the job of courier, but these times can be used to help forge a sense of group cohesion and to reflect on the day's activities.

5 Recruitment

Recruitment for a residential visit can sometimes be difficult and no pupil can – or should – be compelled to attend. Counselling the pupils individually or in small groups can help to reassure and convince the reluctant ones. Home visits may be needed in some cases to explain the purpose and value of the course. Friendship groups are very important to most pupils and teachers may find it helpful to approach these groups to encourage participation.

Pupils can be reluctant to leave home or school even for a short time, for complicated reasons, and the teacher needs to be sensitive about handling this. Once again, the need for adequate preparation is highlighted. If the pupils feel the visit is an important part of their work and they are involved in preparing for it, they are less likely to feel threatened or anxious.

Residential experiences are most valuable when they encompass a wide range of abilities and personalities – this, after all, is one of their main social justifications. There may be value in extending outdoor pursuits skills in a fourth and fifth year option, say, but the entitlement of *all* pupils to benefit from this kind of experience should not be eroded. This does, however, then raise the difficulty about what to do with uncooperative or disruptive pupils. For the sake of a quiet life, many teachers will be inclined to exclude pupils of this kind from the visit. Or they may wish to threaten withdrawal of the residential opportunity, so as to secure good behaviour beforehand. Tempting though this might be, the aims and objectives of the residential experience in terms of personal and social development should be remembered. In some respects, the difficult pupils may be the ones most needing it.

Equally, to threaten misbehaving children with exclusion from the residential visit only serves to undermine its place in the main curriculum, setting it up as a kind of treat or holiday, less educationally justifiable, less like 'work' than maths or English, say. If ORE is to have the same importance as these other subjects, not just at the level of rhetoric, but in practice too, there should be no behavioural justification for withdrawing pupils from it. This may be hard on the teacher – especially at bedtimes – but no-one is arguing that ORE is an easy option!

6 Parents

It will be necessary to obtain parents' written consent for their child to take part in a residential visit. They must certainly be kept informed through letters, meetings, and other detailed, written information. Some parents may want to be involved more extensively and actively and may be willing to assist by taking photographs, or giving specialist knowledge of an area, for example, if they are invited to do so. The importance of keeping parents well informed, not least to protect the children's safety, and as reassurance about the efficient organisation of the visit, cannot be emphasised enough.

7 Insurance

Most LEAs offer insurance schemes to cover themselves against claims for negligence and compensation for injuries. The amount of money allowed in compensation varies from one LEA to another and teachers should investigate additional insurance cover. The Land's End case, however, exposed major ambiguities about insurance cover. Parents were led to believe that the cost of the residential visit included insurance, but this referred *only* to the County Council's own insurance which provided cover only for instances of proven neglect. Personal accident cover of the kind more usually associated with holiday arrangements was not included. Schools should therefore look very carefully at their insurance position, should examine arrangements for additional insurance cover and should communicate these arrangements fully and unambiguously to the parents. The Buckinghamshire County Council (1986) report on the Land's End case strongly advises that approval of Governing bodies should be sought for residential visits. Insurance arrangements should properly form part of these consultations.

8 Equipment

A surprising amount of equipment is necessary for most residential visits. There is, of course, the equipment needed to support the planned activities. Responsibility for some of this can be handed over to some of the pupils. In addition, pupils often have little idea of what is suitable dress for some outdoor activities and a supply of old clothes, particularly extra jumpers and socks, may be useful. An equipment list, sent to parents well beforehand, is essential for heading off the worst of these problems.

9 Safety

As we have seen, safety factors are an extremely important element in ORE. Educating the pupils about safety, taking appropriate equipment, informing the LEA, knowing how to get local information about weather conditions and how to deal with emergencies – these are the most important safety factors of which group leaders need to be aware. Effective planning and preparation to identify potentially hazardous areas and situations is, as we have seen, also essential. Schools are often unclear about safety regulations. Nor do LEAs always have clear guidelines either, although the position on this has improved considerably since the Land's End tragedy. It is as well to check with the LEA on these matters first. The DES pamphlet, *Safety in Outdoor Pursuits* (DES, 1973) has for many years been a useful point of reference on safety issues but is now rather dated. In years to come, it looks as if the most valuable document in this vital area will be a completely re-written version of the old Schools Council document *Out and About*. This has been reshaped and updated by the Schools Curriculum Development Committee, and written up clearly and accessibly by Maureen O'Connor (1987).

10 Practical preparation

Relevant people in school need to be informed well in advance of any outdoor or residential courses. Many schools have established clear procedures to be followed here. Where these do not exist, it is important to have:

- medical details from all pupils and the telephone number of their doctors;
- the school's telephone number and the home number of the head or deputy;
- a telephone number or address where the next of kin of each pupil can be contacted;
- a colleague or parent to be a source of information to others about times of arrival and possible delays – this means only one telephone call will be needed to keep parents informed;
- a First Aid kit to be carried at all times and a person responsible for looking after pupils' medications;
- a list of all pupils in the group for quick roll calls when necessary;
- a card carried by each pupil giving the Centre's address and phone number;
- a set of basic rules understood by all party members – eg a minimum of 2–3 people always to be together when involved in outdoor exercises.

The practicalities of running an ORE course may seem daunting, but adequate planning should avoid teachers feeling overwhelmed. Such pressures can to a certain extent also be alleviated by encouraging pupils to take responsibility for parts of the course where possible.

Conclusion

Given the extent of these practical demands, it is all too easy to get bogged down in the technicalities of ORE and overlook the fundamental aims and objectives of the residential experience. It is this clear sense of purpose, the extent to which the activities and experiences are structured around it, the involvement of pupils in the planning of these activities and experiences, along with a system of effective and continuous review of pupil progress and of the course's effectiveness overall that together are likely to give it a meaningful and worthwhile place in the secondary school curriculum.

The difficulties of funding ORE, and worries about the safety issues surrounding it, threaten to put residential experience in an even more marginal position in years to come than the one it already occupies. Its continuing treatment as a relatively isolated, one-off element of pupils' broader secondary school experience will do little to counter such tendencies. But if ORE is given a clear and recognised place within the secondary curriculum, where its benefits are pursued and made visible beyond the residential experience itself, then schools will have a better case for asserting its educational importance and securing the necessary support from parents and Government alike.

Notes

1   Unless otherwise indicated, all the quoted observations on ORE from pupils and teachers used in this chapter are taken from an exploratory observational study of ORE by one of the book's authors – Henderson (1984). All pupils are aged 14 or 15.
2   This historical section draws on discussions of the Outward Bound Movement in James (1957), Hodgkin (1985, 1986) and Hogan (1968), along with descriptions of private progressive education in Skidelsky (1963), and Gordonstoun School in particular (Brown, 1962).
3   An example of a syllabus for such an option can be found in the appendix to the Schools Council (1980) evaluation of ORE.
4   This example is taken from Henderson (1984).
5   *Ibid.*
6   See Schools Council (1983) for examples of progression in ORE.

5 Personal recording, diaries and log-books

Diaries are normally regarded as a somewhat self-indulgent preoccupation of the furtive or the famous – not something we might consider an important or essential element of young people's secondary school experience. Diaries can supply the raw material for personal memoirs. They can offer opportunities for emotional release, for private confessions. Or again, at infant school level, they can provide a means of passing on news during busy Monday mornings. Diaries have their uses, then. But what do any of these have to do with the personal and social aspects of secondary school experience? This is an important and relevant question, for the use of pupil diaries, log-books and more extensive systems of personal recording has become an increasingly common feature of secondary schooling in recent years, especially for pupils in the 14–16 age-range. Why should this be so? Just how extensive is this development? What explains its emergence? What purposes do personal recording, diaries and logbooks serve? And what contribution, if any, do they and can they make to pupils' personal and social development? Are they a powerful mechanism for heightening personal and social awareness and increasing motivation, or just a sop for the less able – a way of finding work for idle hands? These are the sorts of questions we shall be exploring in this chapter.

Background

In its essentials, personal recording is a simple idea, using simple and easily affordable materials. At first glance, it seems to involve little more than setting aside some time in the week or during a programme of study for pupils to compile a record of their experiences and achievements. Such a record may take one of a variety of forms: it may be open-ended, written on blank sheets of paper; it may consist of entries prompted by questions or statements requiring completion, or it may be part of a systematic scheme, compiled on a series of headed cards. Records of this kind are commonly stored in files or folders which may then be retained by students on leaving school, both to assist them in job applications and as personal mementos.

More extensive systems of personal recording are now well into their second decade in British schools. Over 150 schools are currently involved in one version or another of such schemes. In addition to the extensive 'packaged' schemes, pupil diaries and logbooks are now widely dispersed throughout the secondary system as a constituent feature of Records of Achievement (see Chapter 6); as a stimulus to self-assessment among pupils involved in the Government-sponsored Lower Attaining Pupils Project; or as a means of recording pupils' responses to work and residential experience, especially within the Technical and Vocational Education Initiative (TVEI). The different origins and uses of personal recording can have widely varying implications for personal and social development. The historical background to these linked initiatives therefore merits careful exploration.

Personal recording

The idea of personal recording is a simple one. Like many simple inventions, though – including curricular ones – this innovation actually emerged in response to a range of complex and difficult problems. In the case of personal recording, these were bound up with the educational complexities of the 1960s. While the map of comprehensive education was still unfolding it was announced that the school leaving age was to be raised to 16. Together, these two major upheavals in secondary education served to highlight the plight of the academically less able. As we saw in Chapter 2, many schools developed their own 'Newsom' and 'ROSLA' courses for such pupils, in an attempt to shift the emphasis away from book learning and writing towards more practical and experiential studies. Such measures, it was felt, might meet the needs and offset the resentment of these hitherto less-favoured and potentially disaffected pupils. Whatever the strengths (and weaknesses) of such courses the lack of a recognised qualification at the end of the programme was a serious drawback. It almost inevitably relegated them to the status of second class education in the eyes of pupils and teachers alike.

The poor motivation among low attainers, the lack of an organising principle for a non-academic education, and the absence of a suitable qualification for that kind of education – these were the sorts of concerns that troubled Don Stansbury, one of the pioneers of personal recording, in the 1960s. In response to this range of problems affecting the less able, Stansbury spearheaded the development of the first known system of personal recording in secondary schools: the Record of Personal Achievement (RPA).

In 1966, Stansbury convened and chaired a committee of the Joint Four Secondary Associations in Swindon to consider how secondary schools could adapt to the recent shift to comprehensive organisation and the apparently imminent raising of the school leaving age. Later that year, Stansbury was asked by the LEA to establish a Curriculum Study and Development Centre to coordinate preparations for ROSLA. As part of this exercise, he drew together teachers with experience of Newsom courses and the Duke of Edinburgh's

Award scheme. Neither of these groups, however, appeared to offer 'an organised way of organising and documenting school leavers' (Stansbury, 1980). These concerns prompted a meeting of local teachers, employers and LEA representatives in 1969, which set in motion a new initiative in time for ROSLA in 1972. As a result of the efforts of a working party, a system of personal recording – *The Record of Personal Achievement* – was established. It began operation in four local schools in 1970, and soon spread to a number of other LEAs.

The roots of personal recording were thus clearly fixed in the needs of, and pressures exerted by, less-able school leavers. In Stansbury's terms, personal recording was a 'learning activator' which could provide a motivating force for these young people by touching 'a spring of human action that is deeper and more powerful than the urge to compete. It is the urge to define and declare an identity' (Stansbury, 1980a). Evidently, Stansbury envisaged that personal recording could make a significant contribution to pupils' motivation and to their personal and social development. But for him, these were not its only purposes. He believed that the records built up by pupils could be used to organise and give coherence to non-academic coursework and that they could also ultimately provide a qualification by supplying extensive, descriptive evidence about the young person from which personal qualities could be inferred by an employer or any other interested reader. Motivation, organisation and qualification were thus the touchstone of Stansbury's philosophy; these were powerful claims for a scheme which, on the surface, seemed to involve little more than keeping a chronicle of events and feelings.

Stansbury would be and has been among the first to argue that the complex human processes underlying personal recording are of much greater significance than the simple and sometimes trivial-looking product (Stansbury, 1980b). However, the actual technology of personal recording is by no means irrelevant to the processes it is designed to generate. Indeed, what might appear to be only minor technological differences between the original RPA and some of its successors often reflect important changes in underlying philosophy.

In the case of RPA, pupils selected for it were asked to keep a diary of the most significant events in their lives. Entries were usually completed in 40 minute periods at some point in the school week. A selection of these was later written up on prepared, headed cards – some 29 in all – then stored in a four-part folder.[1] On leaving school, these folders became the property of the pupils, to be used as they wished.

In 1975–76, the Schools Council made an evaluation of RPA (Swales, 1979) and took over the scheme, which they renamed Pupils' Personal Records (PPR). The Council provided modest financial support; enough to assist with the purchase of pre-printed cards and professionally-styled folders as a way of helping generate a sense of pride and value among those who used them. PPR was initially very similar to its RPA predecessor, the major difference being the removal of the diary so that pupils now recorded directly on to the cards. When the Schools Council folded, PPR continued. Though funds had been withdrawn, there was sufficient enthusiasm and momentum for the scheme to continue under the auspices of a new Management Committee, based at the University of Bath.

Meanwhile, in 1974, Stansbury moved to Totnes in Devon. Here, drawing on his three years' experience of RPA, he founded a new scheme of personal recording – the Record of Personal Experience, Qualities and Qualifications (RPE). As with PPR, the original diary was removed. An important innovative feature of the RPE was the introduction of an induction period for pupils at the end of which they could choose whether or not they wished to participate further. This principle of pupil choice about involvement was regarded as a vital ingredient of personal recording; a testimony to its pupil-centred nature.

Perhaps the most important change was a shift in title: from being a record of *Achievement* to one of *Experience*. Babysitting, repairing a friendship, talking to a grandmother shortly before she died – these may not have been achievements, Stansbury argued, but they *were* important formative experiences. Were they not, therefore, equally worth recording?

A third change in RPE was its tighter and more elaborate structure. Pupils were provided with a handbook on the operation of the system. That system as a whole was divided into three stages. In the first, rather than being asked to select from a bewildering range of cards, as had previously been the case, pupils were invited to complete just three: one on an interest (on which 30 hours or more had been spent), one on 'work' (ie a job done out of school); and one on a self-chosen task, designed to illustrate the pupil's best skills and abilities. In the second stage, pupils were additionally required to fill in six of eight headed cards. This gave a clear focus for writing and ensured that the range of recording options was not overfacingly open-ended. Pupils could now develop the skills of recording without having to worry too much about what to write. Only after successfully completing this stage, were pupils allowed to enter the final, more open-ended stage of personal recording.

This more structured system, it is argued, encourages more thoughtful reflection among pupils as they develop the skills of recording. Moreover, it enables personal recording to be conducted with larger groups and therefore allows more pupils to be involved – thus offsetting, to some extent, the problem of personal recording being seen as suitable only for an educationally stigmatised minority (Stansbury, 1980a).

In some respects, then, PPR and RPE – the two main systems of 'packaged' personal recording – are similar derivatives of the original Swindon scheme. Both stress the importance of students having control over their own records. They use similar materials and advise that about 40 minutes per week should be spent on recording. Indeed, if the final product of pupil entries is inspected closely, not a great deal of difference can be discerned between the two systems.

It is not so much the entries themselves, but the processes by which they are produced and the ways in which they are used that distinguishes the two schemes. Since their initial establishment, the philosophical differences between PPR and RPE have become increasingly marked. RPE seems intent on adhering closely to the original tenets of the Swindon scheme – maintaining personal recording as an essentially private and pupil-chosen activity that is valid in its own right. PPR, meanwhile, is developing and strengthening its associations with other aspects of the secondary school curriculum and assessment systems. In particular, its advocates see it playing a key role in the development of pupil Records of Achievment; the diaries and personal records providing the basis for one-to-one discussions between tutor and pupil about progress and personal development (de Groot, 1986). In the most recent handbook of the PPR Management Group (1987: 2), for instance, its authors argue that the handbook itself 'marks the national recognition of the importance of the PPR process as part of current and future developments of pupil profiling'. Stansbury, however, maintains that far from extending the value of personal recording such developments breach its fundamental principles of pupil control and privacy. He regards them as infringements and sacrifices of pupil liberty for the sake of extending school control over and intrusion into pupils' personal thoughts and lives (Stansbury, 1984). We shall return to this controversy shortly.

Further education and training logbooks

A second influence on current patterns of personal recording in schools is to be found not in schools at all but in the further education and youth training systems. Here, logbooks and diaries have been introduced within broader systems of student profiling in vocational programmes like the Youth Opportunities Programme and the City and Guilds 365 course of vocational preparation (FEU, 1982, 1984). The usual practice within schemes of this kind has been for the students or trainees to make daily or weekly records or reviews of what they have been doing, what they have enjoyed or not enjoyed, what difficulties or new and interesting experiences they have encountered, and so on. These records may be entirely open-ended or they may be prompted by questions or phrases. Guidelines for the use of such logbooks suggest that regular time be allocated within the curriculum for entries to be made as a matter of routine (FEU, 1982).

The open-ended nature of the recording, the fact that it is initiated by the student, and the fact that the final document is the property of the student at the end of the course – in these respects, FE-style logbook keeping is virtually identical to personal recording systems in schools. Where the two systems do differ markedly though, is in the content and use of the records.

In terms of their content, school-based personal recording systems are extensive in scope and include the widest possible range of in-school and out-of-school experiences. FE-style logbooks are much more task-focused, however. They may contain statements of broad personal qualities and achievements, but only insofar as these are related to or have arisen from the student's or trainee's programme of study and experience.

Much of the reason for this difference in content has to do with the use to which FE logbooks are put compared with their 'packaged' school-based counterparts. Personal recording systems in schools have mainly been concerned with the declaration and enhancement of young people's personal identity. The open-ended form of the recording, the voluntary nature of the pupil's participation, the discouragement of criticism of entries by tutors, and the protection of pupil rights of privacy in allowing them to choose to whom they wish to disclose their records – all these things emphasise and reinforce the fundamentally pupil-centred nature of personal recording. FE logbooks are, of course, also partly concerned with the development of personal qualities such as self-confidence and reflectiveness. But their most immediate purpose has been to supply evidence as a basis for dialogue between student and tutor about progress and performance. This, in turn, has been designed to lead to the compilation of a grid-like profile, an assessment of skills and qualities revealed during a programme of work or study.

The dialogue, and the evidence that the logbook supplies for it, are seen as supportive to the trainee and as assisting his or her learning process (Pearce, 1981). But in our view the very existence of dialogue gives the logbooks or diaries a very different status from that which they have in personal recording. The FE-style records contain, not so much personal declarations *per se*, but statements to be commented on, scrutinised and amended through the dialogue that eventually leads to the production of the student profile. On the one hand, this kind of dialogue, and the evidence that students or trainees supply for it, can be seen as advantageous: the insights it generates might help the tutor alter coursework, adjust his/her style of supervision, provide appropriate support where relevant, and so on. On the other hand, when diaries and logbooks are incorporated into a wider system of monitoring and assessing progress, this will almost inevitably exert some backwash effect on what it is that students are prepared to disclose; on the depth and honesty of their entries.

Within the school system, not only have logbook styles of recording made an impact in the more obvious areas of 16–19 education – in City and Guilds 365 and the Certificate of Prevocational Education (CPVE) for instance, they have also been adopted within vocationalised parts of the 14+ curriculum. Logbooks have been widely used in a number of TVEI schemes, for example, particularly to enable students to record their responses to work and residential experience.

Diaries and logbooks in records of achievement

In recent years packaged systems of personal recording and FE-style systems of logbook recording have each made their mark on secondary education. While the styles and principles of the two types of system obviously differ, both are contained within identifiable parts of the curriculum and timetable and also tend to provide guidance and support for pupils and tutors alike on how to operate them. The influence of the two systems upon more general uses of logbooks and diaries within secondary schooling has been more diffuse and indirect, however, and in this respect the clarity and strength of supporting structures has been much more variable.

The proliferation of pupil diaries within newly developed systems of Records of Achievement has marked a key stage in the development and adaptation of personal recording. We have already seen how there have been increasing efforts to integrate PPR with more general systems for recording pupils' achievements. The influence of personal recording on Records of Achievement has been even more diffuse. In one pilot scheme for Records of Achievement, for instance – the Oxford Certificate of Educational Achievement – the research and development team has drawn its membership from people with profiling experience in Further Education as well as those with experience of PPR and other personal recording schemes. The expertise that has been drawn on in the development of other pilot schemes has been similarly mixed. This blend of expertise has led to strong recommendations for the use of diaries and logbooks as a basis for dialogue between tutor and pupil in the recording and reviewing process. However, because the principles of personal recording embodied in these two generic systems are to some extent competitive, important questions about how far the integrity of the pupil record should be protected, or how far it should be open to comment and criticism by others, have often been glossed over. Nor, given the principle of granting schools and LEAs autonomy to devise record of achievement schemes that will suit their local circumstances, have procedures and structures for diary recording been made sufficiently clear. It is here, in rapidly emergent systems of recording, where the system is novel, and where teachers may not always be fully committed to it, that the purpose, place and procedure for diary recording are at their most vague. It is here, therefore, that the difficulties of implementing personal recording in a way that will make a real and substantial contribution to personal and social development, are at their greatest.

Summary

Clearly, the keeping of logbooks, diaries and personal records, describes not one kind of activity but several. But at the heart of all of them, it is claimed, lie benefits for personal and social development. Advocates of personal recording argue that it helps to improve teacher–pupil relationships, to broaden and deepen the teacher's understanding of the pupil, and to bring about adjustments in curriculum and teaching to meet the pupil's now more clearly perceived needs. Most centrally of all, though, personal recording is regarded as a source of pride and motivation for the pupil; a means of defining and declaring identity and achievement. Pupils sometimes see personal recording this way too:

> I put it in my folder – sounds dead small – but I managed to clean the terrapins out, you see, and that was an achievement for me, so I wrote it down. It can be big or small – it's just important to me.[2]

> My sister did for options – she did helping this handicapped little boy, you see, and she liked it, and then she kept helping him after the options and then I started helping him and that. I felt really good about helping him so I wrote that down because it was something I really enjoyed doing and I felt I'd done something for somebody else, so I wrote it down.

Personal recording, then, can provide significant opportunities for recognising worth and success. But while personal records have their possibilities, they also have their problems. They may indeed sometimes be avenues for expressing achievement, but they can equally be roundabouts of routine, or cul-de-sacs of control. These difficulties are more than minor technicalities, and need to be examined very carefully.

Issues and problems

Discussion of some of the issues and problems in personal recording is best highlighted by listening to the consumers themselves – the pupils and the teachers. We shall therefore draw heavily on three sources of evidence to illuminate the discussion in this section: the Schools Council's Evaluation of RPA (Swales, 1979); research conducted by one of us in connection with the development of Records of Achievement (Tossell, 1984); and data collected by Paul Philips of Moat Community College, Leicester (though not from his own school), as part of a research project on the use of pupil diaries in the context of Records of Achievement.

Target group

A major issue in personal recording concerns who it is for. Is it apppropriate for all secondary pupils or only for some? Is it suitable only for the less able, or should it be the entitlement of all? Is it best used with older pupils, or should it be employed right across the secondary age range?

The roots of personal recording are in schooling for the less able. The original target group for Stansbury's RPA was low-achieving students in the final two years of secondary schooling. By the time of the Schools Council evaluation, as many as 82% of schools using RPA did so exclusively with less-able students (Swales, 1979: 17). Similarly, the use of logbooks within FE profiling has been concentrated among less-academic, vocationally-oriented groups (FEU, 1982, 1984). TVEI, as part-inheritor of this vocational tradition in schools, has also often used diaries and logbooks with groups which usually exclude the most academically inclined, university-bound students. Where diaries and logbooks have been used in the context of Government-sponsored Lower Attaining Pupil Initiatives, the ability boundaries have, by definition, been drawn even more tightly still.

By contrast, among the packaged schemes of personal recording, both PPR and RPE have urged that if personal recording is of use to the less able, it is equally important for other pupils too. With the support of these schemes, there has been a trend towards the use of personal recording with pupils of all abilities. This has certainly been reinforced by the growth of Records of Achievement – an innovation targeted at the entire age and ability range of compulsory secondary schooling. Where personal recording has been included in, or associated with, this development, this has elevated it to the status of a genuinely comprehensive reform: of relevance to *all* pupils.

In terms of age range, PPR has extended its reach right across the secondary span. A clear shift of policy on this seems to have occurred somewhere between 1981 and 1984. As recently as 1981, the PPR Handbook stated that 'the normal minimum span of recording is four academic terms and the maximum is six', and made it clear that this referred to the fourth and fifth years (De Groot and McNaughton, 1982: 13). Yet by 1984, the new Handbook indicated that 'the opportunity/expectation of engaging in the process could start at any age during secondary education but ideally it is available from year 1' (p 3). This shift of policy interestingly coincided with the Government's announced support for Records of Achievement. While PPR has extended its age and ability reach in part to build a closer association with Records of Achievement, RPE – a scheme that looks less favourably on the Records of Achievement initiative because of the way it allegedly comments on and criticises student entries – has continued to be used with older students only.

There are, then, both exclusive and inclusive versions of personal recording. What are the justifications for each? If the development of self-reflection should be an important part of the curriculum, an essential element of young people's secondary school experience – and we have argued throughout this book that it should – and if personal recording is indeed a valuable means to this end, then there is a strong case for introducing it as early as possible and with as many pupils as possible: across the age and ability range, that is. This case is not a watertight one, though. Consider some opposing arguments.

According to the Schools Council evaluation of RPA, many schools found it difficult to sustain the interest of pupils in personal recording even over the two year period from 14–16. Swales (1979) reported that the quantity of completed record cards often declined as pupils moved into their second year of recording. One reason for this, he suggested, was that competing examination pressures might have forced other, less pressing activities to take a back seat. Certainly, this view was supported by some student comments. As one remarked:

> We have not time to put things down now we are in the fifth year. Examinations
> are coming up and there is the worry about a job.
>
> (Swales, 1979: 52)

Understandably, it was the academic pupils who were most likely to be
dismissive about personal recording. In the face of such criticism and cynicism,
the managerially easier option is to allow more academic pupils to opt out of
personal recording altogether. But what is managerially easier is not always
educationally right. In this respect, we feel there is something ethically and
educationally unsound about confining personal recording to low attainers. To
do so is virtually to say 'Let the academic youngsters take an extra GCSE or
two! And the less able? Let them do diaries!'

A harder, but more justifiable response is for the school to commit itself to
raising the status, importance and relevance of personal recording in the eyes of
all pupils (and necessarily, therefore, in the eyes of their parents too). In this
respect, the credibility and success that personal recording has across the ability
range might well be taken as a measure of how well a school has established
and communicated the balance and range of its educational priorities as
extending beyond the academic domain.

We do not underestimate the difficulties here. Public examinations at 16+
have recently been reinforced and extended through the development of the
GCSE and through the 1980 Education Act's requirement that schools publish
their examination results to help parents choose secondary schools for their
own children. This intensification of market pressure on secondary schools in a
period of falling rolls, where examination results have been made the currency
of survival and success, has made it difficult for secondary schools to innovate
where inroads into the academic education of more able pupils are involved.
Given current policy parameters which require political action beyond the level
of the individual school, the success of schools in establishing status and
credibility for personal recording in the eyes of *all* pupils and their parents is
always going to be limited. In the interim, though, one helpful development
might be the mandatory introduction of Records of Achievement for all
secondary school leavers by the 1990s (DES, 1984; see also Chapter 6) which
might make the existence of personal recording, as a support for the profiling
process, a more 'normal' and accepted feature of the secondary system.

Routine, repetition and boredom

If examinations at 16 explain part of the reason for declining interest in
personal recording among final year students, another factor is undoubtedly
that of boredom, repetition and routine. This is perhaps the most powerful
argument of all against extending personal recording across the secondary age
span. Might not the sameness of personal recording account for at least some
of the fading enthusiasm? Is there not some point in the extension of personal
recording where the law of diminishing returns begins to set in?

The simplicity of personal recording might have managerial attractions, but it can also result in restlessness among students after a while. Within 'packaged' schemes, the selection of cards, followed by writing and filing, can become a monotonous routine. Swales (1979: 56) noted that 86% of students he interviewed were 'indifferent' towards recording. The comments made about PPR by students interviewed by one of us echoed this kind of sentiment. One described how the initial surge of enthusiasm had been followed only by disappointment:

> At first you think, 'Oh great! It's something new!' You think that perhaps you're only one of twelve schools picked for it and you think, 'Oh great. It's really exciting!' And then afterwards you think it's really boring.
>
> (Tossell, 1984: 83)

Nor are less tightly packaged schemes entirely immune from the dangers of routine and monotony. Where diaries have been used fairly extensively in the context of records of achievement, similar problems have been highlighted. As one younger secondary pupil expressed it:

> I've got one (a diary) now, but all I do is put parties in it and people's birthdays. I used to keep one but I've got the same every day – 'Got up. Brushed my teeth. Washed my hair. Did paper round. Went to school. Came home. Paper round. Did my homework. Went to bed!' It was just boring keeping one.
>
> (Phillips)[3]

Similar patterns of response have been found among pupils using diaries within TVEI. In one LEA, for instance, most schools have discarded the diary as part of the recording process, because they 'found themselves filling in the same kinds of things over and over again eg "went to my nan's", "went shopping", "went to science"! There seemed little point in repeating the same information over and over' (Turner, 1986: 4). Under these conditions, diary writing and logbook keeping can easily degenerate into an irksome, repetitive chore. How can this be avoided?

Some schools have attempted to solve the problem by getting away from the rigorous and academic overtones of a 'diary' or 'record', substituting the word 'scrapbook' instead. This has been accompanied by encouragement to use drawings, photographs and memorabilia, as well as conventional writing. We can see that this might motivate and involve some of the less able who perhaps have difficulty with writing. But if such improvements are little more than cosmetic they will do little to offset the doubts and cynicism about personal recording among the more able.

Variety may well be the spice of life, and indeed of recording. But until recently, there were few suggestions in the handbooks about how to introduce it. Teachers had little guidance on how to alleviate the monotony of the cards. The 1987 PPR Handbook has begun to tackle this problem, however. It contains a useful section of exercises and prompt sheets, designed to help get pupils' thoughts moving and to stimulate reflection as a basis for recording, or as a form of recording in itself (PPR Management Group, 1987: 34–52). With suggestions such as these for introducing variety, personal recording inevitably begins to develop closer links with other tutoring and curriculum activities.

The integration of personal recording with other areas of school work is itself a valuable strategy for averting boredom. De Groot (1986), writing on behalf of PPR, has suggested that health education and social education programmes more generally can provide just this sort of context; not least because modern understandings of health education put great stress on the development of feelings of self-worth which are in turn seen to be associated with 'the ability to take responsibility for our own lives, make decisions about lifestyle, and . . . function competently in social situations' (McNaughton, 1982). Some schools have adopted this approach by implementing recording as part of their PSE taught programmes; varying recording with modules of health, political, religious, careers and environmental education. It is not just a question of finding curriculum time for personal recording, though. Recording needs to have a clear context and purpose; one that pupils and tutors alike can recognise. This has a number of implications.

First, personal recording, diary and logbook keeping have often been found to be at their most effective when they are used in connection with a very specific experience, with something out of the ordinary – as in work and residential experience, for instance (Turner, 1986). Here, as we saw in Chapter 4, students will have encountered novel and challenging experiences of an intensive nature that draw heavily on their personal resources and often expose their weaknesses too. Where there is so much that is dramatically new, the student is spared the difficulty of hunting around for something to record. Quite the contrary. With this constraint now removed, and with an agenda now clearly set, the diary or logbook can more usefully be drawn on and developed as a tool of personal reflection; something for pupils to have a dialogue with as they assess their own personal response to the intensive experience they are undergoing. It is for reasons like these that some TVEI schemes have confined diaries and logbooks to the recording of planned intensive experiences, where the purpose and context of that recording are clear. This kind of approach can be especially valuable with older pupils who have had little previous experience of recording; where they are perhaps being introduced to it for the first time.

Another way of giving personal recording a clear purpose is to give it a definite audience. Under most circumstances, the tutor should probably read what the pupil has written. We recognise that this creates all kinds of problems concerning intrusions upon pupils' personal privacy – and we shall return to these shortly – but if what pupils record is *not* read, those pupils can quickly come to feel that it may not be worth recording at all. As two of them complained,

They (the teachers) just don't read it, do they? They just tell you what to put in it!

I just don't like keeping diaries, because if no-one is going to look at them, what's the worth of writing it?

Lack of audience can easily be equated with lack of purpose; lack of involvement with lack of concern. If no one reads the diary, presumably no one cares. That is not an unreasonable interpretation for young people to make. This is why, despite all its very real dangers, we regard the active involvement of tutors in personal recording as exceptionally important. Without some such involvement, it seems to us, personal recording can easily be seen as, indeed be used as, a managerially appealing but educationally valueless time-filler.

One way in which this kind of involvement can be secured is by using personal recording in the context of Records of Achievement. From the pupil's point of view, in the short term, diaries and written records can provide part of the basis for the discussion and review of progress and experience that goes on between pupil and tutor within any particular Record of Achievement scheme. In the longer term, by being linked to a record of achievement, personal records can contribute to the compilation of the final summative statement that pupils can take with them when they leave school. Despite the claims of Stansbury and others, insulated, 'packaged' systems of personal recording have not proved particularly valuable in providing pupils with a meaningful and useful qualification on leaving school. The sheer bulk of the material that pupils have compiled has usually proved too much for employers to wade through (Swales, 1979; HMI, 1983; Hargreaves, 1985). Harnessing personal recording to records of achievement offers one way of bypassing this difficulty; of giving it some role in providing pupils with a qualification.

It is because of these two factors – improving student reflection and teacher–pupil dialogue, and providing a meaningful qualification – that the representatives of one packaged scheme (PPR) now support and encourage links with records of achievement, claiming that 'successful PPR experience provides the bedrock for pupil participation in Records of Achievement' (PPR Management Group, 1984: 1). Despite the problems of privacy, to which we shall return, this development of a closer association between personal recording and records of achievement seems to us sensible – providing a recognisable purpose for personal recording, and a basis for dialogue within records of achievement.

Personal recording can fulfil different kinds of purposes, then – in connection with the PSE curriculum; records of achievement; and specific programmes of work or residential experience. Underlying all these purposes is the even more fundamental one of assisting the pupil in the process of self-reflection; a vital ingredient of personal and social development. Whatever the purpose of personal recording in any particular case, it is surely important that pupils are aware of this. The purpose of diaries, logbooks and personal recording should therefore be clearly communicated to those who use them, and indeed to their parents. The purpose of personal recording, that is, should be clear, and it should be *made* clear too. Pupils will then be much less likely to see it as irrelevant or boring.

Tutor and student roles and skills

We have seen that boredom may come from too much personal recording; from overkill. But equally, it may come from too little; from pupils and tutors having insufficient opportunity to develop and practise the skills needed for undertaking and supporting recording – with the result that it can degenerate into rather aimless and superficial logging of weekly events. Development of and support for clearly defined and well formed pupil and tutor roles in the recording process are essential to its success.

For those more used to the normal run of secondary teaching and learning, the roles required by personal recording can be difficult to learn and adjust to. For example, one of the principles laid down in the early packaged systems of personal recording was that they should be non-directive and non-judgemental. Pupils could select their own content for their records and write about them in whatever way they chose. They could even opt out of recording altogether, if they felt they had nothing to write about. Tutors were urged not to read, comment on, or mark these records unless invited to do so by their pupils. Indeed, if it was the wish of a student to keep a record entirely private, this had to be respected by the tutor. In the words of PPR (1984: 3), the records were thus 'pupil decided' and 'pupil controlled'.

This high degree of student autonomy was the most controversial aspect of these schemes when they first emerged. It ran counter to the general thrust of secondary education with its fixed learning routes through subject syllabi leading towards the judgemental assessments of terminal examinations. By contrast, personal recording required tutors to encourage among their pupils individuality in place of conformity; diversity in place of homogeneity; personal initiative in place of unquestioning compliance. Teachers, accustomed to directing operations from the front of their classrooms through pre-planned lessons and activities, were being asked to change their approach in recording sessions. The last thing needed was planning – at least by the teacher. The teacher's role was to be one of facilitator – enabling pupils to do their own planning, draw up their own agenda for the lesson, think things through for themselves and plan courses of action. Swales (1979) observed how anxious teachers became in these unstructured situations, and also noted their resulting demands for inservice training to help them take a back seat in the classroom!

If the teachers were anxious, so too were the pupils who had themselves become accustomed to receiving the curriculum 'on a plate', as it were, in the form of textbooks, worksheets and dictated notes. For most of their time at school, they had been required to do little more than read, listen to and remember the views of other people. Now, albeit for one session per week, they were being told that *their* preferences, *their* views, *their* values were important

– important enough to record. While in principle this should have been a welcome change, many could not cope with it. Some of this difficulty could no doubt be attributed to the incongruous place that personal recording occupied in the wider context of secondary schooling. Just like group tutorial work and taught PSE courses, it was expecting a lot of pupils – and teachers – to make a dramatic, Jekyll-and-Hyde like switch in character and approach between the rest of their secondary school experience and this one isolated slot. This inconsistency between personal recording and the rest of the curriculum raises problems not just of attitude and approach, but of skill and judgement too. As two teachers interviewed by Swales (1979) noted:

> I would favour a more directive approach . . . Left to their own devices this particular group of children were rather apathetic. I felt they needed more direction in what and when to write.
>
> (p 18)

> There are some pupils who are so limited in reading, writing and drawing or in their imagination for recording of any kind, that they simply cannot do anything requiring these attributes without the immediate active help of the tutor.
>
> (p 40)

Statements of this kind resurrect the perennial questions about the importance of the whole-school context for PSE and for the success of particular PSE initiatives – be they personal recording, group tutorial work, or whatever. Without significant attention being paid to personal and social development throughout the school, across the curriculum, as a major policy objective to which most, if not all staff are practically committed, the impact of particular PSE initiatives like personal recording is, in this sense, always going to be seriously restricted. In addition, particularly in the interim, some positive guidance is needed to help tutors cope with these new patterns of classroom relationships that personal recording demands. Until recently, this has not been supplied in the packaged schemes. Handbooks urged the application of 'razor-sharp awareness of individual need and individual response', the use of 'professional expertise', and sympathised about the 'tutoring tightrope'. But vague statements of this kind were not a great deal of help to the classroom practitioner. Tutors were encouraged to assist pupils to move towards greater self-reliance in recording; but they were also advised against becoming too directly involved themselves. How this difficult dilemma of when and how to intervene was to be managed was not made at all clear.

The most recent handbook for the PPR scheme sets out to deal with some of these difficulties. Like its predecessors, it continues to offer broad advice about the tutoring skills that are required. Tutors should have and show empathy, it says. They should be spontaneous and genuine, warm and open in their relationships with pupils. They should avoid being too directive in their use of language. But in addition to such general advice, useful illustrative examples are also given of the sorts of conversations with pupils that can result when these skills fail to be applied. In addition to this, one long section in the handbook also lists a set of practical, school-based inservice exercises that can be used to promote discussion and awareness of the tutor's role among those involved in personal recording (PPR Management Group, 1987: 10–32).

It is not only tutors that need guidance on the skills of personal recording, but pupils too. The extension of the recording process from the two final years of secondary education to the full secondary span is in part a recognition that pupils are not always naturally equipped to make interesting and insightful self-reflective comments and observations, and that they need to be prepared for such activities. As Pearce (1981) observes:

> Some young people appear to have a natural capacity to reflect upon their experiences and to learn from them, so that each event in their life, whether successful or not, adds to their ability to cope with the next. There are, however, many who, lacking the skill, move from one experience to another as if each were unrelated.

Preparing students to make such connections is often a lengthy process. It requires the tutor's active involvement, and in the early stages, may even necessitate that tutor taking a definite lead until the students have learned to cope with their own autonomy. In these early stages, students may need constant reassurance that their record is valued, they may need advice about content and method of recording and they will need encouragement when they begin to make such decisions for themselves.

It is, of course, important to retain protection of personal privacy in personal recording; to defend its fundamentally personal aspects. We shall deal with such matters in a moment. But in general, we are now talking of a move away from the exclusively 'private document' of earlier packaged schemes and towards seeing 'pupils as partners' in the recording process, as one scheme – PPR – now puts it. Partnership implies sharing, and the sharing of the content of a student's record is an important development in personal recording. We do not want to idealise the existence or nature of this partnership; to gloss over ways in which it might in some instances disguise tutors' attempts to exercise undue influence over what their pupils say and think. Many sins of power and manipulation are committed under the name of partnership, wherever it is used. Our use of partnership in the context of personal recording is, in this sense, a statement of intent, not a claim about current practice. But, ultimately, it is our belief that only through sharing and discussion will the formative benefits of recording be likely to be realised. This we call the interactive approach to personal recording.

Privacy, openness and trust

We have argued that from the point of view of personal and social development, the interactive approach to recording is probably the most appropriate one. Yet we are also aware of the serious difficulties and dangers that accompany this approach. Stansbury (1980a) has offered a poignant description of reading someone's personal record as being like entering their private home. One should enter it, he says, only by invitation, as a respectful guest. In this way, to criticise a record, or suggest ways of improving it, is like criticising your host's wallpaper. It is a breach of good manners, and if you do it, you run the risk of not being invited back, of being excluded forever. Where a (perhaps uninvited) guest who has come to comment on one's personal effects, as it were, is known not to be trusted or as not worthy of respect, the problems for the recorder are especially great. In such cases, having to discuss a personal record with a tutor one dislikes, does not trust, or is suspicious of, is therefore not just an intrusion upon privacy, but by that very fact is also likely to prevent the student from recording anything of worth and value in the first place.

How can this dilemma in the interactive approach to recording be resolved – the fact that it provides necessary support and feedback while at the same time threatening privacy and openness? Some specific measures can certainly be helpful here. First, while tutors can and perhaps *should* comment on what pupils write, they should not, of course, prejudge or insist on what is written. Ultimately, only pupils can take the final decisions about content. No one else can tell them what is significant in their lives. The role of the tutor is to help and encourage them to make that statement of personal identity and not, as in one insensitive case observed by Stansbury (1980a) to instruct them to write about the previous assembly or, as in an instance witnessed by one of us after an outbreak of misbehaviour, about 'Why you are naughty in school'!

More generally, it is helpful if tutors do not make critical remarks about the record as such, but treat it as a basis for wider discussion; as a prompt and opportunity for the pupils to talk about and share wider concerns that might be a source of interest, pride or anxiety.

If the integrity and openness of records is to be protected (despite their being inspected by and discussed with others), there must be qualities of trust, respect and openness in the broader relationship between the tutor and pupil, and indeed, in relationships between teachers and pupils in the school as a whole. This is a tall order, but a vital one. If teachers and tutors are not trusted, the recording process will have no worth or validity. Little of significance will be written or talked about. This is absolutely evident in the comments pupils have made about the use of diaries within records of achievement, where they clearly do not trust their tutors, are suspicious of their motives, and edit what they record accordingly. Some pupils, for instance, take the view that what they write will be used in evidence against them.[4]

> You don't write anything that's too deep 'cause I know the line they'll take – 'Oh, this gives cause for concern, I'll have to tell your mum about that' – 'cause that's what they're liable to say.

> I think one of the reasons why we didn't put much in the diaries was because you don't really put down anything . . . that reveals too much about you or anything . . . It's always about anyone else seeing it. Because you're bound to think things that you vaguely know about yourself, but you wouldn't like to think of putting down on paper, you know, as sort of evidence, if you like.

> It boils down to that you can't trust anyone but yourself. You might as well not write it down, so you might as well keep it all up there (points to head). That way, nobody knows it, so it doesn't matter.

As well as worrying that teachers will use this evidence against them, pupils also suspect that they might share this knowledge with teaching colleagues.

> No man teacher can read it. If there were personal things about teachers, they would gossip. Women teachers wouldn't. You don't see female teachers hanging round gossiping like you do the men teachers. They stand there for ages talking and gossiping about us.

> Say if they read it – for example, if I wrote something really important, see – if they read it and tell all the teachers; that's why I don't like teachers reading it.

> P1: The teachers – they'll gab it all to so many people.
> P2: Bound to, ain't they? All teachers talk to each other. I saw a whole load of teachers – there must have been eight – sitting round there, cups of coffee, cigarettes, nattering about one person.

Pupils have strong perceptions of how such gossip among the community of teachers might work to their disadvantage; how personal recording might have negative, even punitive consequences for them.

> I wrote that English was an f . . . g load of, you know, crap, and, um, the English teacher got it and I got a detention for that, so I threw that book away as well.

> Anyway, a teacher looking at it – you're not going to put, 'I hate this teacher', because then they might go and say to this other teacher, 'Oh, this girl hates you', because of . . . whatever you've written.

> I mean, they might criticise you for what you've put in it, because, say, like I put – 'Social Studies – boring', they'll say, 'Well, why is it boring?' and starting shouting at you, just because you put 'Social Studies – boring'.

> And another thing, say like in a disco dancing competition you came last; you write it in your diary and the teachers look at it – say, like a drama teacher – and they'd think, 'Oh, she won't be able to go in the play', or something like that.

For these sorts of reasons, despite the rhetoric of negotiation, change and partnership that underpins more recent developments in personal recording, some pupils clearly believe that it is not advantageous to make critical remarks about teachers, teaching and what is taught. For them, the curriculum still too often remains absolutely non-negotiable.

It's the sort of thing you think, but you're not gonna write it down. You're not going to say to a teacher that, 'I find French boring because it's mixed ability and I don't like that sort of set-up', because it's not up to us what we like.

Where these perceptions are dominant, pupils find it hard to see that personal recording might serve as a basis for negotiating changes in curriculum and teaching through their tutor (as official policy would have it), but can see it only as yet another device for 'keeping tabs' and 'checking up' on them.

> I think they really want to know what you think about the lessons just to check up on us.

> It's not for the teachers. It's to check up on us. That's why hardly anybody writes anything.

For pupils such as these, the one-sided character of the normal classroom relationship where it is teachers, not pupils, who ask all the questions, and teachers, not pupils, who evaluate the answers, carries right through into personal recording. While diaries might in theory be the pupil's property, they are too often treated as public property, for the teachers, or indeed the rest of the class to look at by right.

> Our teacher . . . wants to look at everybody's and I don't think that's right.

> But some teachers, if they say, 'Oh, would you like to read something from your diary', and you say 'No' because you feel embarrassed, they just in a way, like, make you speak something from it and you wished you'd never volunteered. Some teachers shout at you if you say no.

> Even if you put 'owt on it and you don't want them to see it and put 'Secret' or 'Top Secret' or 'Don't Touch', they just go in it. They don't even notice. I say, 'Can you read on that diary?' They say 'Yes'. And I say, 'What does it say? Top Secret. Don't Look'. They say, 'Oh, that's alright', and just have a look at it. I don't really like it.

Most tellingly of all, perhaps, pupils often grasp the fundamentally one-sided nature of the tutor–pupil relationship that commonly exists where private feelings are being recorded or discussed – a relationship not unlike that found in psychotherapy where the therapist has the right to examine what the patient says and feels, but not *vice versa*.

> They ask us personal questions, but if we ask them back, they think you are being rude.

> If they asked to look at mine, I'd ask if I could look at their diary.

> Mr Z left his diary on the desk, but when he caught us looking at it, he went barmy.

It is in circumstances like this that some pupils see advantages in having two diaries – one absolutely private and secret (with all the developmental and emotional benefits of the confessional), and a more judiciously edited one, to be discussed with teachers (allowing opportunities for advice and feedback without risking undue exposure). First, the case for the emotionally open secret diary:

> You might write it down, but you wouldn't show anyone; not if it was a real problem that was personal. You wouldn't show anyone. If I feel nothing is going right, everything is going wrong – if you write it down, I think you feel better.

Next, the case for the public diary being much more cautious and selective:

> I do let her have a look at it, but I don't put like really important things in the diary . . . That's why I let her have a look at it.

And finally, the case for two diaries, each with a different purpose:

> I think it would be a good idea to have one really personal (diary) to put things you don't like in about teachers and things like that, and then one about school that you can show the teachers – if you had two diaries, perhaps.

What is especially sad about the remarks made by these pupils – many of whom were identified by their schools as having writing or speaking difficulties; the very ones indeed at whom personal recording was originally directed – is that they betray the abject failure of their schools and their teachers to win their trust and respect. Without such trust and respect, these pupils patently regard diary keeping as at best a meaningless and irrelevant activity; at worst a threatening and intrusive one.

There are, of course, exceptions to this. And they are instructive exceptions too. For when particular teachers *have* managed to build a more open, trusting and mutually respectful relationship with their pupils, which the pupils themselves recognise, those pupils come to see very different and much more positive possibilities in personal recording, of just the kind the developers have intended.

> I don't mind showing Mr X because he never does show anyone.

> I got Mr X reading mine because he's quite a nice teacher, Mr X is.

> I'd let her look at it 'cause I know I can trust her and she won't tell anyone.

> I think if he had seen it (the diary), he'd just try to make it so you did understand it and you did like it. But if everybody else liked the way we were doing it and I didn't, then it would be difficult because he couldn't change the whole lesson just for one person. But he would try to make it so that you could do it.

> Sometimes the (diary) can't change the teachers' ways 'cause sometimes kids keep it to themselves. They don't let the teachers look. But if you let them, it might change their ways a bit.

> Teachers' attitudes are hard to change, but they will eventually and the (personal recording) things will help.

What you put in your diary, then, can work in your favour, or it can work against you. Where diaries are discussed with tutors, the potential in either direction is powerful and real. As one pupil put it most succinctly:

> It's really a gamble. If you show them, they might lean on you like anything. Or they might improve. You've got to take your chance really.

As we have seen, though, many pupils are obviously much less brave than this individual. They are not prepared to take the gamble. They cannot open their hearts and minds to a community of teachers they do not trust; to teachers who, in their view, might gossip about them, check up on them, even punish them for things they might record. They cannot entrust their feelings, thoughts and deeds to teachers who will transform their private revelations into public news, who will expect pupils to open out and change yet show little willingness to do this themselves – to reveal their own points of vulnerability, something of their private selves, perhaps even some readiness to change too.

Despite all the arguments in favour of using personal recording in the context of records of achievement where tutors are involved in discussing what has been recorded, the pupil comments here suggest that until more trust, openness and respect can be injected into teacher–pupil relationships in general, personal recording is likely to have only the most limited educational value. In some instances, its influence might even be anti-educational.

Is this not a case for returning to the earlier versions of personal recording of the type sponsored by Stansbury, as an entirely private process with minimal teacher intervention? This is a tempting solution. It would retain the confessional benefits of recording without undermining it with the supervisory and inspectorial activities that often accompany the discussion of records with tutors in more formalised systems of Records of Achievement. Yet, as we shall see in the next chapter, one clear purpose of records of achievement is precisely to open up the teacher–pupil relationship, to make it a more genuinely two-sided affair. Here we have the classic 'Catch-22' that afflicts most PSE initiatives. Personal recording, when combined with records of achievement, is intended to bring about more openness and trust in the teacher–pupil relationship. At the same time, its very effectiveness in this respect presupposes the presence of those qualities which recording is itself designed to create. How can this deadlock be broken?

One strategy is simply to muddle through; to recognise that we have to start somewhere and take the kind of gamble the pupil we quoted earlier did. In this case, we somehow hope there will be enough success to be noticed, and that it will spread. This could just work. But it could have the opposite effect; a widespread, contagious sense of failure could create disillusionment and suspicion among pupils and teachers on a scale that could take years to undo. This is just too great a gamble to take.

Neither a return to private recording nor a sudden and widespread commitment to recording in the context of teacher–pupil discussion therefore seems satisfactory. In our view, some kind of phased introduction to interactive recording and to extending the recording process looks like a safer, more productive option. There are various ways in which this might be done. Introducing recording within very specific programmes of activity – like work and residential experience – where the agenda is clear and relationships with tutors are already rather different from those found in most classrooms, is one that we have already discussed. Developing recording within particular parts of the curriculum, where the commitment to personal and social development, not least among those who teach it, is already very strong – is another. The development of personal recording within the context of PSE taught courses can be useful here. On the same principle, introducing personal recording with one particular year team of committed and enthusiastic tutors can equally create a base of successful experience and practice on which further development can be built. Personal recording can, in this sense, benefit from the strategies that have often been used to introduce tutorial work more generally (see Chapter 3).

In the early stages of introducing personal recording, or where pupils are experiencing it for the first time, there may be something to be said for compartmentalising it and making it rather private in nature – in the style of the earlier packaged schemes. This can be a valuable interim strategy – giving pupils experience in the skills of recording, a supportive format for doing it, and protection from evaluation and misuse of what they have recorded. In our view, this really ought to be an interim measure only, otherwise, as we have seen, boredom will probably set in. If used in addition to this, none of the opportunities that personal recording offers in terms of recognising and rewarding achievement, or improving the teacher–pupil relationship, will be grasped.

Until trust has been secured, another way of protecting privacy might be to have two diaries – as some pupils have indeed suggested: a secret one of an entirely personal nature, and one with a more carefully selected edited range of comments and observations for discussion with tutors. This could, of course, become burdensome and time-consuming, but if the use of two diaries were offered on an optional basis, our guess is that many, in practice, would not take it up. The important principle of having an outlet for recording 'secret' and highly personal information and observations would thereby be protected, without this leading to 'diary fatigue'.

Even when trust has been reasonably well secured, an important principle for maintaining and sustaining it will still be the existence of procedures which demonstrably respect and protect pupils' rights of privacy. Preservation of the right to contract out of personal recording on *emotional* or *ethical* grounds (but not academic ones of the 'Can I do a second language instead?' sort), is probably important here. This would give personal recording the same kind of moral importance and ethical standing that religious education enjoyed many years ago, before its position in the secondary school system weakened. Critics might want to argue that making personal recording optional in this way would undermine its status and credibility, especially among the more able. We recognise this danger, but feel that the principle of opting-out instead of opting-in, along with the acceptance of ethical reasons only for such opting-out, will go some way towards offsetting it.

More important still, perhaps, is the establishment of rules and procedures designed to recognise the privacy and confidentiality of what is shown to and then discussed with the tutor, so that it will not be used thoughtlessly or expedientially for other school purposes – to service the discipline and referral systems, for instance. Possible procedures of this kind, with their massive implications for whole-school policy, are discussed in the next chapter. Without formal recognition and upholding of the principle of privacy and confidentiality, along with a set of procedures for dealing with these things, it is indeed extremely unlikely that the degree of trust required to operate an effective and worthwhile system of personal recording will ever be secured.

Conclusion

One of the recurring themes of this book is that PSE is part of the curriculum, not an appendage to it. Personal recording is an important element of PSE, and to set it aside as a discrete activity, conducted once a week with no connection to other curriculum activities is probably a mistake, except perhaps as an interim strategy. Swales (1979) noted that under such conditions, pupils failed to make any connections with other parts of their school experience; most of their recording was about out-of-school activities and very little about the remainder of the curriculum. For these reasons, it seems sensible to link personal recording to other school activities – to taught PSE courses, to tutorial programmes, and to records of achievement – throughout the period of secondary education.

More interactive uses of recording do, of course, carry with them very real dangers of the kind that are pervasive in PSE as a whole: threats to privacy, to liberty and human dignity more generally. In particular, such uses of recording depend on those qualities of trust and openness in the teacher–pupil relationship which their very introduction is designed to develop. We do not underestimate the seriousness of these difficulties; but we believe that by phasing in personal recording gradually, and by securing clear protections for pupil privacy and confidentiality, they may be surmountable. And that would be a good thing, for the potential contribution of personal recording to personal and social development is very great indeed.

Personal recording began as a response to some of the major educational developments of the 1960s – to the need to give pupils a role in their own learning, the need to value pupils for whatever strengths they bring to the school community, and the need to provide a means of qualifying pupils on the basis of those strengths. Initially, these needs were identified with older, less-able pupils, for that was where policy demands and the threats to school order were most pressing.

In the 1980s, as discussion about the principle of comprehensive education has extended beyond the mere provision of common buildings (as in the earlier stages of reform), to discussion about common entitlements to similar educational experiences, the relevance of personal recording (like PSE more generally) to *all* young people, is coming to be recognised. In this respect, the status and acceptance of personal recording as an entitlement of *all* pupils is being greatly enhanced by the Government-sponsored development of Records of Achievement for all. Despite the dangers we have outlined, it is understandable that personal recording should increasingly have taken on an interactive cast and linked itself more closely with this major policy initiative. Clearly, in the next few years, the fate and effectiveness of personal recording will be very much bound up with the fortunes of Records of Achievement more generally. This is the subject of our next chapter.

Notes

1   Examples of the cards and the headings used for cards in connection with different personal recording schemes can be found in Balogh (1982), Goacher (1983) and HMI (1983). In the latest version of Pupils' Personal Records, there are no longer card headings as such; only suggested titles. These are:

Art, craft and design	Following instructions, inter-
Attendance	preting instructions
Away from home	Jobs, part-time employment
Day visits	Oral work, talking with people
Films, television and radio	Personal experience
General activity assignments	Reading
Group project work	Service to others
Hobby, interest and personal	Sports, physical activity
project work	Work visits, work experience
Illustrations and display	Writing

2   These quotations are from data collected by Paul Phillips in connection with his research on pupils' interpretations of diary keeping in the context of Records of Achievement.

3   Quoted in PPR Management Group (1984).

4   All ensuing examples in this section are drawn from Phillips' research.

6 Records of achievement and pupil profiles

In July 1984, the DES published an influential policy statement on Records of Achievement (DES, 1984). It announced that:

> The Secretaries of State hope it will be possible to establish throughout England and Wales, arrangements under which all young people in Secondary schools will have records of achievement and will take with them when the leave school a summary document of record prepared within a framework of national policy which leaves scope for local variations.
>
> (Para 8)

It was envisaged that these records of achievement would contain three components: an external examination component where conventional public examination results would be recorded (eg GCSEs, B. Tech and possibly also such things as Duke of Edinburghs' awards and swimming certificates); a record of internal continuous course assessments which would document pupils' achievements in a number of school subjects; and a personal record component which would record pupils' experiences and achievements beyond the conventional academic curriculum, both within and outside school. It is this personal record component, along with all its possibilities and problems, that we will discuss here.

This major policy initiative, as the DES itself recognises, is not entirely new to education. In many respects, as we shall see, it is the culmination of a whole spate of more localised developments over recent years. All the same, the Government's intervention has added significantly to the scale and importance of records of achievement in the secondary school system. Of all the approaches to PSE we have reviewed in this book, the Records of Achievement initiative is the only one to have received Central Government backing. This has taken the form of a published policy statement (DES, 1984), the allocation of ten million pounds to fund and evaluate nine pilot schemes in the area, and the stated intention to have all secondary schools operating some kind of record of achievement by the 1990s. Nor does Goverment interest end there. Pupil profiles are also a widespread feature of the Lower Attaining Pupils Project (LAPP) and the TVEI, and are a mandatory requirement of the Certificate of Prevocational Education (CPVE). There is no doubt that in profiles and records of achievement, we are dealing with an innovation of national scope and significance. Good or bad, its implications for PSE are substantial.

This chapter will review the claimed benefits of profiles and records of achievement for young people's personal and social development. Then, by looking at the historical background to profiling, it will try to explain why profiling should have generated such intense political and professional interest. Lastly, it will raise a number of key issues and problems. The chapter will be a long one – much the longest in the book. But we hope you will bear with us on this; profiling is a fairly recent development and a highly diverse one – so we will need to present a good degree of information as well as analysis to illustrate the range of what, for many people, will be unfamiliar practice, to identify the varying nature of the problems that can be encountered, and to explore different possible solutions for dealing with them.

Purpose and rationale

Records of achievement and pupil profiles are designed to serve many different purposes. There are many justifications for their use. Much of their strength and popularity comes from their apparent capacity to meet many of these purposes simultaneously. In this section, we will examine some of the more commonly stated reasons.

1   Records of achievement propose to *give genuine recognition to the whole range of pupils' abilities and achievements*, not just academic ones. Conventional public examinations at 16, it is argued, assess only a narrow range of what pupils achieve inside and outside school. They tend to focus on what the Hargreaves Report for the ILEA (1984) called just one aspect of achievement – cognitive–intellectual achievement; knowledge of the sort that is easily remembered, regurgitated and written on demand. Such examinations have not been so good at assessing and recognising practical achievements of a making, doing and designing kind (though the GCSE is aiming to rectify this to some extent). And they are even less good at assessing and recognising personal and social achievements.

School reports have traditionally suffered from the same kinds of drawbacks (Goacher, 1984). They have supplied summary grades and terse comments on a narrow range of curricular achievements or their absence, that give parents only the most minimal information about how their children have responded to their school experience. 'Good work', 'makes little effort', 'must try harder' – these things say little about the vast array of pupils' personal and social experiences and achievements in school.

In the early stages of development in profiles and records of achievement, this is where much of the attention focused – on the compilation of a final document of personal record which can be presented to employers and other 'users'; on the benefits of a more extensive and comprehensive system of recording and reporting what young people have achieved in school.

Discussion about such a *summative* document or report and the form that it might take is, however, often allowed to obscure what may well be the more educationally significant *formative* stage in assessing and recording pupils' experiences and achievements; the continuous process of appraisal and review where educational experiences and the pupils' personal responses to them are discussed, evaluated and negotiated, and where new targets are set and agreed for the future. It is this process of continuous appraisal and review of personal experiences, achievements and difficulties, designed to increase pupils' involvement in and raise awareness of their own learning, that perhaps forms the very core of records of achievement. This principle lies at the heart of all its other claimed benefits.

2   *By recognising and assessing personal and social achievements* in particular, it is hoped that records of achievement will draw greater attention to them; *give them more emphasis in the school curriculum*. Public examinations have often been accused of being an unfortunate tail that wags the curriculum dog – narrowing the curriculum, and cramping teaching and learning styles (D. Hargreaves, 1982; ILEA, 1984; HMI, 1979). Advocates of profiles and records of achievement acknowledge the principle that assessment determines the curriculum, but turn this principle to different ends. By assessing and recording personal and social experiences and achievements, they hope to increase the educational importance attached to these things. Different tail – different dog! That is the intention.

3   By broadening the areas of achievement that are recognised, rewarded and assessed, it is hoped that profiles and records of achievement will also help *motivate* pupils more in their schoolwork, *by giving them greater experience of genuine* (not contrived)[1] *success*, and by recognising such success when it has been achieved. If you broaden the definition of achievement, you increase the likelihood that individuals will experience it, and you reduce the likelihood of certain individuals being overwhelmed by the experience of persistent failure. Records of achievement are therefore seen as a way of *motivating* young people, particularly those traditionally regarded as 'low achievers' or 'academically less able'.

4   Such motivation, it is felt, will also be enhanced by *giving pupils the opportunity to define and declare their own identity* as a way of *increasing their self-awareness and independence*. This will be helped by pupils comparing their performance against themselves; not against one another. These advantages surrounding the development of pupils' awareness of personal worth along with the provision of opportunities to state it, hold much in common with the more long-standing aims of personal recording (see previous chapter).

5   A common view is that pupils' motivation will also be assisted by *involving them more in their own assessment*. This will not only increase self-awareness, it is claimed, but encourage pupils to *take more responsibility for their own learning* also, if they themselves see that they have some positive and influential stake in it.

6   Self-assessment does not only boost pupil motivation. It also helps teachers *diagnose* their pupils' *learning needs*. We can teach people much more effectively when they are in a position to tell us about their commitment, understanding, and so on. Good doctors seek this kind of information all the time when making diagnoses. They don't tell us 'You have a pain!', they are astute (and indeed polite) enough to ask how we feel first, to involve us in order to improve their diagnosis. Yet in teaching, we often make judgements of this kind. We presume we already *know* how pupils are thinking and feeling – and this is reflected in the way we talk to them and in the way we comment on their work: 'You don't understand', 'You're not listening', 'You haven't tried', 'This is not your best', 'Concentrate, will you' etc. We rarely ask pupils first. A more formalised system of pupil self-assessment, and a way of making these assessments available to teachers, will, it is hoped, help teachers improve their diagnoses of pupils' learning difficulties; and make teachers more effective in their daily work.

7   As the routine, day-to-day importance of self-assessment is grasped, and these assessments are discussed between pupils and teachers, schools and teachers begin to realise that assessment is no longer simply something that takes place when a piece of learning has been completed. It is more than just an examination grade, a test score, or a mark and comment on a piece of homework. *It becomes a part of the learning process* itself; a way of providing the teacher with extra information to help the pupil; and a way of providing the pupil with feedback to help improve his or her performance.

8   Self-assessment involves reflecting on one's own achievements and shortcomings, as we have seen. But to do this realistically, one has to *assess the context of* those *achievements* too, of what one is achieving *at*, how much help is being provided, and so on. This means that pupils will increasingly become involved in assessing the nature and quality of what is being offered, of what is being taught and how it is being taught. Poor attendance at school but not on work experience may say more about the school than the person failing to attend it. Lack of interest in reading may be identified as following on from a dislike of reading round the class, or pulling plots to bits so that all their spontaneity is lost, for instance. Consider the comments of these pupils to their teacher on aspects of their English teaching, collected during pilot work for a self-assessment scheme in that subject.[2]

(a) I enjoy reading because its a good, no effort hobby. I usually read at night if I'm bored and sometimes during the day if I've got a book I can't put down. I like reading about people's experiences during the war. I quite like reading historical studies as well . . .

Reading in school is boring. A whole class of thirty reading the same book. When I was in this position, I'd read on and almost finish the book while the teacher was still droning out chapter 5. Also, you can't concentrate or listen properly with twenty nine other people around you because not all of them are interested in the story . . .

The fourth year literature course has really annoyed me. We sit and read books at home or in class and then have to go and write an essay on the tiniest, most unimportant point you can think of. All it does for me is spoil the enjoyment of a book I may have liked . . .

(b) I can read quite well when I want to I read a lot on my hobby and I read the news paper quit a lot. and I read some magazines. I most read in my spear time. if im not in the mode for reading I wont read. I have to be in the mode for reading. but if I want to find something out in a book I go on and read it. I most read about my hobby – racing pigeons I read that almost every day for about an ahuer or more some days I dont read if I have to do something else. or if I go to bed late it all depends. I like to read about the deaseses that pigeons can cach . . . and how you should look after them. I dont like reading much in school because im not usuealy in the mode to read in the day time because I need to be in the mode to read. and another reason is the school havent got the stuf I like.

What these comments indicate is that once *genuine* dialogue begins about how pupils interpret their educational experience and their response to it, this is bound to raise questions about the quality and suitability of that experience, of the curriculum, of the teacher's own teaching. This poses fundamental challenges to the teacher–pupil relationship, to the teacher's traditional classroom authority. It makes the teacher more vulnerable. It puts him or her in a continual position of having to assess the worth or appropriateness of what and how he or she is teaching. When thirty children tell you quietly and independently that they get very little from reading round the class, it is hard to resist the feeling that you really should do something about this. In this sense, profiles and records of achievement are a sort of Trojan Horse. On the face of things, they appear, innocuously enough, to be a useful aid for improving and extending the reporting system. Once brought inside the school, though, they have the potential to transform the entire teacher–pupil relationship.

9 Equally, as pupils become more independent and take more responsibility for their own learning, it is anticipated that they will have more of a say in that learning, in deciding what they are taught, in making choices about their own curriculum. In this sense, as we shall see, records of achievement imply large scale *changes* – not just in the teacher–pupil relationship, but ultimately *in the*

entire curriculum and organisation of secondary schooling (Burgess and Adams, 1985).

10   Last, but not least, profiles and records of achievement promise (or threaten) changes of the kind we have outlined for more than just particular, identifiable groups of pupils. In the DES policy statement, they are not seen as a reform that should be restricted to the 'less able' (unlike LAPP); nor are they specifically targeted at the broad middle ability range of pupils (as most pupils opting into TVEI programmes are turning out to be); nor are they intended solely for middle and high attainers (unlike the GCSE). Rather, they are a reform targeted at all secondary pupils, whatever their age and ability. In this sense, of all recent Goverment initiatives in education, records of achievement is the most *genuinely comprehensive*.

Summary

The rationale behind profiles and records of achievement is exceptionally broad. Indeed, it is this apparent capacity to solve many educational problems and needs simultaneously that gives the records of achievement initiative its appeal. Some of the arguments have been brought together succinctly in a statement on Records of Achievement by the Junior Education Minister, Bob Dunn.[3] He supports the development of records of achievement partly because of the benefits a summary document would have in providing 'a more rounded picture of young people's achievements and abilities than can be provided by a list of examination results and a testimonial', and partly because

> We must do justice to pupils' efforts – to recognise and give credit for what they have achieved; we must help schools to identify the all round potential of their pupils and to develop their curriculum and teaching in ways that will best do justice to this potential. And we must contribute to pupils' personal development and progress by improving their motivation and helping them to develop such qualities as self reliance and self assessment . . .

Similarly, in its policy statement on Records of Achievement, the DES outlines what it takes to be its four main purposes for the initiative. Records of Achievement, it says:

> . . . should recognise, acknowledge and give credit for what pupils have achieved and experienced, not just in terms of results in public examinations, but in other ways as well . . . They should contribute to pupils' personal development and progress by improving their motivation, providing encouragement, and increasing their awareness of strengths, weaknesses and opportunities . . . (They) should help schools to identify the all round potential of their pupils . . . (and they should provide) a short, summary document of record which is recognised and valued by employers and institutions of further and higher education.

> (DES, 1984: 3)

This, then, is the scale of what is being proposed and implemented in the name of records of achievement: a reform encompassing a broad range of achievements for all pupils, designed to boost their motivation, increase their independence and self-awareness, and make them active, negotiating partners in the teacher–pupil relationship and in shaping the secondary school curriculum. It is a reform designed to give confidence, purpose and sense of success to young people; and to transform the curriculum and teacher–pupil relationship in secondary schools in such a way as to make these things possible. It is a reform that treats personal and social development not as something peripheral to or isolated from the rest of the schools's curriculum and organisation (as in the approaches to PSE we have discussed so far), but as something that is absolutely central to the entire educational process; something that is inextricably intertwined with curriculum, organisation, teaching style and assessment. It is a daring reform, more wide-ranging, radical and penetrating in its implications than almost anything we have seen in secondary schools since comprehensive reorganisation.

For some tastes, the initiative may, in some of its guises, even be a little *too* radical, as the Junior Education Minister hints when he says[4]

> Some even see records of achievement as the heralds of an educational revolution in the classroom. Perhaps this may prove to be so in the long term. But we must not allow ourselves to be carried away . . .

How, we might ask, has a development of such professed revolutionary implications come to receive such firm Government support and widespread professional interest? What track record did profiling have before the DES began to take a substantial interest in it? And why, if the benefits of profiling have been evident for some time, should the DES suddenly take an interest now, in the 1980s?

To answer questions of this kind, we need to look at the historical background of profiles and records of achievement, to examine some of the purposes for which they were originally designed, and identify some of the problems they were intended to solve. When we do that, we may find reasons behind the support for profiles and records of achievement other than the officially professed ones; and in identifying those reasons, we may be able to locate the nature and source of some of the issues in profiling that people are now having to confront.

Background

Notwithstanding the DES's recent interest, the idea that young people should be provided with a rounded statement of their achievements on leaving secondary school is not new. The 1944 Education Act placed an obligation on schools to ensure that 'every pupil on leaving secondary school should be provided with a comprehensive school report containing the fullest possible information about him and his abilities and potentialities'. Almost twenty years later, the Newsom Report echoed this statement when it said that 'boys and girls who stay at school until they leave at 16 may reasonably look for some record of achievement when they leave'.

The change of wording from 'report' in 1944 to 'record' in 1963 is significant. *Report* implies an intentionally judgemental document which may be positive or negative in character. *Record*, however, suggests a more open-ended collection of evidence on which readers can base their own judgements. The introduction of the word 'achievement' is also notable since it invites positive rather than negative comments. The idea of the very term 'records of achievement' was therefore already in currency by the early 1960s.

At that stage, though, the meaning of records of achievement was narrower than it is now. It referred to some kind of final leaving statement that young people would collect when they completed school – to the end-point or *summative* stage of educational assessment. In this early use, no mention was made of the long process by which such records might be produced through a continuous review of pupils' progress and experience over the course of their secondary education, in which pupils themselves played an active part. The contribution of records of achievement to the *formative* process of educational assessment was not an issue in the early 1960s.

Whether we are looking at formative or summative aspects, though, little progress was made in the development of profiles and records of achievement for fifteen years or so following the Newsom Report. For quite some time, little became of those records which were to be the right of every student leaving school at 16. Yet, if the general commitment to profiles and records of achievement throughout the 1960s and 1970s was weak, there were, nonetheless, a number of localised initiatives and experiments during this period which in effect supplied influential guidelines and precedents that later, more widespread developments would often follow. What were these developments? And what lessons would be learned from them?

1 Personal recording: the Swindon scheme

The contribution of personal recording to more recent developments in records of achievement was discussed in Chapter 5. There, we saw that personal recording was an initiative originally designed for older, less able pupils in the context of comprehensive reorganisation and the raising of the school leaving age. The bulkiness of the extensive dossier proved too overfacing for employers. But for the pupils themselves, the scheme provided an avenue for them to develop and declare a personal identity. The scheme was almost entirely open-ended. The words and thoughts were the pupils' own. And in principle, what was recorded belonged to them too. It was to be shared with their teachers only with the pupils' consent. The rights of authorship and ownership belonged to the pupil – emphases which have persisted in some modern versions of records of achievement.

2 Pupils in profile: the Scottish initiative

A second initiative – one that would prove highly influential for the profiling movement in years to come – could hardly have had a more different emphasis. This was the *Pupils in Profile* project, developed by a working party of the Headmasters' (later Headteachers') Association of Scotland in association with the Scottish Council for Research in Education (SCRE) from 1972 onwards. Like personal recording, *Pupils in Profile* was also precipitated by the raising of the school leaving age. The Association established the initiative, it said, because its members were 'concerned about the non-certificate pupils who would leave school at 16 without a national certificate' (SCRE, 1977: 1). Its primary purpose was to devise a pattern of assessment appropriate to these pupils; 'to supply an incentive and a recognition of a goal which is relevant and worthwhile to those who will leave school at 16' (p 2).

On paper, the goals that were later agreed for this new assessment initiative were not all that different from the goals of personal recording. It was hoped that the development would 'provide users with useful information, orientate teachers towards a guidance model, support the schools in their programme of total education and enhance pupils' self knowledge' (SCRE, 1977). Beyond this level of generally stated goals, though, the similarities with personal recording end.

First, the format was different. Basically, it was a grid which allowed teachers to tick their assessments of pupils on a 1–4 scale. The assessments were of cross-curricular skills like listening, reading and physical co-ordination; of subject performance in terms of knowledge, reasoning, presentation, imagination and critical awareness; and of two 'work-related characteristics' – perseverance and enterprise. While there was also some space for teachers to add more open-ended comments where appropriate, generally speaking, the *Pupils in Profile* format was much more systematised than the one adopted in personal recording.

Second, teachers had much more control over the records and the recording process than in personal recording. Teachers assessed pupils. Pupils made no assessments or records of their own. Nor were the assessments the basis of any negotiation between teachers and pupils. Assessment was something done to pupils by teachers. Pupils had no continuing involvement in it themselves. The only exception here was that the profiles were meant to help discussion between pupils and their guidance teachers – but these discussions were infrequent and were not held with the teachers who had made the assessments. This lack of pupil involvement in and control over the profiling process extended to their rights of ownership too. Pupils owned only their own final leaving statement (though it has to be said that this was a significant advance on the previous system of confidential references). Pupils did not, however, either own or have any say in the compilation of their interim profiles. Indeed, the profile could be retrieved and consulted at any time by the guidance teacher or class teacher without the pupils' permission. Pupils' ownership rights were therefore severely limited; their authorship rights non-existent.

Third, much of the profile was designed with the interests of employers very much in mind. The simplicity and economy of the final report was meant to serve employers' interests in providing something they could rapidly scan when considering applicants. In addition, the section of the profile dealing with personal qualities had a much more powerful and explicit vocational thrust than did personal recording. 'Work-related characteristics', the profile called them, which perhaps explains why, out of all the qualities that might be relevant to personal and social development, only perseverance and enterprise were picked out for comment. This emphasis was deliberate. The Head-teachers' Association categorically stated that it wanted to concentrate on assessing 'behaviours that might be relevant to further education and employment on leaving school' (SCRE 1977: 14).

In Scotland, the impact of *Pupils in Profile* was minimised and over-shadowed by developments in 16+ certification as a whole (Broadfoot, 1986a, b). In England and Wales, though, it left important legacies. Widely cited in more recent profile developments, the Scottish initiative established the principle that profiles should be of simultaneous benefit to teachers, schools, employers and the pupils themselves. It made the point that this process should be available to all pupils, not just the less able (even if that was where its efforts were first directed). Its grid format was widely emulated in further develop-ments for a number of years. Lastly, the vocational backdrop to profiling, so prominent in the SCRE project, remains in more recent schemes even though they are more ostensibly preoccupied with personal and social development as such. The tones of that backdrop are merely rather more subtle and faded. One way in which that backdrop remains is in the continuing unquestioned accep-tance of the fact that employers should be involved in profile development.

3 Further education and training: negotiated grids

Outside Scotland, most of the early running in profile development was made in the Further Education (FE) and Youth Training sectors. In the late 1970s and early '80s, FE experienced a rapidly expanding intake of young people on non-award-bearing courses, opportunities programmes and training schemes. Pressure was building in the low status end of the educational market in FE just as it had in schools when the leaving age was raised. Many of the new programmes and courses were experiential in nature, yet there were no ways of recognising and recording how well young people were responding to that kind of learning (Pratley, 1982). These sorts of considerations prompted the DES supported Further Education Curriculum Development and Review Unit

(FEU) to launch a pilot programme for developing student profiles (FEU, 1979); a programme from which many further developments would soon follow.

The creators of the new FE profiles took into account existing developments in Scotland and Swindon (Mansell, 1982) but these were not regarded as appropriate for the special requirements of the FE sector and of training this particular group of young people. For one thing, the world of employment was of paramount importance in the development of any profile for youngsters beyond school leaving age on courses with a strong vocational element. This lent greater importance (even more than in the Scottish case) to the final summative document and its accessibility to, and credibility among, employers. This helps explain the widespread adoption of various kinds of grids in FE schemes. One of the most widely used and influential of these has been the grid adopted from early FEU pilot work by the City and Guilds of London Institute (CGLI) for its '365' Vocational Preparation Course, which involves students, with their tutors, shading in how far along a thermometer-like scale they have developed mastery of a selected range of skills.

The second special feature of FE in profiling terms is that its expanded intake of youngsters would demonstrably not be easy to teach. Many had not fared well with their teachers in the ordinary school system with its conventional patterns of curriculum, assessment and teaching style. Nor, unlike the traditional system of day-release and evening classes, could compliance be secured by providing skills and certificates that had demonstrable benefits for trainees' and apprentices' existing jobs (Mardle and Gleeson, 1980). Training the young unemployed created new needs and new control problems. Any new assessment structure would need to be motivating, to engage students' interest and involvement, if it was to cope with them. The use of student logbooks, a leaf out of the personal recording book, went some way towards meeting these needs. The key assessment strategy for dealing with this particular group of youngsters, though, was profile *negotiation*.

Profiling would not be something done *to* students by teachers (as in the SCRE scheme), nor a predominantly private preoccupation of the student (as in personal recording), but a process where assessment and progress would be discussed and negotiated between student and tutor together. Tutor-compiled profiles might form a basis for such a discussion, as might student logbook entries, but any eventual statement would be negotiated, signed, and if possible agreed by both parties (Stratton, 1986). Pratley (1982: 30) has put it this way: 'the curriculum is made explicit to the learner, and in this respect the profile acts as a focus for the negotiation of learning agendas'. This might also involve identification of and agreement on *learning contracts* for the future between tutor and student as goals are discussed and shared, and the curriculum is increasingly tailored to the students' needs (FEU, 1981: Para 88).

While the gap between the rhetoric and reality of profile negotiation is often great, as we shall see later, and while negotiation in FE has been largely restricted to the formative stage, the principle of it has probably been the FE sector's chief contribution to more recent developments in records of achievement at school level, along with its demonstration of the ways in which profiling can be integrated into the curriculum as a whole. Its further development of the grid format has been less influential and is out of tune with DES recommendations on the issue – though its contribution has served to reinforce the more general principle, still widely accepted, that *some* method should be found to record personal and social skills and qualities in a hierarchical way. One last point: if profiling has seemed to some as being easier to implement in FE than in schools, that is because time and staffing are more flexible commodities in the former. This is a point worth remembering by those keen to transplant FE profile models into the school sector.

4 School-based developments

The origins of pupil profiling are very much of a grassroots nature. Nowhere is this more evident than in a number of isolated but influential experimental schemes undertaken in individual schools. The reputation of some of these within the profiling movement is now almost legendary. Evesham High School is among the best known. This school pioneered the *criteria checklist* system of profiling which required pupils to tick off, on a kind of checklist, when they had mastered particular descriptions of skills, and then have these entries stamped and verified by a teacher. Under personal and social skills, for instance, were items such as 'Is normally and cleanly dressed for school', 'Can work well as a member of a group', 'Can swim 25m'. Because of mounting reservations about grids of the SCRE kind, checklists (a variant of them) have not been widely adopted in subsequent developments. The kinds of qualities and skills considered worth recording and the principle of employer involvement have, however, had some influence on later practice.

Much more directly influential, though, have been the steps taken by a small number of schools in developing more open-ended systems of student self-assessment, not just in tutor periods but within mainstream subject teaching too. In these instances, the recording and reviewing process was being developed as an integral feature of the curriculum, not something added to it. Work in this area at Comberton College, Cambridgeshire, for instance, involved pupils being given periodic opportunities during their last two years at school to reflect on their achievements and experiences in order to build up a picture of themselves. Teachers could discuss the pupils' statements with them, if the pupils so wished, but could not decide what they wrote about. As one of the teachers responsible for the development put it, 'it is for them (the pupils) to write as they choose, knowing that what they write might affect the teaching they receive'. Having made a series of interim statements, the students then wrote a final statement about themselves which they knew would be for a public audience. They therefore selected items they thought it important for other people to know about them. At the same time, the tutors independently wrote statements about the students. The final record of achievement showed both statements alongside one another.

Bosworth College in Leicestershire took this one stage further by having teachers reply to student self-reports, then using the two as a basis for negotiation (Marcus, 1980). Thus, the principles of open-ended self-assessment were combined with those of profile negotiation (see also Fletcher, 1980). These two elements have been widely adopted in more recent, large-scale record of achievement schemes.

5 Profile consortia

By the end of the 1970s, the collected experience of profiling consisted of a wide range of disparate initiatives, innovative in design but usually modest in scale. This was not quite the 'armada of little ships' that one commentator (Broadfoot, 1986b) has suggested; more a small flotilla. As Janet Balogh found, reporting for the Schools Council as recently as 1980, fewer than 1% of all secondary schools offered anything more than a structured testimonial. Indeed, scarcely 25 schools met the Council's own criteria for a profile: that it should be *non-confidential*, available to *all* pupils, include references to *cross-curricular skills and personal qualities*, and be in a *structured format*. Progress until that point, it seems, had been very slow indeed.

From that still very recent point of modest growth, though, profiles have proliferated at astonishing speed. In 1981, the Schools Council followed up its evaluation of existing profile schemes by commissioning Brian Goacher (1983) to undertake a development project with a number of schools (26 in the first instance). This was set up with 'some questions posed to us by Lady Young, then Minister of State at the DES' very much in mind (Goacher 1983: 5). This signalled the DES's development interest in the area. The Schools Council went on to support and report on other assessment initiatives in Manchester (Sutton *et al.*, 1986) and Surrey (Dean, 1987). Meanwhile, in 1981, HMI (1983) undertook a review of record of achievement schemes in ten secondary schools. This involvement of the Schools Council and HMI, together with the spread of profiling through the new TVEI and CPVE, added considerably to the public prominence of profiling.

It was in a growing number of co-ordinated initiatives between schools, LEAs and Examination Boards, though, that progress was most startling. These consortia, with their pooling of resources and expertise, had a powerful impact on the development of records of achievement. One such consortium-based scheme originally emerged from schools in Clwyd, was later adopted by other Welsh LEAs, and was eventually transformed into a nationally agreed profile scheme for the whole of Wales. This, the Welsh National Scheme (Schools Council Committee for Wales, 1983), had a record of achievement booklet that listed a number of skills or qualities, on each of which the tutor then wrote a comment about the particular pupil in question. The comments were not freely chosen, though, but selected from a small bank of statements arranged in a hierarchy of levels. All that was required was for the letter and number code to be selected for the required comment, and this could then be entered into and processed by the computer. As a result, from a specific range of limited items entered into the computer, a continuous prose statement could be produced. Processed like this, the comments appeared as if they were individually tailored to the student. They had a definite personal touch about them. But at root, they remained graded selections from predecided categories. Essentially, then, these *comment banks* were and still are wolfish grids in woolly prose clothing.[5]

Comment banks have enjoyed continuing popularity among developers of profiles and records of achievement because they retain some of the desired characteristics of grids, particularly in the sense of their being rapidly processable by teachers, while having a more human, personalised feel about them, than a few ticked-in boxes or shaded-in charts can convey. Their savings of teacher time, not least because of their amenability to computerisation, are especially valued. As the Welsh profile developers have themselves noted, 'the best use of teacher time was a major factor in influencing the design of this profile' (Schools Council Committee for Wales, 1983: 9). In some cases, the comment bank principle has extended to the formative stage of profile negotiation too, where students and teachers independently select what they consider to be appropriate descriptions of the student from a hierarchy of statements, which provides a basis for negotiation between them – as in the Warwickshire Profile which we shall return to later. In one case at least, in order to deal with the objection that schools and teachers resent having to choose from lists of comments devised by others that may not be appropriate to their own situation, a computer programme has been developed to enable teachers and schools to construct and modify their comment banks as they see fit (eg Bedfordshire). There are problems surrounding the use of comment banks, as we shall see, but they have undoubtedly become one of the most favoured technological means for recording personal achievements.

Another widely-used approach is the open-ended prose summary. Owing much to developments in pupil self-assessment, to earlier experiments in profile negotiation in FE and elsewhere, and to personal recording as a basis for profile discussion, the greatest advances in the development of this type of approach have been made by the Oxford Certificate of Educational Achievement (OCEA). OCEA arose from a consortium of four LEAs (Oxfordshire, Coventry, Somerset and Leicestershire), the Oxford Delegacy of Local Examinations, and the Oxford University Department of Educational Studies. The certificate contains three components; now closely mirrored in the DES policy statement. One of these – Recording and Reviewing – is explicitly concerned with personal and social development (OCEA, 1987). In this component, the final prose statement, and indeed, interim ones compiled throughout a pupil's secondary education are negotiated between tutor and pupil, and describe the pupil's experiences and achievements. There is no prescribed format for how this is to be done; no set list of pre-written comments from which selections have to be made. But there are general, stipulated criteria which the recording process must meet.

Statements must be positive, not negative; in the pupil's own words as far as is reasonably possible; refer to out-of-school experience as well as in-school ones; arise from dialogue between teacher and pupil; be based on specific descriptions of things done rather than on attributions of general qualities; and so on. More radically still, the criteria extend far beyond the technicalities of the recording process itself to aspects of the curriculum, organisation, and pastoral provision of the school as a whole. For instance, they make it the school's responsibility to provide opportunities for pupils to develop and practise those skills and capabilities that will allow them to take full advantage of the recording and reviewing process. The criteria require the school to provide a variety of opportunities for personal and social development and achievement and to demonstrate that it recognises and values the significance of activities and experiences outside the range of school or college provision (OCEA, 1984: 9). Further still, the criteria declare that the school should 'design and deliver its curriculum in such a way that students are involved in a constructive planning and reviewing process' (OCEA, 1984: 10). Such criteria, still being developed through pilot work at the time of writing, will be set and maintained by a widely constituted Accreditation body whom schools will need to satisfy if they wish to join and remain in the scheme. If this approach is successful, it offers the prospect that the approaches to PSE reviewed in this book will, for the first time, become part of the mainstream of school life; no longer fringe activities conducted by enthusiasts, but a central part of the curriculum.

Another advantage of setting broad criteria is that while they are designed to stimulate far-reaching change in the curriculum and organisation of secondary schools, they do this in a way that offers maximum flexibility to individual schools in constructing approaches to suit their own special needs and circumstances. This flexibility is important; not least because, for schools and teachers, it maximises their own involvement in and ownership of their own schemes. That is regarded as a vital source of teacher motivation in facilitating their commitment to change – a key strength of the OCEA scheme in its developers' eyes.

The open-ended nature of the final prose record is designed to increase pupils' sense of ownership and authorship too. For if the record is in their own words, based on an agenda that has importance for them, and rooted in a continuous personal record or diary that is seen as a source of pride and identity, then the importance they attach to it is likely to be all the greater. Ownership, authorship, wide-ranging change and local flexibility – these, then, are some of the key principles embraced by the OCEA development.

Summary

The consortium arrangement is now making most of the headway in the development of records of achievement – and with it the implementation of comment banks and open-ended prose records as the dominant preferred options. Nine of the consortia are being funded by the DES from 1985–88 so that, in the words of the DES, it and others can 'gain more experience . . . with a view to establishing the greatest possible degree of agreement on the main issues'. Moreover, the national steering committee responsible for monitoring and evaluating these nine schemes is being asked to offer draft guidelines for the proposed national introduction of records of achievement by the end of the decade (DES, 1985: 46). The different models now being tested within the nine DES projects and beyond are therefore critical for what looks likely to be a nationally agreed or imposed scheme of records of achievement in the future. There is much to learn from the problems and dilemmas encountered by those working in current and previous schemes of records of achievement.

In this section, we have tried to show that if you want to be adequately forewarned of troubles ahead, to some extent you need to go 'back to the future'. In this sense it is important to recognise that while the days of the school and college-based cottage industry in records of achievement are now clearly numbered, many of the principles which they pioneered and assumptions on which they were founded have been incorporated into more recent consortium-based schemes. Among the early principles that are now common-place in profile schemes are those of negotiation, prose based records, self-assessment, the integration of profiles into the learning process, their availability to *all* pupils, and so on. Some of the assumptions built into earlier schemes that have also left their traces in more recent developments include the (sometimes unspoken) bias towards vocational values, and the use of profiles to control and motivate potentially difficult pupils. These vocational and controlling elements, so strong in the history of profiling, are often at odds with those centred more closely around pupils' personal and social development, as we shall soon see. Before we explore these dilemmas of profiling and their practical implications more closely, it might be useful to remind ourselves of the main types of profiles and records of achievement that are now available.

Range of schemes

Building on a typology first outlined by Hitchcock (1986), six main types of profiles can be identified.

1 *Grids* Brief, summary descriptions of general qualities (perseverance, punctuality etc) or task/social competencies, presented in the form of an

easily-scanned set of numerical grades, ticked boxes, or blocked-in charts (eg SCRE, City and Guilds 365).

2 *Checklists*   Ticked lists of tasks or activities completed or skills shown (eg 'Can swim 25m') verified by an appropriate adult, which are assumed to be indicators of underlying skills or qualities (eg Evesham High School).

3 *Comment banks*   Preselected statements of qualities and abilities, ringed as appropriate by tutor and/or pupil, and later combined to form what appears to be a freely written prose statement (eg Welsh National Scheme, West Midlands Examination Board Record of Achievement).

4 *Personal recording*   A system where pupils make extended entries of their own choice on a variety of headed cards which are then stored in a voluminous file, access to which is controlled by the pupil (eg PPR, RPE).

5 *Subject self-assessment*   A procedure for allowing pupils to reflect on their own learning in particular parts of the curriculum. Pupil assessments may sometimes be juxtaposed with separately written teacher ones. A third, negotiated statement might then be produced on the basis of the first two (eg Comberton and Bosworth Colleges).

6 *Open-ended prose summary*   A leaving statement expressed in succinct, prose form and in a more open-ended way than comment banks allow. This is designed to facilitate and encourage pupil involvement in recording activities and experiences that are significant to them, in their own words (eg OCEA).

Elements of virtually all these are detectable in current records of achievement schemes, though the comment bank and open-ended prose summary are now the two dominant ways in which summative statements are presented. Much of our discussion of the issues and problems of profiling will therefore revolve around the relative merits of these two alternatives.

Ulterior motives?

Records of achievement, we have seen, can potentially meet a wide range of different objectives. In the interests of securing broad agreement and support, these objectives are often presented as complementary – not least by the DES itself (DES, 1984). In fact, though, as writers like Goacher (1983) have recognised, the objectives are often contradictory. We have already pointed to some of the positive educational justifications for records of achievement – recognition of achievement, enhancement of pupil motivation, curriculum renewal, transformation of teacher–pupil relationships, and so forth. Yet, in addition to these positive purposes, records of achievement serve other ends also, whose educational value might well be regarded as more debatable. There are at least three of these:

1 Gratuitous vocationalism

In one sense, profiles and records of achievement mark one further stage in the intrusion of industrial, vocational interests into the educational process. The make up and format of some profiles seems to be founded less on a concern to develop personal and social qualities as such, than on a concern to develop those qualities that employers value. We have seen this with the SCRE profile and its emphasis on 'work-related characteristics'. FE developments too have been highly cognisant of employers' interests. When jobs were still around, or the group being profiled would soon be moving directly into the labour market, this representation of employers' interests might have been entirely appropriate. But with so few young people now going directly into work at 16, it is arguable that employer involvement in the design of records of achievement does not so much reflect the actual extent to which they will *use* these records, as the ways in which schools are increasingly coming to embrace, and to be seen to be embracing, the values and priorities that employers hold. Such gratuitous vocationalism, and the values and habits it fosters, is not always demonstrably in tune with the requirements of personal and social development.

2 Social control

Much of the impetus for records of achievement comes from the intensifying difficulties surrounding the education of older and less able pupils with few examination prospects and little hope of employment. Despite their comprehensive rhetoric, it is often as a response to this group and the control problems they generate for their teachers that profiles and records of achievement have been developed. The concerns of ROSLA pupils, the young unemployed, and so on, were certainly uppermost in the earlier profile initiatives. Despite their claimed advantages for personal and social development, then, records of achievement can, intentionally and unintentionally, be turned to a very different set of purposes – as instruments of control and surveillance; operating for the school's and the state's benefit more than for the pupil's.

3 'A nice little earner'

What was it about examination boards, bodies not known for their reformist zeal or their interest in personal development, that led to their becoming involved in the development of records of achievement? Was it a turn in their educational conscience; some Damascus-like change in their educational outlook, perhaps? This is, of course, a possibility. Even examination boards are not entirely immune from changes in the climate of educational opinion. At least as important, though, has been the income crisis facing examination boards in the 1980s as pupil numbers in secondary schools have been falling and with them, the total entry fees paid to the boards. Like all financially threatened enterprises, examination boards have learned that you must diversify to survive. By including more pupils in the public assessment process, examination boards can offset their anticipated losses. For examination boards, profiles are, in this respect, 'a nice little earner'!

Recognition of this fact is more than just a matter of gossip. The success of more open-ended types of records of achievement depends on the firm application of broad criteria to ensure that individual schools participate in the innovation in more than a perfunctory way. If the criteria are applied too loosely, if they have no teeth, then such schemes are unlikely to meet the standards they set themselves. One worrying implication here is that strict application of criteria threatens income. Will accreditation bodies apply these criteria regardless of the income implications, we wonder? In this respect, it is interesting and perhaps a little disconcerting to note that at the time of writing, in the CPVE – another development being initiated in a similarly broadbased way – no school has yet failed to meet the criteria (Radnor *et al* ., 1988).

The wide range of purposes that profiles and records of achievement can fulfil helps gain them support, right across the political spectrum. But what gains them public support also creates private difficulty for the teacher. For it is at the level of the school and the classroom that the different and often contradictory objectives must be worked out; the tensions between vocational values and personal development, the choice between pupil independence and institutional control. What specific problems do these broad dilemmas create? And how might teachers and schools deal with them? We now go on to examine these very practical problems by posing and responding to a series of questions that people involved in profiling might ask.

Issues and problems

Who is the record for: the pupil or the employer?

Two of the main purposes of records of achievement, as the DES makes clear in its policy statement (DES, 1984: 3), are that they should motivate pupils by drawing on experiences and achievements not normally valued by traditional forms of assessment; and at the same time, express these items in such a way that employers will accept them as valid qualifications. The first purpose is one of motivation; the second, one of selection. In many respects, these two purposes are incompatible. There is a tendency for pupil motivation to be improved only at some cost to efficient employer selection, and vice versa (Hargreaves, 1985).

For instance, employers tend to prefer easily-scanned boxes and grids which give a quick breakdown of employee-related qualities (Jones, 1983; SCRE,

1977). Yet, by using unclear categories which might make expectations difficult to meet, by including negative as well as positive ratings and comments, and by denying pupils the opportunity to record achievements and experiences they consider to be sigificant *in their own words*, box and grid profiles can just as easily depress pupil motivation as raise it, especially where pupils are involved in 'agreeing' this statement of what may sometimes turn out to be their own apparent personal and social incompetence. Perhaps it is as well, then, that the DES has advised that such systems do not play a major part in records of achievement in the future:

> . . . any such assessment (of personal qualities) is likely to carry more weight if it includes concrete examples of what the pupil has achieved or experienced. The greater the extent to which personal qualities and skills can be inferred from such concrete examples, the more valuable it is likely to be to users . . . The assessment should take the form of sentences written for each pupil, not ticks in boxes, or numbers, or letter gradings. Such sentences are likely to be fairer to pupils, more useful to users, and less open to misinterpretation.
>
> (DES, 1984: 6)

In our view, this advice might usefully be extended to some comment banks as well, for in the interests of saving teacher time and standardising the comments made across different schools (perhaps with employers in mind), the pupils' *authorship* of their records is taken away; the stamp of their personal identity removed. Selecting comments from other people's options and agendas is unlikely to do much for pupil motivation – especially where those agendas are more to do with the kinds of qualities that employers might value than with things which are important to the pupils themselves.

By contrast, more extensive systems of personal recording are often a great boon to pupil motivation, especially among the less able, but are almost worthless to employers as a guide to job selection. They are too unwieldy. Once again, the motivational and selective purposes of records of achievement appear to be in conflict.

The succinct prose summary, produced through teacher–pupil negotiations, perhaps resolves this dilemma to some extent. But even here, difficulties are still likely to be encountered in the negotiation process itself. As long as the activities and experiences that pupils wish to record imply qualities like persistence, loyalty, enterprise and obedience, of the kind that employers value, there is unlikely to be any problem. Girl guides, choirboys and school prefects need have nothing to fear. But where pupils declare activities that suggest dissent or non-conformity, there is a problem. Should they declare their interests and identities, however unconventional, even at the risk of prejudicing their employment prospects? Or should they edit, select, or even distort their records a little so as to present a good impression to employers, at the cost of suppressing or falsifying important aspects of their own identities?

How will tutors deal with pupils who want to mention their interest in

Rastafarianism or breakdancing? How will they deal with pupils who belong to groups who believe that breaking the law is sometimes justified – CND, animal rights, or Greenpeace, for instance? How will they, indeed how *should* they, resolve these dilemmas? We would like to suggest the following possible courses of action as things that teachers and schools might consider.

1 Make as clear a distinction as possible between the formative stages of assessment and recording which will be centred very much on the pupil, and the summative stage which will involve preparing a statement with external 'users' (including employers) very much in mind, ie those who might be expected to view the statement from a particular angle. Such a solution may help overcome the problem of using a private record for a public purpose. The record would remain confidential, but the pupil would know that the summative statement would be for a public audience and would be able to decide which elements of that record to reveal (eg Comberton College and OCEA).

2 Related to the last point, use part of the formative process, and programmes of personal and social development more generally, to develop in pupils the skills of 'playing the system' – not in the formative process itself, of course, but where external audiences are involved. Learning when not to voice their views too publicly, learning how to adjust what they say to the expectations of their audience, and so on, might be valuable exercises in educating pupils in how to present themselves in their final document of record.

3 Educate employers to accept less than they would ideally like. Why should we assume that *their* expectations for records of achievement cannot be changed when employers are constantly expecting schools to make changes of a very substantial nature? In this respect, the expectation that employers should accept the open-ended prose summary format of recording as against grid-and-box or comment bank schemes would not be unreasonable.

4 Reduce employer involvement in the development and use of records of achievement at 16 so as to minimise their impact on the recording and reviewing process, and therefore on the promotion of pupil motivation. We have already seen that with large-scale youth unemployment, employers' involvement is scarcely justified by the very limited use they will actually make of these records. Their presence, rather, seems to result from gratuitous vocationalism more than anything else; a thin pretext for an intrusion that often undermines the processes of motivation and personal development that records of achievement are designed to foster.

What qualities should be assessed?

How far are the criteria and categories in your school's profile there to record and facilitate pupil development, and how far are they there to meet employers' interests or the school's norms of attendance, punctuality, tidiness, completion of homework and the like? How far does the profile and those who use it value qualities like 'asserting oneself', for instance (as in the ILEA Profile) that will make pupils less rather than more compliant? (ILEA, 1985: 14). It is no use having a high flown rhetoric about pupil autonomy and personal development when you are operating a profile that is actually preoccupied with and gives priority to things like attendance, appearance, dealing with authority, and so on.

The Warwickshire Profile – a multiple choice, comment-bank system – is one scheme that falls into this trap. We shall return to this scheme from time to time as an example of the issues surrounding comment banks. The very first page of the profile – significantly entitled SELF – actually begins with a question about whether the pupil likes school. This is followed by further questions about whether the pupil takes pride in how he/she looks, whether he/she remembers books and equipment, whether he/she can work without being supervised by the teacher, and how well he/she responds to teacher criticism etc. This opening page, it seems to us, has very little to do with *self* and the pupil's interests at all, but a lot to do with the school and its interests.

A clear decision must be taken here. Either profiles are for the pupil, or they are not. If they are not, if they are for preventing misbehaviour, keeping pupils in order, giving employers information on personal qualities that they value etc, then we should be absolutely honest about this and not camouflage our real aims in a deceptively benevolent rhetoric of personal development.

Schemes with pre-set agendas of the comment bank type are, of course, more open to these sorts of weaknesses than ones with a more open-ended structure. Even so, those who work in more open-ended systems are by no means immune from these problems. It is not difficult, when negotiating a profile with a pupil, to impose the school's concerns or priorities, or to overstress the kinds of things that employers value, or to devalue or disvalue pupils' own concerns and commitments – especially where such pupils are outside the cultural and political mainstream. For these reasons, teachers need to be sensitive to, aware of and open about their own values, and not impose unwarranted or unintended censorship on what pupils can record or discuss. The discussion, clarification and review of staff and school values should in this respect rank as a high inservice priority – and be returned to at regular periods.

How much detail should we go into?

Although most of the earlier profiles dealt with personal qualities and skills in a general way, there has been increasing disquiet about the usefulness of this approach. One criticism is that general and vaguely phrased descriptions often fail to convey accurate information to the reader. The early City and Guilds 365 grid, for instance, used categories like 'Can interpret simple signs and indicators', 'Can assess own results with guidance' and 'Can reliably perform basic manipulative tasks'. But as the evaluators of this and a range of other FEU schemes have noted, how does a reader know how simple is 'simple', or how much guidance has been allowed, or what is meant by 'basic' (Education Resource Unit for YOP, 1982)? Another criticism is that the steps between different skills and levels are often uneven and sometimes formidably huge. Under *Everyday coping skills*, for instance, the FEU 'sets out an uneven series of domestic skills like making tea and then jumps to a magnificent "self-reliant, could fend for him/herself, even in unfamiliar surroundings"'. In the words of the evaluators of this profile, this is like going 'from Brooke Bond to James Bond' (Education Resource Unit for YOP, 1982).

If it is hard to describe skills with precision and accuracy, attitudes and personal qualities present even greater problems. Judgements about personality, qualities or attitudes are highly subjective and depend very much on the perceptions or 'personal constructs' of the person doing the assessing. For this reason, statements about general personal qualities like perseverance and punctuality are, when taken out of context, unreliable and ambiguous. Pupils may show evidence of perseverance in some lessons but not in others, for instance – in art, but not in maths, perhaps. Much depends on the subject and the teacher.

One of the best ways to test whether a profile of the comment-bank type is ambiguous or not is to fill it in about yourself. If, when you have answered questions about how you react when you are embarrassed, or whether you like school etc, you mainly say 'it depends' – then you know it is not a very useful profile. This activity can provide a useful base for staff discussion when profiles are being considered.[6]

For the reasons we have outlined, we share HMI's (1983) doubts 'about both the propriety an the wisdom of assessing personal qualities'. And we agree with the DES (1984: 6), that it is more helpful to provide concrete examples from which personal qualities can be inferred, than to make assertions about those qualities as such. This is not only more accurate, but it is also fairer to the pupil. It makes the pupil less vulnerable to the judgements and prejudices of others; those who perhaps have the school's or the employer's interests at heart more than the pupils'; those who are mainly concerned with how well the pupil will 'fit in'.

An example will demonstrate the point. Take attendance. Of all the general qualities and behaviours that might be commented on, surely this is the most indisputable, the least open to subjective interpretation! Would not a general comment like 'good' or 'poor', or even just a simple numerical score be perfectly self-explanatory here? The point seems to be so obvious as to be scarcely worth labouring, until more extended pupil comments on their pattern of attendance are considered. Here are two of them.[7]

> In the first, second and third year, I didn't have one single day off. Now in the fourth, and just a few weeks ago, we had a (teachers') strike and I missed a few lessons then, but that is only because there was too far to walk back to school (after lunch).

> Usually my attendance is fine, yet at school it is slowly sliding as many teachers get me down. At work, I am always on time: usually early. At school, I am always late as I wait for my cousin in the morning. I am never late for appointments. If someone is late when I have arranged something, I am very moody and have a fit at them.

How much more informative these descriptive statements are than 'poor' or 'satisfactory'. How much more effectively they protect the pupil against assumptions of fecklessness or low commitment that usually accompany the designation 'poor attendance'. For what the descriptions make clear is that poor attendance (like poor behaviour, boredom etc) can sometimes reveal as much about the institution as the pupil. It all depends on the circumstances. Descriptive sentences protect the pupil by making the circumstances clear. Statements about general qualities open him or her up to the subjective judgements and controlling interests of others.

Should statements be positive or negative?

Should the comments and descriptions in the profile or record of achievement be positive or negative in nature? The DES (1984) is quite clear about its own position here: '. . . the assessments should concentrate on evidence of positive qualities . . . the final document of record should not refer to failures or defects'. In our view, it is right that this should be the emphasis. After all, we are speaking of a record of *achievement*. Records, like references, with a possibly negative element would retain the teacher's power to censure, along with the control 'benefits' of that ('If you don't behave, I'll put it on your profile'). To have such records peppered with negative comments would confer no pride upon those who owned them. The records would lose their capacity to motivate.

At the formative stage, the discussion of weaknesses and shortcomings has a more legitimate place. Indeed, without this it is difficult to see how the skills of self-reflection can be developed and progress in learning be made. But such discussion can and should be conducted in a supportive, non-intimidating way. Some approaches to profiling clearly do not do this. They contain within them a negative, even a punitive element. They proclaim the institution's standards and threaten to punish those who deviate from them with bad grades and adverse (possible demeaning) comments.

Conventional grids are especially guilty of this – which is one reason why they incur the DES's disapproval. Grids that are particularly open to criticism here are those which include rather patronising and insulting descriptions of skill achievements (or their lack) at the lowest end of the scale. When pupils do not progress much beyond the first stage in most aspects covered by such a grid; when their achievements are described as 'Can use equipment safely to perform *simple* tasks under guidance', 'Can follow instructions for *simple* tasks and carry them out under guidance' etc – it is hard for the pupil not to conclude that he or she is, in fact, *simple*! (Education Resource Unit for YOP, 1982).

Comment banks are open to the same kind of objections when the last item in the list of options to be coded is always the 'nasty' one. Again, if we return to the Warwickshire Profile and put together the last statement from all the items on the first page, we get a description where the negative nature of the judgement being made is all too apparent. Such a statement would read:

I don't like school much.

I am not bothered how I look.

I don't care whether I have (my books and equipment) or not.

I only work when the teacher keeps me at it.

When I have to make up my mind about something, I do the first thing that comes into my head.

If a teacher criticises my work, I am too fed up to bother again.

If something embarrassing happens to me, I get upset or cannot control my feelings.

Perhaps the presence of these comments on the profile is designed to 'smarten up' pupil behaviour before the time for filling it in comes up. Perhaps they are meant to provide an opportunity for tutors to use the profile 'discussion' to discipline their pupils about their behaviour or their attitude. Whichever is the case, they seem to be designed more with the school's interests in mind than the pupils'.

More worrying still is that, in our view, not all these last-option statements are as self-evidently bad or wrong as they first appear, though their consistent placement in last position very much conveys the impression that they are. For instance, is it always wrong to be too fed up to bother again if a teacher criticises your work? Surely this depends on who the teacher is and how constructively the criticism is made. Similarly, is it wrong if you 'get upset' when something embarrassing happens to you? Indeed, are *not getting upset* and *controlling one's feelings* generally accepted virtues that everyone would value and admire, or part of the emotional hypocrisy of never showing one's feelings that makes up 'polite' middle class society? Our complaint here, then, is not just that negative judgements are being made about pupils' personal qualities, but that these judgements are being made from a particular point of view, of an undeclared class-biased nature. In cases like these, profiles could well be not enhancing personal development, but steering pupils into middle class morality. They could be less about care than control.

Who writes this stuff anyway?

How much opportunity do pupils have to write things about themselves in their own words? How much are they expressing their own concerns or responding to other people's? How much *authorship* do they have of their profiles or records of achievement? Is it a declaration of identity or a completion of someone else's questionnaire? The more that authorship rests with the pupil, the more likely it is that the record will be a source of pride and motivation, and will not be dominated by the control-based agendas of schools and employers.

There are limits to this argument, of course. Too much writing in one's own words can be counterproductive, especially for the less able. Profiling can too easily become one more monotonous chore for these pupils. Yet more writing! Where pupils are diffident about recording, where they have difficulties with speaking or writing – the demands of authorship can be not an opportunity at all, but an intimidating imposition. In such instances, there is a case for more structure in the recording process to help get pupils started. *Prompt sheets* can be useful here: a set of open-ended questions, sentences requiring completion, or possible keywords that might be used. These things can start the ball rolling as the pupil reflects on and discusses what he or she has done.[8]

Prompt sheets are not the same as comment banks, though. Comment banks provide limited options of statements on a fixed agenda which close discussion down and remove the rights of authorship. Prompt sheets provide starting points for discussion on a looser agenda as a means of opening discussion up. They offer support for diffident pupils (and diffident teachers too!) in discussing and negotiating progress.

Pupils who have difficulty with speaking and writing can also be helped if the recording process, particularly the business of self-assessment, is extended beyond the written form. The use of computers, audio and video tapes can be particularly helpful here and can also assist the integration of profiling into the curriculum in areas like information technology and media studies, for instance – especially if pupils play some part in assessing one another. Whatever supports are provided, though, the principle of protecting the pupils' author-ship of their records, as far as possible, remains an important one. Grids, boxes and comment banks do not permit this.

Does the format matter?

Our views on profile formats for the final statement and indeed for interim ones should now be clear. Summary descriptions of general qualities, presented in easily-scanned boxes, grids or charts have some attraction for employers. They are often preferred by schools and LEAs too on the grounds of cheapness, ease of use, and overall efficiency and simplicity – although increasingly this preference is for comment banks in particular; grids in disguise.

Our concern, based on existing evaluations of profile schemes (Education Resource Unit for YOP, 1982; Balogh, 1982; HMI, 1983), is that grids and their lookalikes are descriptively inaccurate because they make subjective judgements about behaviour and personal qualities out of context; are often demotivating for pupils registering at the lower end of the scale, especially where the descriptions of these lower levels are patronising or demeaning; and by denying pupils authorship of their own statements and setting an exceedingly tight agenda for discussion, they often sacrifice pupils' personal development needs to the needs of the institution or of employers. We therefore agree with the DES's recommendation that grids be dispensed with and suggest this be extended to comment banks also – certainly in the area of personal and social development.

Dispensing with highly structured formats for recording and review does not, however, automatically dispense with all the difficulties surrounding that process. Not all the problems of profiling are technological. Improvements in the technology of profiling only widen the scope for and the possibility of sensitive human judgement. They give no guarantee that this will happen. In the process of one-to-one discussions with pupils, we have already seen how tutors can easily be drawn into serving the interests of schools and employers more than those of the pupil; into imposing institutional and vocational values rather than helping pupils declare their own. This need for awareness of and sensitivity about whose values are being served extends to other aspects of the recording process also. Personal privacy is one such area.

Are profiles an invasion of privacy?

Profiles and records of achievement widen the areas of pupil performance and development that are open to assessment. Not just performance but emotions, behaviour, personal relationships too – all are now subject to evaluation, appraisal and intervention, to the teacher's all-seeing eye. There are, of course, sound reasons for this. One chief aim of records of achievement is to recognise, reward and record achievements and experiences in the personal and social domain. This means that teachers will need to know what happens there if they are to do their pupils credit. But there are times when this proper concern can be extended so far as to amount to an unnecessary invasion of privacy. There is a sinister side to the fact that pupils are open to assessment wherever they go, whatever they do; that there is no space or activity which is protected from the teacher's surveillance. And this is especially worrying where it is not just the intellect that is being continually assessed, but behaviour too. More of the pupil is assessed for more of the time.

From studies of progressive primary and middle schools, we already know how apparent increases in pupil autonomy can in practice be undermined by the teacher's quiet and unobtrusive, but also persistent and all-encompassing, surveillance (Hargreaves, 1977, 1986; Bernstein, 1975). Research in this area has also shown how the not-so-polite and less-than-deferential working class pupil can come off badly when informal day-to-day evaluations of behaviour become scrambled up with judgements about academic attainment (Sharp and Green, 1975). Records of achievement are also open to these dangers of assessing and recording things that may not be their proper concern, in a way that may be biased against and therefore disadvantage working class and ethnic minority pupils.

Worries about profiles becoming instruments of surveillance and invasions of privacy are particularly strong where they are extended into family life. On the one hand, we think it right, as part of the principle of improving the partnership between home and school, that pupils be given the opportunity to record out-of-school experiences and achievements, *if they so wish*. But it is a serious abuse of that notion of partnership to have young people's behaviour out of school compulsorily appraised, evaluated and rated. One of the more extreme instances of this kind of abuse is to be found in the Warwickshire Profile. Section 5 of this profile is called *Out of school*. Figure 6.1 gives its first seven questions.

Questions such as these, to be filled in by parents, invade privacy in two senses. First, by assessing aspects of pupils' life at home, they are assessing the quality of that home life too. The parent is being assessed as well as the pupil. And again, this assessment seems to be being done according to a narrow, 'white' middle-class yardstick. Is it really so bad to be impulsive with your pocket money rather than a cautious middle class saver? And is not to some extent racist to evaluate the parents of Muslim boys according to ethnocentric, Anglo Saxon standards of who should help with domestic chores? It is questionable whether these things can be judged in a culture-free way, and indeed whether it is any of the school's business to judge them at all.

Second, by getting parents to fill in details about their pupils' behaviour at home, the school is, in effect, having parents 'spy' on their children. This is not the development of an active partnership between schools and parents, as when parents are invited to comment on and contribute to the assessment and planning of their children's learning (ILEA, 1985: 11). It is a way of using parents to collect information that will be useful to the state (of which the school is a part) in controlling its subjects. In recent years, we have seen the state extend its influence into aspects of people's private lives over which it should properly have no jurisdiction and in which it should have no interest. Profiles of the sort we have just described can very easily become a part of this widening web of state control. Schools and teachers must ask themselves seriously whether that is what they really want.

Personal privacy, as we have emphasised throughout the book, is a vital

5.1 ☐ You manage to get yourself up in good time

☐ You need a lot of calling and then have to rush around

5.2 **You make your bed and leave your room tidy:**

Yes No

☐ ☐

5.3 **You help with:—**

	Yes	Sometimes	No
Washing up	☐	☐	☐
Dusting and tidying up	☐	☐	☐
Vacuuming	☐	☐	☐
Preparing the vegetables	☐	☐	☐
Laying the table	☐	☐	☐
Shopping	☐	☐	☐
Looking after a pet	☐	☐	☐

5.4 ☐ You have prepared a full meal for yourself

☐ You have cooked yourself a hot snack

☐ You make a good cup of tea or coffee

5.5 ☐ I trust you anywhere on your bike

☐ I trust you on quiet roads

☐ I only trust you on your bike in our street

5.6 ☐ You keep your bike in good repair

☐ You have to be reminded to look after it

☐ Your bike is never working properly

5.7 ☐ You usually plan what you spend your pocket money on

☐ You spend your pocket money on the very first thing you see

Figure 6.1.

human right – for young people just as much as for adults. It should be breached only for reasons of the highest social importance, and certainly not on a routine or casual basis. A good test for when your own school's profile or record of achievement is in danger of invading privacy is again to *fill in the profile about yourself*, adjusting the question slightly to your own more mature interests where necessary (by substituting car for bike, for instance). If you would regard being required to complete these answers, and having other people see them (perhaps your head as part of a staff appraisal process), as an unnecessary invasion of your privacy – if, for instance, you would deem it none of your head's business to know whether you kept your car in good repair, if you were prone to running up overdrafts, or how conscientious you were with the housework – then the profile is probably an unethical breach of young people's privacy too. The only exception might be if you want to assign different human rights to yourself from those you apply to your pupils – but any such extra moral privilege must be rationally decided, not simply presumed.

Comment banks are particularly susceptible to the difficulties we have described in this section. But more open-ended systems are not entirely immune. We saw in the previous chapter how pupils were often anxious that information committed to their records might be used in evidence against them and communicated to their homes. Such difficulties can be minimised, though, if teachers are made continually aware of the problem; if the disclosure of home-based information is made optional and not required by a predecided value-based format; and if there are strict, carefully observed and publicly recognised procedures for profile ownership. It is these issues of compulsion and ownership that we raise next.

Should the recording and reviewing process be compulsory?

The exploration of personal feelings and emotions with someone else can increase self-awareness and give valuable insights into one's own personal development. But when this process is *compulsory*, a statutory part of school experience, again we have worries whether this process will be altogether beneficial – the difference between voluntary and compulsory psychiatric care, perhaps.

In one sense, the regular nature of the recording and reviewing process is one of the most distinctive benefits of records of achievement. It gives young people entitlement to a timetabled opportunity to review and discuss their own progress and set targets for the future. Yet if a system is, in its essentials, fundamentally control-oriented; geared to the school's interests, not the pupil's; concerned with normalising, not developing young people – then the regular nature of reviewing as a compulsory requirement can turn into an overhanging threat (like the old reference). It can become a way of heading off trouble before it starts. The pupils' knowledge that they will be subjected to inescapable future reviews can simply work to suppress misbehaviour before it arises. It is no accident that this type of regular reviewing is a common feature of control regimes in disruptive units, institutions for young offenders etc. Compulsory review can be an excellent device for behavioural control.

Given these ethically disturbing aspects of *compulsory* review, schools perhaps need to consider whether pupils should be given the right to contract out of this process if they wish – even if only in extreme cases. Where the system remains compulsory or virtually compulsory, it is especially important that the recording and reviewing process be pupil-led; raising issues of concern and importance to the pupils, not to their teachers or to employers; giving them an opportunity to discuss their development, rather than offering the school an excuse to exercise its control.

Who should own the records?

If, for all the reasons we have mentioned, there is a lack of trust in the system; if profiling becomes a process of rating pupils in relation to how well they conform to what schools and employers want; if it is not primarily designed to declare success and experiences in the personal and social domain – even unconventional ones – then pupils will become suspicious of the diffuse ways that profiling operates, of its nebulous, ever-present nature, of the fact that anything they might say now could later be used in evidence against them.

All this raises questions about the ownership of profile records. Most of the public debate here has centred on the ownership of the final document of record. This, the DES recommends, should be owned by the pupil him/herself. We agree with this. It is not, however, the only issue as far as ownership is concerned. Equally important, if not more so, is the question of who owns and controls the interim formative statements that are produced throughout a pupil's school career.

Can teachers in the pastoral and guidance systems consult these records at will, without the pupil's consent, if there are enquiries from police or social workers, if the pupil gets into trouble, or if his or her parents are coming to make a complaint, for instance? Might not the availability of records on computer be a temptation for teachers wishing to collect relevant information about 'problem' cases?

Schools may feel that, as large and bureaucratically complex institutions, rapid access to relevant information is essential when pastoral problems arise. They may feel that if ownership is passed to pupils and their consent is required before records can be consulted, this will cause great administrative inconvenience (if the pupil is absent, for instance). We sympathise here, but feel that the principles of consent and confidentiality should be protected all the same; for without these things there is no trust (evidence may *indeed* be used against them); and without trust, it is doubtful whether anything of value will be recorded in the first place. We therefore agree with Stansbury (1984) when he says:

> One most important rule is that the recorder must control the record . . . Take that right of ownership away and what would be left could be rather nasty – the negotiated record, summarised and distilled by the teacher and sent away to some authority to be validated, copied and returned. Little snippets of private information revealed in all innocence and sifted out, stored away and copied. A record of the private life of every child and of much more about family and friends. A record to contemplate in 1984.

When Stansbury made these remarks, he was speaking of summative records. They apply to formative ones equally well, if not more so. The maintenance of confidentiality, trust and pupil ownership are vital for the success of records of achievement. We believe that adoption of some of the following procedures might help protect these precious things.

1   Printed recognition that everything discussed between tutor and student during the review process is private and confidential and should not be divulged to any other party, however casually, without the pupil's consent. If there are to be any exceptions to this rule, if teachers are to be slightly less than priests or doctors in their treatment of confidences, these excepted categories should be made clear to pupils at the outset through profile guidelines. Information which brings to light breaches of the law might be placed in this category, for instance.

2   Clear procedures for access to negotiated statements that arise from the review process. Here, especially where information is stored on computer, schools may find it useful to classify it according to different levels of confidentiality. Some of that information, like name or date of birth, will be uncontroversial for most pupils and should be open to all. Some information, regarding family circumstances, or relationships with other teachers, for instance, may be somewhat sensitive and should only be available with the prior permission of the tutor who has negotiated the statement with the pupil (they will be the only ones to have the access codes or 'passwords' for this information). Finally, some information will be so confidential that access to it should be granted only via the pupil him or herself, who alone should know the computer password that would release it. The pupils themselves ought to be the ones who, after discussion with their tutor, decide which information is allocated to each category.

In these ways, pupils retain ownership of and control over their own data. This helps ensure that information gathered for one purpose (personal development) will not be used for another (institutional control). This in turn helps protect the trust and confidentiality vital to a recording and review process designed to foster personal development. On paper, the access procedures we have described sound cumbersome and time consuming. Occasionally, they may be, though this is a small price to pay for human dignity. In practice, however, since statements will largely be written positively, we would expect very few pupils to require personal clearance before access to their records can be achieved. In virtually all cases, we would expect them to delegate this responsibility willingly to their tutor. But it *is* important, all the same, that the principle of confidentiality and ownership is demonstrably protected – that trust is patently built into the system. Such trust is at the heart of effective and meaningful negotiation of profiles between pupils and their tutors; our next consideration.

When does negotiation become manipulation?

The completion of many early profiles and records was a heavily one-sided process. The Scottish Profile was teacher dominated. Personal recording was almost entirely pupil centred. Important breaks with these traditions were made by schools like Bosworth College, but it was the FE sector which made the most significant moves towards profiles being compiled jointly by tutor and student together (Pearce, 1979). The word the FEU (1979, 1982) used to describe this process was *negotiation*. This term remains common within other 16+ initiatives like B.Tec and the CPVE, but its use at school level has roused some hackles and created considerable anxiety. Within OCEA, for instance, the term has proved highly controversial and has been dropped. The DES has similarly shown little enthusiasm for it. Increasingly, the idea of 'dialogue' or 'discussion' has been preferred instead. In our view, this shift of terminology is unfortunate. It is based on a misunderstanding of what is meant by *negotiation*, and by substituting *dialogue* and *discussion*, it misrepresents some of the fundamental aspects of the profiling process.

Understandably, some teachers associate *negotiation* with the uncompromising self-interested nature of management–union bargaining and would not want to describe what they are doing in those terms. But this is only one view of negotiation. Woods (1983: 133), writing about teacher–pupil relationships in general, calls it *closed negotiation*,

> . . . where the parties independently attempt to maximise their own reality in opposition to and conflict against the other, and each makes concessions begrudgingly, and only if forced.

There is another sense in which negotiation can occur, though, which Woods describes as *open negotiation*. This

> . . . is where parties are aware of the contract, move some way to meet each other of their own volition and subsequently arrive at a consensus.

This comes close to the *Oxford English Dictionary* definition of to *negotiate* as to 'confer with a view to compromise or agreement'. This is more than mere 'exchange' – one definition of *dialogue* – or 'conversation' (another definition). Pupils and teachers come to the profiling process from different starting points; with different experiences and insights. They also arrive in a position of unequal power that sets limits on the degree of openness that can be achieved in the teacher–pupil relationship. These differences in power, experience and interest and the difficulties they unavoidably create in some cases are neatly captured by the term *negotiation*. They cannot be washed away with emotionally soothing and descriptively inaccurate terms like *dialogue* and *discussion*. The difficulties need to be confronted and dealt with positively, not evaded by changes of vocabulary. *Negotiation* serves to remind us of this continuing need; a gritty reminder of the professionally taxing realities of the profiling process.

From the point of view of personal development, *open* forms of negotiation are clearly preferable to closed ones. Much of what goes on in profiling is, however, often tightly closed. Goacher (1983) found instances of this in his report on the Schools Council profile development project.

> Where self-assessments had to be countersigned by a teacher, a number of pupils encountered difficulty. Where teachers' views did not coincide with those of the pupil, a number of teachers put considerable pressure on pupils to 'alter' their assessment. 'Persuading' pupils to improve their own ratings appeared to be rather more common than attempts to have them lowered. Some pupils found the process 'funny'. Others were angry about it.

This kind of coercion is sometimes present in less obvious ways than direct confrontation or 'persuasion'. Where schemes are lengthy and highly structured (as the Warwickshire Profile is, for instance), this can sometimes place so much pressure on the teacher to 'get through' and 'complete' the profile in the limited time available, that pupil responses can be reduced to a string of yesses and nos. In these cases, the tutor often virtually ends up writing the statement for them. This danger is, of course, particularly acute where pupils lack confidence or are not especially articulate.

Contracts present another problem for profile negotiation. Many schools have incorporated learning contracts into the profiling process; agreements between teachers and pupils about the changes that are needed and will be attempted in the period up until the next review. If profile negotiation is to involve change in the teacher–pupil relationship and to allow adjustments of learning requirements and support to individual pupils' needs, these contracts should frequently be two-sided in nature, involving agreed action on *both* the pupil's *and* the teacher's part. Many that we have witnessed, though, have been unambiguously one-sided – amounting to little more than written undertakings by pupils to write more neatly, work harder, not be late, and generally not misbehave. These are less like contracts than signed ultimatums.

Contracts of this kind seem to have much more to do with social control than personal development.

Negotiation, then, can often turn into manipulation by teachers skilled in the use of the language of persuasion and the gentle imposition of their superior authority. But not all the blame for manipulation rests with the teachers, by any means. Pupils have considerable expertise in this area also. Profile negotiation and the written processes that support it present excellent opportunities for braggarts, cynics and sycophants to exercise their considerable talents.

Traditional forms of assessment do not and cannot offer pupils a platform for their views. It is therefore prudent to warn teachers that, in the early stages at least, pupil statements under new forms of assessment will be far from predictable. At the sycophant end of the spectrum are pupils who readily absorb and conform to the teacher's values, lacing suitably acceptable comments with liberal doses of flattery. Often these are glaringly unsubtle, as in the case of a pupil who wrote in her mathematics diary, 'You have probably already read Susanna's diary and know that I like you' (Tossell, 1984). So blatant is the ingratiation here that the teacher would almost certainly regard such gushing comments with great suspicion. Other pupils, however, have more subtle methods of playing the system, as in the case of the pupil who confessed to one of us that he always deliberately under-rated his performance as a way of 'fishing for compliments'. As a result, he believed that his reports from his teachers were always good because they were led to believe that he needed to have his confidence boosted (Tossell, 1984).

Clearly this type of assessment gives some pupils the opportunity to gain advantage by means of the comments they make. There are, however, others who cannot calculate such advantages at all. Indeed, because of the bluntness of their comments, they often unintentionally offend teachers and place themselves, potentially, at a serious disadvantage. Teachers need to accept that once pupils are given the chance to assess their own performances, it is only a matter of time before they criticise the context of those performances too – the syllabus, the books, the lessons, and the teachers. This, indeed, is a major justification for records of achievement, as we argued at the outset. But pupils will not always present these criticisms with the tact and aplomb their teachers might prefer. Here, for instance, in a humanities diary, a pupil is critical of the lack of resources.

> I like doing topic work but didn't enjoy doing the last one because the book didn't provide the information needed and the books that did provide the right information weren't about a lot. But the main reason why I didn't like that topic was that there weren't any films to collect information from.

And in this mathematics diary, both the teacher and the amount of noise in the classroom are criticised:

I finished the booklet then went on to do the test. I managed to do half of it but I was distracted by the noise then me and Delan went into a small room to choose the project but after a while (the teacher) came and told us off for being so long.

We have spoken to many teachers who admit to having felt threatened in these situations, as their traditional authority seemed to be undermined. However, if teachers can guard against over-reacting to the *way* in which criticism is made, even the most tactless of pupils can provide valuable feedback. If handled sympathetically, even the outpourings of a bored 5th form maths pupil can be used as a basis for negotiating a positive way forward, as this example from one pupil diary demonstrates:

Student
Lesson boring. Done work well a bit for what (it's) worth. Could have done a lot more if some people hadn't opened their Big Gobs as normal. Just the same old Boring class so what if I don't work? Even when I do nobody ever notices so I don't bother any more. (You think I'm a B criminal or something to that extent anyway). So don't ask me why I don't work because one day I'll tell someone very rudely.
'You haven't done that'
'That's not good enough'
'You've got to do more than that'
'Come on Mark'
'It is disgraceful the amount of work you do'
For what it's worth I just can't not be bothered any more.

Teacher's Reply
Since you wrote this, Mark, things seem to have settled down better. Perhaps I did tend to pick on you that day but you had to make yourself *very noticeable* to start with and so one tends to carry on noticing you! When you are in the mood, you can do quite well. *I* think you are brighter than *you* think at Maths and if you tried harder you would do so much better. You must try to be less aware of people around you so they don't distract you and you don't distract them. Believe me, I don't enjoy moaning at people, but time is *so* short to get through your CSE course and I find that most people do need pushing – which I was trying to do (on that day) – but not successfully! *If you behave I promise not to nag.* Show me your project so that we can work out what needs to be done over the holiday to make it better.

When one of us spoke to this teacher, she confirmed that Mark was hostile to both teacher and subject. When he wrote this statement, it was on a day when the tension between himself and the teacher was especially high and eventually he had stormed to the shelf where the diaries were kept and had angrily poured out his feelings. This proved to be a useful, if temporary safety valve. The benefits went further than this, though. Because the teacher had formed the habit of replying to pupils' comments in their diaries, Mark knew that his action was not a futile gesture and that his criticisms would be answered. The teacher's reply began with a justification for her actions on the day (the tone is, indeed, a little officious here), but it moved on to be more conciliatory and ended by offering practical advice. The teacher explained that both she and the pupil later discussed the two statements in a calmer atmosphere and established the basis of a working relationship to take them through the remainder of the academic year. Interestingly, Mark's later entries in the diary were markedly different in tone. The strident comments and expressions of indignation disappeared and there was evidence that he was beginning to enjoy overcoming small challenges in the subject.

This is an example of a move towards the kind of open negotiation we have been describing: the acceptance of different starting points, the recognition of and attempt to overcome difficulties and obstacles (rather like negotiating river rapids!), the working towards agreement, and the ultimate improvement of the relationship as a result. Closed negotiation is the easy option for teachers and pupils alike. It is less time consuming, less personally intrusive, and less emotionally taxing. Open negotiation is much harder to secure but *can* be approached, given the right circumstances. These would include:

- *knowing the pupil* you are negotiating the profile with;
- doing this *in private*, in quiet surroundings;
- allowing sufficient *time* for open-ended negotiation to develop;
- securing maximum *confidentiality* for what is being negotiated and making these confidentiality rules clear;
- being as *accepting* as possible of what the pupil says and how he or she says it; avoiding being pious or overly judgemental;
- avoiding schedules and comment bank systems that do not permit pupils to have an *independent voice*;
- providing *support for diffident and inarticulate pupils* in the form of prompt sheets, etc;
- providing a *programme of personal and social development* in which pupils can develop skills of negotiation.
- providing *INSET support* so that teachers can develop the special skills of one-to-one negotiation too.

In addition to these specific measures to help teachers and pupils move successfully towards open negotiation, the most important principle of all is that such openness should be in evidence elsewhere in the teacher–pupil relationship too. What takes place in profile negotiation should as far as possible be consistent with what the pupils are experiencing elsewhere in their school lives. Without that consistency, pupils will simply not trust their teachers. And without trust, everything of value in records of achievement breaks down. Closed negotiation persists. And everyone – pupils and teachers alike – expends wasted energy and time on a bureaucratic chore, on a system that cannot meet the expectations set for it. Consistency is therefore vital. This raises important questions about the relationship of profiling to the rest of the secondary school curriculum.

Conclusion: profiles in context

We have argued that profiles and records of achievement are likely to have only limited value if they are treated as separate from or extra to what is already going on in school – as an additional chore. For these reasons, we believe that profiles and records of achievement should involve more than an extended reporting system; more even than a series of private one-to-one reviews between students and their tutors about progress. Their success, as outlined at the beginning of this chapter, will depend on the extent to which they pervade the curriculum as a whole. It will depend on how far profiles and records of achievement become the subject teacher's responsibility as well as that of the form tutor – through subject self-assessment, for instance. And it will depend on how far new patterns of assessment can be accommodated by and integrated into imaginative new curriculum and learning structures.

The development of modular curricula might prove particularly important here. The construction of shorter modules of study of a few weeks each can be rounded off by the negotiation of a statement at the end of each module. This forms a natural conclusion to that part of the learning process. Such records can also be torn off and sent home as a report to parents at the same time. This modular arrangement could usefully replace the conventional curriculum and assessment system with its long one-to-two year haul in a subject leading to a final examination. It might also replace the usual one-off report to parents by a more continuous stream of information and feedback on which parents can themselves comment.[10]

Such things, together with the use of curriculum time in areas like information technology to begin the process of profile compilation, can bring curriculum, learning, assessment and reporting together into a unitary whole. They can begin to meet the usual objections, so often encountered in 'bolted-on' versions of profiling, about where the time is to come from, how duplication with the reporting system is to be avoided, etc. In short, profiles and records of achievement are only likely to be successful in terms of learning and personal development if they are part of a broad and bold change strategy in curriculum and reporting sytems as a whole.

Like PSE more generally, profiles and records of achievement cannot be effective if they are 'bolted on' to an unsympathetic school structure. One of the most unsympathetic of such structures is the public examination system. It is the persistence and dominance of that system which so often turns profiles and records of achievement into a brittle appendage to the mainstream academic curriculum. With the continuing high priority attached to public examinations through the development of the GCSE and the requirement that schools publish their results, anything that does not directly contribute to that goal is widely treated as being of secondary importance.

Records of achievement, along with other Government initiatives, are requiring that teachers take their retraining, and their reappraisal of priorities, seriously. It seems to us that the DES and the examination boards should also go through that process. They should clarify for themselves the importance of records of achievement and their relationship to public examinations, for the process leading to public examinations is not necessarily compatible with that leading to a record of achievement. Moreover, there are questions as to how seriously teachers can take records of achievement when the examination-related demands on their time and commitment are being increased. In this respect, the almost simultaneous introduction of Records of Achievement and the GCSE seems to us a move of the most monumental professional insensitivity – oblivious to or disregarding the extraordinary demands that innovation on this scale makes on teachers' time and commitment. Already, we are beginning to hear remarks in school staffrooms of the sort: 'I can't do much with these records of achievement, I'm too busy trying to sort out my new GCSE syllabus'. The GCSE forms one arm of current Government policy. By contrast, records of achievement are not so much another arm of that policy, as a little finger. As these two become locked in professional arm-wrestling within schools, it is not hard to predict which will be victorious!

Such conflicts of interest require some rethinking about the amount of time and resources which a school is expected to allocate to examination ends as part of its overall work. This in turn requires a national reappraisal of the quantity of certification which it is necessary for students to attain. With so few students now going directly into work at 16, the continuation of public examinations at that age is looking increasingly irrelevant, particularly where the taking of some eight or nine certificates is involved. In the long term, we may well have to choose between records of achievement and public examinations. In practice, many hard-pressed teachers and schools are already doing this – but not in the direction those concerned with pupils' personal and social development might perhaps regard as best.

Our great fear is that because of time and cost implications, because of the desire not to threaten or erode the hegemony of the subject-based, publicly examined, academic curriculum, and because of political anxieties about there being too much of an educational revolution in the classroom, Government may come to make its choice between examinations and records of achievement earlier than we think. And we worry that this might well be a choice that will limit records of achievement to manageable, safe, confined areas of the curriculum – to little more than extended systems of reporting for all pupils, and to formative processes of negotiation and self-assessment only with the lower achievers. We believe these are options that schools should avoid. The potential of records of achievement for PSE, curriculum and learning as a whole is far-reaching and radical. This principle requires political protection and professional support. We hope it can be secured.

Notes

1 The contrast we are making here is with the kinds of contrived success that are offered through graded assessments in subjects like mathematics and modern languages. Here, it is the certificate received for reaching a particular level of achievement that is meant to be the motivating factor; not the nature or quality of what is learned itself. Nor is the reaching of a particular grade always an achievement as such, although that is how it is presented. This is because the lower levels of achievement are actually constructed in such a way that the vast proportion of the relevant age group will already be able to achieve them without making any additional effort. For a critique of the motivational aspects of graded assessments, see Hargreaves (1988a).

2 This material was collected in relation to the development of assessments in English in the Oxford Certificate of Educational Achievement.

3 Speech given by Mr Bob Dunn to the London Education Business Partnership, 11.11.86.

4 Ibid.

5 However, comment banks are less easily interpreted by employers if they do not know what grades are behind the comments.

6 Other valuable inservice activities which illustrate the highly subjective nature of personal judgements are set out by Law (1984).

7 We are grateful to Don Amphlett of Drayton Secondary School, Banbury, Oxfordshire for making this material available.

8 Examples of such prompt sheets are reviewed in Law (1984) and OCEA (1987).

9 The remaining examples in this section were collected by one of us in connection with research on self-assessment and records of achievement (Tossell, 1984).

10 There are some problems with modularisation, however. Modules can disguise the process of educational selection from parents and pupils alike until, from their point of view, it is too late. See Hargreaves (1988a) for a development of this point.

7 Conclusion: whole school policy

In this book, we have examined different approaches to personal and social education; different organisational ways in which schools can attend to this important area of young people's development. In doing this, whether we have been looking at taught courses, tutorial work, residential experience, personal recording or records of achievement, we have, in slightly different ways, kept returning to an enduring set of issues and questions that pervade the whole area. These concern the values underpinning PSE, the purposes it serves; and the status of the area, the importance it manages to attain within the curriculum and organisation of secondary schools. We want to return to these issues and questions and analyse them in more detail now, for they highlight the fact that schools and teachers face choices and challenges not just in relation to the organisational ways in which PSE might best be presented, but in relation to the fundamental purposes and priorities that are attached to the area also. In particular, we want to address the following questions:

- What are the basic values and purposes that underpin the teaching of personal and social education? Are they genuinely concerned with the *care* of the individual pupil and the enhancement of his or her personal and social development, or are they more concerned with exerting and increasing *control* over young people's behaviour to make it more socially acceptable and manageable?
- Does PSE predominantly concern itself with the affective aspects of learning and development, and does it, because of this, open itself to charges of emotional indoctrination? Or is there a more rational, cognitively rigorous side to PSE too, which stresses moral reasoning, rigorous argument and thoughtful criticism?
- What are the arguments for dealing with PSE separately within the school curriculum, as against integrating it carefully with other aspects of school life?

Care or control?

In our discussion of traditional pastoral care systems, we noted some striking disparities between the rhetoric and reality of provision in this area. The 'conventional wisdom' of pastoral care was that it was centrally concerned with the care and individual welfare of pupils (Best, Jarvis and Ribbins, 1977). In practice, though, pastoral care was often overwhelmingly preoccupied with administration, discipline and punishment (Best, Ribbins, Jarvis and Oddy, 1983). This was certainly how most teachers understood the place of pastoral care in their own schools. As the authors of one study of teachers' perceptions of pastoral care concluded:

> There is little evidence . . . that the institutionalisation of pastoral care roles necessarily leads directly to a greater concern for pupil welfare. Indeed, teachers seem more likely to perceive such roles in terms of their resolution of problems of teacher control and administration.
>
> (Best, Ribbins, Jarvis and Oddy, 1980: 268)

In making these observations on the reconstruction of pastoral systems around the concerns of control rather than care, we do not want to imply that we regard control or discipline or punishment as necessarily bad things. While we hold very strongly to the view that some approaches to punishment and discipline are extremely damaging to the welfare and personal development of young people (and we shall take this up in more detail later), we recognise that even in the most caring institutions, pupils will still misbehave and arrangements will still need to be made to admonish them, withdraw their privileges, contact their parents, refer them to outside agencies, and so on.

We are not therefore arguing that punishment and discipline should, or even could be removed from schools. On the contrary, along with writers like Emile Durkheim (1956), we regard the development of discipline through the establishment of moral rules whose rationality and fairness young people can recognise and appreciate, as an essential element of their personal and social education into responsible adulthood. Discipline, understood as the development of self-discipline rather than frequent, arbitrary and weakly justified punishment, is at the heart of the educational process where young people are concerned. However, we do want to draw attention to the fact that pastoral systems formally established to care for the welfare of young people, have too often become preoccupied with administering, controlling, disciplining and punishing them instead.

The need for much of that control has arisen from the expectation that the main purpose of the pastoral system is to provide 'back up' for the academic system within the school (Best, Ribbins, Jarvis and Oddy, 1980: 257–258). Yet it has often been the inadequacies of this academic system, of the curriculum and tasks that children have been set in the first place that has been the source of the problems with which the pastoral system has then been expected to cope. Under these circumstances, pastoral care has often been turned into what Williamson (1980) calls *pastoralisation* where the tutor frequently uses the relationship of mutual trust . . . to deflect legitimate grievance away from the inadequate types of learning experience offered within the school.

(Williamson, 1980: 172–173)

Within traditional pastoral systems, such confusions of purpose between care and control are undesirable. Dual responsibility for individual pupil welfare and for discipline and punishment were built into the role from the very beginning. With more recent PSE initiatives, this has not been the case. Teachers of PSE courses, for instance, have not been formally expected to take any responsibility for discipline and punishment as such. Care and control have not both been written into the job description from the outset. Have more recent developments in PSE therefore managed to avoid becoming enmeshed in the business of institutional and social control?

David (1983: 12), in his influential review of PSE in secondary schools, is sceptical:

Improved pastoral care and personal and social education appear sometimes to have been devised merely to contain a difficult age group and to enforce discipline and social control rather than with more positive and more imaginative aims in view.

As we have seen, this charge could certainly be applied with considerable justification to the early Newsom and ROSLA courses, specially designated for older, lower attaining pupils. With more recent initiatives, aimed at the entire ability range, this somewhat conspiratorial view that discipline and control have perhaps been part of the very conception, planning and design of PSE developments, seems a little harsh.

Discipline and control, we have seen, do have a persistent and often unfortunate presence within PSE initiatives. But that is not necessarily because the school or the LEA or the teachers intend it to be that way (though we recognise that this sometimes happens). Often, rather, discipline and control are aspects of PSE that hard-pressed, busy teachers, short on time and opportunities to reflect, find themselves drifting into. Adopting a tendency to move towards discipline and control rather than towards more challenging and professionally unsettling interpretations of PSE is literally the line of least resistance to take in the immensely demanding and stressful environment of secondary school teaching. As teachers, that very busy-ness perhaps also makes us a little less aware than we should be of the realities of how pupils see us and the relationships we have with them. The evidence of Chapter 5, for instance, points to the likelihood that even when we are trying to work in genuine and open partnership with our pupils, we are probably still overestimating the trust that they are prepared to place in us, and underestimating the effects that the authority of our position, our capacity to judge, to evaluate and to punish, has upon those pupils and what they are prepared to disclose in our company. This is why we have emphasised the importance of creating regular planning and in-service opportunities for teachers involved in PSE to evaluate what is taking place so that the fundamental values and purposes that are in practice underpinning the whole area can be subject to open discussion and continual review.

Control will sometimes be consciously intended by those who are involved in PSE. Often its presence will intrude unintentionally. And even where teachers are consciously working against it, their pupils, drawing on their wider experience of relationships with teachers, will tend to act as if control were still influential – maintaining their distance, holding back their trust.

Although it may not have been the intention, we have seen how tutorial work, for example, can become very preoccupied with the coping skills of social adjustment rather than the transforming skills of social change. We have also seen how it can present particular versions of middle-class manners and morality as if they were universal principles of socially desirable human behaviour on which everyone would agree. In Records of Achievement, we have seen even more powerful and pervasive possibilities for the fulfilment of control and disciplinary interests over and above those of personal and social development. Through what, for pupils, can be an overarching threat of repeated and regular review; through what, in power terms, is inevitably a rather imbalanced and somewhat one-sided process of contractual agreement on learning targets and future goals; and through extended intervention and intrusion into the hitherto private world of the pupil's family and community life, records of achievement can be turned into profoundly disturbing instruments of social surveillance and informa-tion gathering which open up the personal and private worlds of children and their families to continual inspection, regulation and interven-tion.

Many of these control consequences in PSE initiatives are cruelly ironic. Teachers and schools often do not intend them. Many begin with very different purposes in mind. They embrace personal and social development aspects of PSE initiatives with passion, commitment and sincerity. But the stresses and routines of day-to-day life in school often mean that innovations originally intended to meet the personal and social development needs of pupils can quickly be transformed into efforts to meet, or at least not threaten, the smooth and orderly running of the school and the perceived needs of the employers. They come to serve, or at least not to challenge, the teachers' and employers' interests rather than the pupils'. They become concerned with institutional and social control more than with individual care.

It is the busy-ness of schools, more than conservative conspiracies among their teachers, that sustains this ever-present tendency for the interests of control to intrude into the practice of PSE. That is why it is imperative that the discussion of values should not cease with the original planning phase of PSE initiatives but be a continuing part of school life; supporting and encouraging reflection and vigilance among all those concerned about the purposes that PSE initiatives are actually serving, not just on paper, but in practice too.

Affective or cognitive?

One way of protecting children from being excessively vulnerable to the controlling interests of others is to help develop in them the powers and skills of autonomous, critical judgement. Such a requirement calls for a rigorous, cognitive component in PSE, devoted to the improvement of thinking and reasoning in relation to personal and social issues and experiences. If anything, though, the emphasis within many PSE initiatives has been more towards the affective rather than the cognitive domain of human experience, towards the realm of feeling and emotions than that of thinking and reasoning.

Given the circumstances in which PSE has emerged in secondary schools, this kind of emphasis is, perhaps, understandable. When comprehensive schools were established, they tended to take over the curriculum of the grammar schools they superseded. In order to establish and protect a reputation as 'good schools', their curriculum, their interests and many aspects of their organisation became heavily skewed towards academic learning in the intellectual-cognitive domain (D. Hargreaves, 1982: 51). Learning in other domains like the affective-emotional and the personal-social was comparatively neglected.

Recent research supports these observations and points to some of the social consequences of excessive academic emphasis. In a region of South Wales where one part of the area went comprehensive and the other did not, Reynolds and Sullivan (1987) found that, because of their academic aspirations and pretensions, the new comprehensive schools became more like the grammar schools than the grammar schools themselves. This had serious implications for their social outcomes. In terms of rates of truancy, delinquency and vandalism, for example, the comprehensive system fared less well than its selective, grammar/secondary modern counterpart. Undue academic emphasis appeared to be having adverse consequences for the personal and social development of many young people.

The strong cognitive emphasis in the new comprehensive schools meant that the more affectively and emotionally-based aspects of secondary education were allotted less time. They were effectively being relegated to second class status. From across the political spectrum, from the Conservative Secretary of State to the incoming Chief Inspector of the Inner London Education Authority, calls were made to redress the balance, to increase the amount of time and attention devoted to the more affective areas of educational experience.[1] Indeed, some of the most significant initiatives in PSE have been justified in just these terms. Baldwin and Smith (1983: 37), for instance, argued

that their widely adopted *Active Tutorial Work* programme was developed
because:

> . . . the value system of schooling has been dominantly linguistically, cognitively
> and intellectually based with little emphasis on the emotional, intuitive, practical
> and experiential aspects of human development.

Greater emphasis on the 'affective domain' has therefore begun to redress a
long-standing imbalance in the secondary school curriculum. But can this
'affective domain' properly be equated with personal and social education?
When we speak of personal and social education, are we also speaking about
affective areas of experience rather than cognitive ones; about feeling rather
than thinking? Some writers certainly do appear to equate the two (eg
Broadfoot, 1986b). And in practical terms, some versions of PSE seem to be
mainly preoccupied with affective aspects of learning and development rather
than cognitive ones. We have seen that some kinds of group tutorial work, for
example, have just this kind of emphasis. The importance they attach to
experiential learning in staff training as well as in the classroom, the stress they
put on personal growth and development within the supportive context of the
small group, and the priority they give to the attitudes and skills of caring and
sharing, trust and support – all these things are good indicators of the affective
loading within tutorial programmes.

For many people, social, personal and moral development is indeed essentially a question of feeling. Some teachers too believe it more important that
their pupils feel for others and act well towards them, than that they can think
reflectively about moral questions. After all, people do not necessarily act on
what they think, still less on what they say. Isn't it what they *do* that is
important? Shouldn't PSE therefore be mainly concerned with educating young
people to accept and be committed to commonly accepted norms of behaviour,
and to feel and act appropriately?

Plausible as it sounds, we believe that there are problems with this position.
First, the feelings we have concerning other people are of a different order than,
say, feeling tired or feeling hungry. They are not already there from the moment
of our birth. They have to be learned. The feelings we learn are therefore
influenced by what feelings are regarded as socially important or desirable. Of
course, some feelings and dispositions – like concern for others or tolerance –
seem, within our culture, to have an unarguable social importance. But what of
feelings or dispositions like patriotism and loyalty? These are somewhat more
contestable. The feelings we value, the dispositions we develop towards others,
therefore depend, in part, on social judgements about what are proper and
worthwhile ways of relating to others. These judgements, like judgements of
right and wrong, are not self-evident. They are contentious. For that reason,
they deserve serious, rational discussion of a cognitively rigorous kind – both
between teachers and pupils and among teachers themselves.

Second, and even more importantly, we make value judgements not just about different kinds of feelings or disposition, but about the things to which we attach those feelings. To take loyalty as an example: is loyalty to one's friends the same as loyalty to one's school or one's country – good or bad, right or wrong? Should we not sometimes question the worth of what it is we are being asked to give our loyalty to? And does this not mean that we should consider suspending our loyalty when arguably higher moral principles are at stake like honesty or fairness? In this respect, it is perhaps salutory to note that Mussolini's first Minister of Public Instruction, Gentile, was very much an educational 'progressive' who favoured state schooling giving high importance to spiritual development. Expressing his confidence in Gentile's reforms, Mussolini himself proclaimed that 'from the future fascist schools and universities, the nation's new and ruling class would issue' (quoted in Entwistle 1979: 185). Such are the possible consequences for political indoctrination of too strong an emphasis on the affective, emotional or spiritual aspects of children's education! As Entwistle (1979: 82) puts it, 'an innovative, democratic society requires not merely "spontaneity" but also citizens who are well informed'.

PSE which excludes or plays down rational and rigorous cognitive appraisal of the value of different feelings and dispositions, and of the value of what we feel or are encouraged to feel disposed *towards* is in our view more akin to indoctrination than education. Approaches to peace studies or world studies that place undue reliance on the emotive power of drama or role play; work experience that has no place for rigorous appraisal of the organisation of the workplace or the norms of enterprise culture themselves; or experiential activities in group tutorial work that open children's private feelings to public exposure and create a kind of vulnerability and inner doubt which makes them overly suggestible to new beliefs or commitments advanced by the teacher – all these things are examples of the kinds of political and moral indoctrination that concern us.

Yet, if PSE can have too strong an affective bias and run the risk of indoctrination, it can also become too cognitively inclined, too rationalist in its emphasis. Here, the risk is not one of indoctrination but irrelevance. Developing the intellectual capacity for moral reasoning may help create rational and morally autonomous human beings, equipped with the thinking skills to come to their own independent moral judgement (Hare, 1952; Kohlberg, 1976). But, by failing to engage the emotions, and by not relating directly to the practical lives of pupils, a rationalist presentation of PSE can come to be seen as uninteresting and irrelevant by many young people – just one more facet of that academic curriculum with which they have already become profoundly disenchanted.

Even where it does successfully engage young people's interests, the effectiveness of this rationalist approach to moral education is still open to question – for how people *think* about moral issues, the intellectual games they play in discussing moral questions, has no necessary implications for how they will *act* in relation to such issues. It is not just words, but deeds too that are a vital part of PSE. The rationalist approach has at best a limited capacity to deal with them. This is where long-running tutorial programmes, for instance, with their stress on developing self-awareness, cooperation, trust and mutual support within the living relationships of the class group, have very real strengths.

The cognitive and affective aspects of PSE are therefore equally vital. On the cognitive side, it is important that PSE should convey factual information on health issues, sexuality, subject choices in school, the world of work, the state of the arms race, and so on – to provide a basis of knowledge around which feelings can then be explored (Marland, 1980). Such programmes should also help young people make rational, autonomous decisions about themselves and their world. They should help the pupils question and think; a requirement, one would imagine, not just of PSE in particular but of education itself. On the affective side, PSE should be organised in such a way as to engage, explore and enhance young people's emotions – to foster caring, concern and commitment in relation to other people and the world around them. PSE, that is, should develop a sense in the young person of being not just a morally autonomous person, but a morally responsible and committed one too.

The cognitive and the affective, thinking and feeling, head and heart: these things necessarily go together in any programme of or approach to PSE which strives to be both rigorous and relevant; which engages with pupils' emotions and commitments while also protecting them intellectually from the dangers of indoctrination. Ultimately, therefore, we agree with John Tomlinson when he says that:

> It is too often implied that the educational needs of children can in some way be divided into cognitive and affective areas ... In fact, the two kinds of development are inter-dependent.
>
> (Tomlinson, 1983: 5)

Integrated or separate?

Whatever the emphasis of PSE, decisions still have to be taken about how to provide for it in school. Those decisions can have far-reaching consequences for its effectiveness. One of the most managerially attractive options for introducing PSE is to make some kind of separate provision for it – in addition to the school's existing curricular and organisational arrangements. A taught course, a tutorial programme, a residential week – such innovations ensure that provision is made for PSE, that someone has clear responsibility for it and, not least, that there is minimum disruption of, or challenge to, what the school is already doing.

Separate provision, then, can ensure coverage, allow allocation of clear responsibilities and, by not threatening what is already going on, smooth the path of innovation. Throughout this book, however, we have also seen that separate provision, when it is the only provision, can seriously undermine the status of PSE, placing it on the margins of school life and at the tail end of staff and pupils' priorities.

As we have seen, PSE taught courses are constantly vulnerable to lowered prestige compared with the mainstream curriculum, in the eyes of teachers, pupils and parents. This affects not just the dignity and professional respect of teachers involved in the area. It has immense implications for the coherence and effectiveness of those programmes too. In Chapter 2, we saw that the lowered status of PSE courses often brought with it problems of recruiting suitable staff, difficulties in securing appropriate timetabling, lack of opportunity to meet like 'real' subject departments, and difficulties in getting suitable accommodation for the more open-ended kinds of teaching that PSE requires. The existence and visibility among the other staff of many of these problems then tends to reinforce the low status which gave rise to those problems in the first place.

Similar problems, we found, affect the provision of residential experience too. If isolated from other parts of pupils' education, whatever benefits are gained from the experience can be short lived. And the contribution of the participating teachers, not fully understood but regarded instead as little more than going on 'trips' and holidays, can be devalued.

Where virtually all teachers are given some clear responsibility for PSE in some way, the problems that come with such isolation are minimised. But they are by no means eradicated. If responsibility for PSE is confined to a small number of relatively limited, clearly bounded tasks, located in particular parts of the timetable, other problems of lowered status are likely to arise. Almost everyone may in some measure be dealing with PSE, but if they are doing this for but a small part of their time, and if this has little connection with the other things that the teachers concerned are doing in school, then their commitment to the area, the priority and importance they attach to it, will not be great. We have seen how such status-related problems of lowered commitment and priority in comparison with work in the mainstream, academic, examination-based curriculum, can prejudice the success of tutorial work and records of achievement, for example.

Separately provided PSE, mounted aside from the remainder of school life, therefore looks likely to be an ill-fated venture. Not everyone agrees with us on this, though. Taking a pragmatic stance, some writers argue that the alternative strategy – whole-school commitment to and support for PSE – is exceedingly difficult to coordinate managerially, and without the support of the head, this may not be forthcoming at all (eg McNiff, 1985). Under these circumstances, they conclude, it is better to do something, even if it is imperfect, than to do nothing at all.

We have some sympathy for this view: one that arises, in some respects, from frustration with the little more than tepid support of many heads for PSE and with the current trends of Government policy which are offering increasing financial and legislative support and direction to change and development in the mainstream academic curriculum, and therefore to teachers' commitments in that sphere. The separate route of PSE development may be the only realistic one for interested teachers in many schools. And we would not want to discourage more modest, less wide-ranging initiatives of that sort. Indeed, on some occasions, isolated new initiatives can present models of good practice that others then wish to emulate elsewhere in the school. But this is not the usual pattern and we would want to warn teachers and heads who wish to or feel they have to take the route of separate development, that they will almost certainly meet a host of difficulties of the kind we have outlined in this book. This in turn will undermine the success of their innovative efforts.

PSE is an area of such all-encompassing relevance to the life and development of young people that high expectations for its success call for high commitment not just from an enthusiastic few, but from the majority of a secondary school staff. Repeatedly, we have found that the coherence and effectiveness of any particular PSE initiative depends on wider support for and commitment to PSE throughout the school as a whole. We therefore came to the conclusion drawn by several other writers in this area, that effective provision for personal and social education requires it to be a central feature of the educational policy and commitment of the whole school.

But what do we mean when we speak of the need for a whole school policy on PSE? Obviously, this must amount to more than a commitment on paper within the overall aims of the school. Yet if we are looking for a more practical kind of commitment, what form should this take? We want to close our discussion by outlining three aspects of whole school policy that we believe are important to the effective development and delivery of PSE in secondary schools. These concern mechanisms of coordination, principles of consistency, and particular sorts of school ethos.

Coordination

There is no substitute for having a coordinated approach to personal and social education across all aspects of secondary school life. PSE is more than just an extra subject on the curriculum. It deals with a huge slice of young people's educational and human experience. Coherence between the different parts of that experience is essential. So too is orderly, year-by-year progression in the learning that pupils undertake in this sphere. Effective coordination in this area is therefore vital to reduce fragmentation, eliminate duplication, achieve coherence and secure progression.

Coordination is needed between specific PSE initiatives – to ensure that the tutorial system neatly dovetails with the taught PSE course, for instance. It is needed to give greater coherence to the teaching of PSE content within the remainder of the curriculum, to ensure, for example, that what is provided in relation to sex education in biology, health education, social studies and childcare classes amounts to a coherent set of educational experiences. Coordination is required to ensure that newly provided PSE content does not duplicate or conflict with treatment of similar content within the existing curriculum. Most importantly of all, if the status of PSE and all that goes with that is to be protected, its place in the overall management of the school needs to be secured by coordinating it at an appropriately senior level with the other major aspects of secondary school organisation – most notably, those concerning curriculum and assessment.

As Marland (1980: 159) points out, whole school policies are 'difficult to start, to implement and to monitor . . . The more complicated you get, the more difficult it is to make sure the work is actually being done'. Because of this, the task of coordination requires a clear and recognised place in the management structure of the school.

At the top, the support of the head is vital (McNiff, 1985: 110). Research on English teaching has indicated that the strength and imaginativeness of English departments is strongly associated with the interest in and support for the subject shown by the head (Ball and Lacey, 1980). Research on PSE departments has revealed similar patterns (Rose, 1986). Status, coherence and effectiveness have been difficult to achieve without firm backing from the head. Where PSE is seen as something that bears on all aspects of school life and for which every teacher in the school holds some responsibility, that support is even more crucial.

Next, there should be at least one person in the school with designated responsibility for pulling together and giving coherence to a school's PSE provision in the way we have outlined. At the very least (and this is increasingly becoming the favoured pattern), this person should have responsibility for the PSE department (and any associated tutorial programme) and be appointed at Head of Department level. That appointment should reflect the scope and importance of the area and therefore be made at a level equivalent to the leadership of other large departments in the school.

We regard this kind of appointment as only minimally adequate, however. PSE is more than just another subject, and although awarding Head of Department Status to its coordinator would certainly elevate its position above that which it has already managed to attain in many schools, even that status would not adequately reflect the importance and scope of the whole area, reaching as it does into the pastoral system, the assessment system, and the existing curriculum.

One way of recognising increased status and importance for PSE would be to include it within the wider job description of one of a school's deputy heads. Indeed, the existence of deputy heads (pastoral) in many comprehensive schools sets a clear precedent for such a move. But we have already seen, in Chapter 2, that where PSE is embraced within a deputy head's wider range of responsibilities, it can become obscured by these other concerns and receive rather less attention than it deserves. Moreover, as we saw in Chapter 1, combined responsibility for PSE with some of the more traditional pastoral duties involving punishment, administration and discipline can ultimately have adverse consequences for PSE.

Where, then, should the PSE Coordinator be placed? Within the context of existing school management structures, this is a tricky question. Those structures do not necessarily reflect the educational needs and priorities of the late twentieth century. If we really are committed to reappraising and upgrading the place of personal and social education within the overall curriculum and organisation of secondary schools, then such reappraisals should presumably be reflected not just in additions or adjustments to the existing curriculum, or in a reshaped tutorial system, but in a reshaped management structure too.

Personal and Social Development is neither a new subject, nor a fashionable reconstruction of what we have conventionally understood as pastoral care. It is a major dimension of young people's educational experience, equivalent in significance to those things we call curriculum and assessment. We therefore recommend that responsibility for coordination of PSE should be designated as having the same status and seniority as responsibility for coordinating curriculum and assessment. This suggests the appointment of three senior coordinators – at senior teacher level, perhaps – for curriculum, assessment, and personal and social education respectively. Together with the head and possibly a reduced number of deputies, these three coordinators would make up the school's senior management team, bringing together and giving coherence to the school's educational provision as a whole.

The boundaries between these coordinators' responsibilities would not be watertight. We have shown that much PSE can be found within the existing curriculum, and that many recent assessment initiatives like pupil profiles have improvements in personal and social development uppermost in their priorities. There would certainly be overlaps in the coordinators' roles, and rightly so. But their starting points, their areas of priority, would be very different. Together, though, this triumvirate of coordinators could help establish a secure, senior and coherent place for PSE in the overall curriculum and organisation of the secondary school.

A Coordinator of PSE appointed at such a level would need to liaise frequently with heads of faculty, heads of department and pastoral heads too. We believe, though, that one of the most powerful and influential links would be with the heads of year. Indeed, we believe it is appropriate for year heads to be allotted a significant coordinating responsibility for PSE in their own right. For this responsibility to be discharged effectively, though, the role of Head of Year will need to be broadened considerably beyond its present interpretation in comprehensive schools.

The role of Head of Year in the comprehensive school has developed largely in the context of the pastoral system and has therefore encompassed responsibilities for individual pupil welfare, punishment, dicipline, contact with parents, referrals to outside agencies and so on (Corbishley and Evans, 1980). In recent years, this role has often been extended to include responsibility for the development and coordination of tutorial programmes too. Only rarely, where secondary schools have established foundation programmes of integrated studies with their lower years, have heads of year moved beyond coordinating *pastoral* work to coordinating *academic* and other curricular work across the year.

There is no reason or sound educational justification why the responsibilities of heads of year should be restricted to pastoral and administrative duties. The reasons why the role should have developed that way are largely historical and have to do with the need for efficient systems of administration and discipline in the large, impersonal, bureaucratic and academically-slanted institutions that comprehensive schools became. The career interests of reorganised secondary modern teachers of some seniority were also implicated in this development. In addition, the existence of a powerful subject departmental system has made it difficult and often unthinkable for Heads of Year to encroach upon what has conventionally been understood as academic territory. The role of Head of Year as it is currently understood has therefore developed in the context of the academic–pastoral divide which in many respects, comprehensive reorganisation both created and sustained.

This pastoral model of year leadership is the dominant one in the mainstream secondary system. Within other parts of the comprehensive system, however, alternative models of year leadership which have bestowed upon it a more imaginative and wide-ranging set of responsibilities, are available. In 9–13 middle schools (which are officially designated as secondary schools by the DES) heads of year have traditionally taken on responsibility for coordination of both the pastoral and the academic sides of pupils' lives in school. This has provided a smooth system of pastoral administration and an impressive lateral system of curriculum coordination too, which has secured a measure of coherence between different parts of pupils' work (Hargreaves, 1986b). In middle schools, the year team, led by its coordinator, has come to work together not just as a pastoral team, but as a curriculum planning team as well.

This model of curricular and pastoral integration is worthy of emulation in the mainstream secondary system. Research on the early years of secondary education has shown that pupils who have developed and been expected to exercise personal and social skills and qualities like choice, initiative and collaboration in primary school, are given little opportunity to exercise them when they transfer to secondary school (Measor and Woods, 1984). Rectifying this would involve extending the role of the year head far beyond that of dealing with misbehaving pupils, developing new report procedures, and so on, to the very core of teaching itself; to teachers' preferred methods of working.

Change in such matters is fundamental and can only be achieved through close teamwork, staff involvement, mutual support and collective review. The subject department is not the best managerial unit for dealing with these matters that bear on the overall coherence of the pupils' educational experience and personal and social development. It sees and deals with only fragments of the pupil. Coordination and integration must therefore rest with some other staff unit. Drawing on the middle school experience, we can see that the year team and its coordinator is capable of taking on this task and well placed for dealing with it.

This reconstructed interpretation of year leadership would extend responsibility for PSE beyond the business of pastoral administration and tutorial provision, to coordinating and reviewing its place within the main part of the curriculum too. With such widened responsibilities, the year coordinators, as they should perhaps be called, would prove a valuable point of contact with the senior PSE Coordinator (and indeed with the other coordinators as well). Such responsibilities would, of course, require extra time, but much of this could be created by transferring a good deal of the existing burden for pastoral administration and school discipline on to the form tutors and class teachers – a point we shall return to later when we discuss school ethos.

Contemplating changes like these (which are not without precedent in the existing secondary system) helps us appreciate that the task of coordination involves considerably more than bringing together what is already there in secondary schools. It involves development as well as coordination. And if this development is to be part of a process of increasing the priority and significance attached to PSE, it must involve changes in the managerial structure of secondary schools, in order to reflect and secure the heightened status of the area. In this respect, we find once more that meaningful change in personal and social education involves substantial change in education itself.

Consistency

The task of coordination, as we understand it, is a broad and a demanding one. It extends far beyond the bringing together of different bits of PSE provision, to the core of the teaching process itself. For specific PSE initiatives are unlikely to meet with any great or lasting success if what they teach and what they encourage is contradicted by what a pupil learns, understands and experiences in the remainder of his or her school life. One of the most important tasks of the PSE Coordinator is to try and secure some consistency in the personal and social qualities, skills and understandings that, explicitly or implicitly, pupils are being encouraged to develop across the whole range of their school experience. There are at least three areas that are worth examining here.

First, are the official messages relayed through the overt content of PSE courses and initiatives being supported or contradicted by what the pupil is experiencing elsewhere in school? If studies of law and order emphasise justice, fairness and the principle of innocence until proven guilty, is this what pupils themselves experience in their relationships with teachers and in their encounters with the pastoral system? If their daily experience of school rules is that many of them seem unnecessary, or that they are poorly justified, or that they are applied with arbitrariness, haste and inconsistency – will this not perhaps teach them much more about 'the rule of law' than any discussion of such matters in PSE classes?

Second, are the *processes* of personal and social learning and development in PSE initiatives at one with the processes of such learning and development elsewhere in the school? Pupils will find it hard within PSE courses and tutorial classes to participate in group discussion and talk about social issues open-endedly if, within the mainstream curriculum, open discussion is not encouraged, pupils' own contributions and initiatives are suppressed and their role is largely confined to 'guessing' then reproducing the teachers' predecided 'right answers'. They will experience difficulty in working cooperatively in groups if this experience is largely confined to PSE classes. And they will be diffident and suspicious about entering into open relationships of partnership with their PSE teachers if such behaviour is treated as punishable cheek, over-familiarity or precociousness by most other school staff.

Third, as well as problems of inconsistency between the content and process of particular PSE initiatives on the one hand, and the remainder of a pupils' school experience on the other, there are also sometimes problems of inconsistency in the behaviour of individual teachers who have some involvement with PSE. Is the behaviour of teachers in specific PSE contexts broadly consistent with their behaviour in other aspects of their teaching? If it is not, how are pupils to respond to these Jekyll-and-Hyde like mood swings in their teacher's relationship with them? How are pupils to respond to teachers who, as their form tutors, encourage openness, discussion and collaboration, but as their subject teachers, demand passive absorption of predecided knowledge? What trust can pupils invest in teachers during one-to-one discussions of profiles, if those teachers deal with them impersonally, hierarchically, and perhaps even unsympathetically in the normal run of class teaching? And how long is the trust and informality carefully established between teachers and pupils during an intensive residential experience likely to last, if teachers revert to their traditional, more distanced classroom role on return to school?

To say that personal and social education affects almost everything that goes on within school is more than just a hollow cliché. Failure to recognise and act on this principle leads not only to limited changes in PSE throughout the curriculum and ethos of the school as a whole. By doing that, it also undermines the effectiveness of more modest and localised PSE initiatives. This is why it is ultimately essential that the coordination and integration of PSE should extend beyond tidy packaging of pieces of curriculum content to the establishment of some consistency in the processes, relationships, and styles of teaching and learning that run through the whole school. This, of course, begs the vital question of what form those processes and relationships should take – which leads us to the third and final aspect of whole school policy: school ethos.

School ethos

Fostering of worthwhile personal and social education is not simply achieved through lessons with an explicit personal and social focus. It is in the everyday fabric of school life; in its rules and regulations, its attitudes and expectations; in the entire range of relationships within the school community, that most personal and social learning takes place. Such things, taken together, are usually understood as making up the ethos or climate of a school. A school's ethos, it is widely claimed, has immense implications for the personal and social development, and indeed the intellectual achievement, of its pupils. If this is indeed the case, it will be valuable to know what kinds of ethos are most beneficial for personal and social development. To answer this question satisfactorily, though, we need to be a little more precise about what this nebulous thing we call 'ethos' actually is.

The notion of the ethos or climate of a school is indeed a vague one. It is something we know, 'in our bones' to be there, something we realise has a powerful and pervasive effect on childrens' and teachers' lives, and because of this, something we yearn to understand more fully. Yet ethos or climate appears to defy clear, precise description. Users of the concept speak allusively of 'amorphous environments' (Stewart, 1979), of 'atmosphere' and 'tone'. Or they fall back on persuasive yet equally imprecise analogies such as Halpin's (1966: 131), 'personality is to the individual what ... climate is to the organisation'. Michael Rutter and his team (1979), in a section explicitly concerned with the concept of ethos, have spoken loosely of 'group norms' and of the fact that 'any relatively self-contained organisation tends to develop its own culture or pattern'. Elsewhere, they allude to 'broader institutional effects', to 'style and quality of life at school' and so on, but such phrases add little in the way of clarification.

Norms, culture, pattern, tone, style – these things and others have at different times, in different places, been advanced as constituents of and synonyms for school ethos. Vagueness and confusion abound. The dictionary definition of *ethos*, derived from the Greek, is no more helpful, referring as it does to 'the characteristic spirit, prevalent tone of sentiment of a people or a community'. Evocative as such existing interpretations are, they supply few clues as to what an ethos comprises and therefore, more importantly, as to how that ethos might be changed.

Attempts at more precise definition have not been encouraging either. Some have equated school ethos with statements made about a school by its head (eg Sharp and Green, 1975). This overestimates the accuracy with which heads wish, and indeed are able, to present their school to outside audiences. Others (eg Rutter *et al*., 1979), despite their characteristically vague definitions of ethos in general, have in practice tried to construct some understanding of what a school's ethos might amount to, and what influence it might have, from the bottom up, factor by factor, variable by variable.

This second approach has rather more to commend it. Whatever else school ethos refers to, it certainly encompasses school processes – patterns of human relationship and the institutional mechanisms that bind them together. Much of our understanding of school ethos along with its educational importance for pupils' learning and development has therefore emerged through research on school effectiveness, where measures have been taken of a whole host of school processes, and then correlated with further measures of those schools' academic and social outcomes in terms of examination success, truancy, delinquency and so forth.

Despite the greater promise of this approach in terms of trying to pinpoint particular elements of school ethos, its weakness is that it has tended to treat the processes of schooling that might make up a school ethos individually, as if they were disconnected, unrelated to one another. It has often been left to the reader to deduce what the ethos might be, by adding together those process factors that the research concerned has identified as being associated with a school's academic and social outcomes. Such extra details, with their vast conglomerations of relevant process factors, do not enhance our understanding of school ethos. They clutter it. The most promising way forward in school ethos research would therefore seem to be through conceptual simplicity rather than numerical complexity. As Anderson (1980: 411–412) argues, after undertaking an extensive review of the school climate literature:

> The need now is for conceptually-based research aimed at improving models of school climate effects rather than merely adding to the already long list of separate variables or reaffirming their association with climate or outcomes.

Even so, becoming aware of some of the processes that seem to influence academic and social success or failure, creates a useful base for developing that kind of understanding. What are some of these processes then, that appear to be important in influencing the social outcomes of secondary schooling? Some of the most consistent findings of school effectiveness research (summarised in Reynolds, 1982; Reynolds and Sullivan, 1987; Galloway, 1985) point to the following as being particularly important for personal and social development.

- involving pupils and encouraging their active participation in lessons, as well as allowing and encouraging pupils to intervene and initiate lines of enquiry and discussion themselves.
- involving pupils and giving them responsibility in the wider aspects of school life through clubs and societies, and monitor and prefect systems. This is most effective when such involvement extends right across the ability range and is not restricted to the academic few.

- devolving maximum responsibility for pastoral care and discipline on to the shoulders of the class teacher and form tutor, and shifting it away from the higher echelons of the pastoral and administrative system. This includes dealing with and taking responsibility for most disciplinary issues in the classroom, and only referring pupils to senior staff in the most exceptional cases. It also entails class teachers and form tutors taking more responsibility for direct contact with parents over their pupils' welfare.

- creating a pattern of relatively relaxed and informal relationships in the classroom where confrontations are avoided if possible, where there is a warm and often joking quality to teacher–pupil relations, and where there is tolerance of a certain amount of pupil posturing in relation to such matters as smoking and chewing.

- keeping the number of school rules to a minimum, especially in relation to such matters as school uniform, chewing, jewellery, lining up, and so forth. As a matter of definition, the more rules a school creates, the more deviance it creates also – and the more it needs to deploy sanctions and punishments as a result.

- emphasising positive rewards through praise, certificates and other incentives, rather than penalising pupils through pervasive and frequently applied systems of discipline and punishment in terms of criticism, detentions, physical punishment and the like.

These things are not declarations of our own personal values. They are summaries of the findings of educational research. They are empirically grounded statements of the sorts of processes that appear to be associated with positive social outcomes from schooling. These processes have profound implications for pupils' personal and social development. Within most educational research, they have been picked out individually, one-by-one. But we believe their significance is greater than might be deduced from simply adding them together.

The processes we have described and reviewed seem to us to be fundamentally interrelated. They reflect and reinforce patterns of human relationship that recognise and respect the dignity of pupils as people. They recognise and respect the rights and needs of human beings to develop and express their personal autonomy – to make their own distinctive mark on and contribution to their social surroundings. They recognise and respect the value of people being involved in, taking responsibility for, and therefore having some sense of ownership of their own learning, along with the educational environment in which that learning takes place. And they recognise and respect the fact that feelings of self-worth and value are likely to be enhanced more by processes of praise, encouragement and support, than by punishment, blame and indifference.

Deregulation of the school rule system and de-escalation of the pastoral system shifts responsibility for all these processes towards the class teacher and form tutor. It trusts and values them to trust and value their pupils. It grounds responsibility for personal and social development more and more within the ordinary classroom relationship. Just as with learning and achievement; welfare, discipline and personal and social development increasingly become recognised as the class teacher's responsibility and cannot easily be displaced elsewhere. Giving pupils more involvement in and responsibility for their own personal and social development therefore entails increasing the class teacher's responsibility for these things also.

This raises an additional and important finding of school effectiveness research. Schools with positive social outcomes are not only schools that place a premium on involving and giving responsibility to their pupils. They are schools that maximise responsibility among their teachers as well. Effective schools are schools which involve their staffs in curriculum planning and school decision-making. They are schools which delegate as much responsibility for pastoral care and discipline as possible to the classroom teacher. They are schools which recognise the worth of their teachers, value their contributions, and actively involve them in the process of change and review. In short, they are schools which recognise that academic and social success is ultimately grounded in the quality of the classroom relationship, a relationship for which ordinary teachers have prime responsibility.

In all this, one can see excellent justifications for delegating almost all the responsibility for personal and social development and pastoral care to the class teacher and form tutor. One can also see good reasons for involving all a school's staff in the development of a whole school policy for PSE – not just as a way of securing cosmetic agreements on paper, but also as a way of ensuring that the policy is implemented consistently and with a sense of ownership and responsibility by the teachers concerned at classroom level. Clearly, a school that values the personal and social development of its pupils must also value the personal and social development of its staff.

It is in this principle that we can finally grasp what school ethos is. School ethos is not just an elusive, ethereal quality. Nor is it what heads proclaim their schools to be. Nor is it the sum total of a disconnected set of educational processes. It is a set of qualities that underpin and organise a consistent and systematic pattern of human relationships throughout a school – among pupils, among teachers, between pupils and teachers and, not least, between all these people and the school's head. In the case of effective schools producing positive social outcomes, these are relationships which respect and seek to develop human autonomy and independent judgement, which encourage people to take maximum responsibility for their own learning and development, which emphasise involvement and ownership as a way of increasing commitment and effectiveness, and which value praise and support as a way of fostering these things. They are relationships that apply to pupils and teachers alike. For that reason, the personal and social development of pupils should almost certainly be preceded and accompanied by initiatives designed to promote the staff development of teachers. Children do not develop well socially in schools where their teachers do not.

Conclusion

The test of a school's commitment to PSE is ultimately to be found not in the separate provision it makes for this area, but in the quality and character of its classroom relationships. Securing change of that range and depth requires whole school commitment to PSE on the lines we have indicated: through a managerial coordinating structure that adequately reflects the area's status and significance, and through a process of teacher involvement that secures staff agreement on and commitment to the practical changes needed in classroom relationships. Clear and firm support from the head for all these things is essential.

Without such support and involvement from management and colleagues, even the most ardent and enthusiastic innovator must accept that the impact and effectiveness of separately provided PSE initiatives will probably be very modest. Occasionally, initiatives like pupil profiles may lead to wider reviews and changes of what the school is doing in relation to PSE. But in the main, if the route of separate development is adopted, the most likely outcome will be frustration and disappointment. The separately mounted PSE initiatives will almost certainly be undermined by the allocation of greater commitment and priority to the mainstream subject-based, examination-oriented curriculum. Current Goverment policy on national curriculum reform, and the use of public examinations as a base for parental choice in a deregulated educational market-place will, if it persists, do little to offset these tendencies which are prejudicial to the development of PSE.

As part of a whole school commitment to PSE, specific and separate initiatives do have an important contribution to make to the school's overall provision in this area. Taught courses can provide a clear place to explore politically controversial and emotionally sensitive issues with a group of suitably skilled and committed staff. Tutorial programmes can provide the pupil with a firm and familiar home base where, within the developing, supportive context of a real class group, that pupil can reflect on and take responsibility for his or her personal and social development. Residential and other kinds of direct experience can provide pupils with powerful challenges in a real life context, where the skills and qualities they develop and exercise have immediate, practical and significant implications for themselves and for others. And personal recording and pupil profiles can increase awareness of personal and social achievements, encourage more emphasis to be placed on those sorts of achievements, deepen teachers' knowledge of their pupils and their potential, and enrich the teacher–pupil relationship.

Such a programme of personal and social education, efficiently coordinated, widely supported by a school's staff and its senior management, closely harmonised with a surrounding and supportive school ethos, committed to care rather than control, and to critical thinking as well as emotional adjustments, could well provide one of the major educational challenges of the 1990s. The choice for teachers, schools and Goverment itself is whether they seriously want it.

Note

1   Sir Keith Joseph, Secretary of State for Education and Science, commented on these matters in his speech to the North of England Education Conference in Sheffield, in January 1984. David Hargreaves' views were published in *The Challenge for the Comprehensive School* (1982) and in the ILEA Report, *Improving Secondary Schools* (1984), published shortly before his appointment as Chief Inspector to the Inner London Education Authority.

Bibliography

Anderson, C. (1982) 'The Search for School Climate: a review of the research', *Review of Educational Research*, Vol. 52, No. 3, Fall.

Apple, M. (1979) *Ideology and Curriculum*, London, Routledge and Kegan Paul.

Armstrong, A. (1986) 'Urban Studies and Community Education' in Brown, C., Harber, C. and Scrivens, J., *Social Education: Principles and Practice*, Lewes, Falmer Press.

Assessment of Performance Unit (1981) *Personal and Social Development*, London, DES.

Atkinson, P., Rees, T., Shone, D. and Williamson, H. (1982) 'Social and Life Skills: the latest case of compensatory education' in Rees, T. and Atkinson, P., *Youth Unemployment and State Intervention*, London, Routledge and Kegan Paul.

Baglin, E. (1984) *A case study of a social education department*, dissertation for the Special Diploma in Educational Studies, Department of Education, University of Oxford.

Baldwin, J. and Smith, A. (1983) 'Uncertain Futures: an approach to Tutorial work with 16–19 year olds in the 1980s', *Pastoral Care in Education*, Vol. 1, No. 1.

Baldwin, J. and Wells, H. (1981) *Active Tutorial Work: Books 1–5*, Oxford, Basil Blackwell.

Ball, D. (1986) Report on the 1986 National Association for Outdoor Education Conference on *The Outdoors and Gender*, in *Adventure Education*, Vol. 13, No. 2.

Ball, S. and Lacey, C. (1980) 'Subject disciplines as the opportunity for group action: a measured critique of subject subcultures' in Woods, P. (ed), *Teacher Strategies*, London, Croom Helm.

Balogh, J. (1982) *Profile Reports for School Leavers*, York, Longman.

Banks, O. (1955) *Parity and Prestige in English Education*, London, Routledge and Kegan Paul.

Barnes, D. and Shemilt, D. (1974) 'Transmission and Interpretation', *Educational Review*, Vol. 26, No. 3.

Bates, I. (ed) (1984) *Schooling for the Dole*, London, Macmillan.

Belshaw, P. (1985) 'Outdoor and Residential Education within TVEI: an HMI view', address to Conference on Outdoor and Residential Education within TVEI, Losehill Hall, Castleton, 23–27 September, 1985.

Bernstein, B. (1970) 'Education cannot compensate for society', *New Society*, 26th February.

Bernstein, B. (1975) 'Class and pedagogies: visible and invisible' in *Class, Codes and Control Vol. 3*, London, Routledge and Kegan Paul.

Best, R., Jarvis, C. and Ribbins, P. (1977) 'Pastoral Care: Concept and Process' *British Journal of Educational Studies*, Vol. XXV, No. 2, June.

Best, R., Ribbins, P., Jarvis, C. and Oddy, D. (1980) 'Interpretations of teachers' views of "pastoral care"' in Best, C., Jarvis, C. and Ribbins, P. (eds) *Perspectives on Pastoral Care*, London, Heinemann.

Best, R., Ribbins, P., Jarvis, C. and Oddy, D. (1983) *Education and Care*, London, Heinemann.

Blackburn, K. (1975) *The Tutor*, London, Heinemann.

Bolam, R. and Medlock, P. (1985) *Active Tutorial Work: training and dissemination – an evaluation*, Oxford, Basil Blackwell.

Bridges, D. (1986) 'Dealing with controversy in the curriculum: a philosophical perspective', in Wellington, J. J., *Controversial Issues in the Curriculum*, Oxford, Basil Blackwell.

Broadfoot, P. (1986a) 'Assessment Policy and Inequality: the United Kingdom experience', *British Journal of Sociology of Education*, Vol. 7, No. 2.

Broadfoot, P. (1986b) 'Profiling and the Affective Curriculum' *Journal of Curriculum, Studies*, Vol. 19, No. 1.

Brown, A. A. (1962) *Unfolding Character – the Impact of Gordonstoun*, London, Routledge and Kegan Paul.

Buckinghamshire County Council (1986) 'School Visit to Cornwall by Stoke Poges Middle School', report of the Chief Education Officer, Buckinghamshire.

Bulman, L. (1984) 'The Relationship Between the Pastoral Curriculum, the Academic Curriculum and the Pastoral Programme', *Pastoral Care in Education*, Vol. 2, No. 2.

Burgess, R. (1983) *Experiencing Comprehensive Education*, London, Methuen.

Burgess, R. (1984) 'It's Not a Proper Subject: it's just Newsom' in Goodson, I. and Ball, S., *Defining the Curriculum*, Lewes, Falmer Press.

Burgess R. (1987) 'The Politics of Pastoral Care', paper presented to the *International Sociology of Education Conference*, 5th–7th January, Westhill College, Birmingham.

Burgess, T. and Adams, E. (1985) *Records of Achievement at 16*, Windsor, NFER-Nelson.

Button, L. (1981) *Group Tutoring for the Form Teacher*. 1. *Lower Secondary School*; (1982) 2. *Upper Secondary School*, London, Hodder and Stoughton.

Button, L. (1983) 'The Pastoral Curriculum', *Pastoral Care in Education*, Vol. 1, No. 2.

Cannon, C. (1964) 'Social Studies in Secondary Schools', *Educational Review*, Vol. 17.

Central Advisory Council for Education (1963) *Half Our Future* (The Newsom Report) London, HMSO.

Coates, B. M. (1983) 'School Reformers Have a Lot to Learn', *Sunday Telegraph Colour Supplement*.

Cohen, P. (1984) 'Against the New Vocationalism', in Bates, I. (ed) *Schooling for the Dole*, London, Macmillan.

Cooper, B. (1985) *Renegotiating Secondary School Mathematics: a study of curriculum change and stability*, Lewes, Falmer Press.

Corbishley, P. and Evans, J. (1980) 'Teachers and Pastoral Care: an empirical comment' in Best, R., Jarvis, C., and Ribbins, P. (eds), *Perspectives in Pastoral Care*, London, Heinemann.

Countryside Commission (1980) *Groups in the Countryside*, Dartington Amenity Trust Report, October.

Cox, C. and Scruton, R. (1984) *Peace Studies: a Critical Survey*, Occasional Paper, No. 7, Institute for European Defence and Strategic Studies, London, Alliance Publishers.

Crick, B. and Porter, A. (eds) *Political Education and Political Literacy*, London, Longman.

David, K. (1983) *Personal and Social Education in Secondary Schools*, Schools Council, Programme 3, London, Longman.

Dean, J. (1985) *Where Am I Going: a study of pupil goal setting in three Surrey secondary schools*, London, SCDC.

De Groot, R. (1986) 'Pupils' Personal Records' in Broadfoot, P. (ed) *Profiles and Records of Achievement*, Eastbourne, Holt-Saunders.

De Groot, R. and McNaughton, J. (1982) *PPR Handbook*, 1st edition. Department of Education and Science (1973) *Safety in Outdoor Pursuits*, London, HMSO.

Department of Education and Science (1983) *Teaching Quality*, London, HMSO.

Department of Education and Science (1984) *Records of Achievement: A Statement of Policy*, London, HMSO.

Department of Education and Science (1985) *Better Schools: evaluation and appraisal*, Conference proceedings, Birmingham, 14–15 November.

Devon County Council Education Department (1982) *Personal, Social and Moral Education*, Exeter, Devon County Council.

Drasdo, H. (1972) *Education and the Mountain Centres*, Bangor, Welsh Universal Press.

Dudley Education Authority (1985) *A Framework for Residential Experiences under TVEI*, Dudley TVEI Project, Dudley Teacher's Education and Development Centre.

Durkheim, E. (1956) *Education and Sociology*, Glencoe, Illinois; Free Press.

Education Resource Unit for YOP (1982) *Assessment in Youth Training: made to measure*, Glasgow, Jordanhill College of Education.

Eggleston, J. (ed) (1982) *Work Experience in Secondary Schools*, London, Routledge and Kegan Paul.

Elliot, J. and Pring, R. (1975) *Social Education and Social Understanding*, London, University of London Press.

Entwistle, H. (1979) *Antonio Gramsci – Conservative Schooling for Radical Politics*, London, Routledge and Kegan Paul.

Fletcher, C. (1980) 'The Sutton Centre Profile' in Burgess, T. and Adam, E., *Outcomes of Education*, London, Macmillan.

Foster, P. (1985) 'The Transmission of Values in Social Education Curricula', M.Sc. Dissertation, School of Education, Open University.

Further Education Curriculum Development Unit (1979) *Active Learning*, London, FEU.

Further Education Curriculum Review and Development Unit (FEU) (1979) *A Basis for Choice*, London, FEU.

Further Education Curriculum Development Unit (1980) Project Report 4, *Beyond Coping: Some approaches to Social Education*, London, HMSO.

Further Education Curriculum (1982) *Profiles: a review of issues and practice in the use and development of student profiles*, London, HMSO.

Further Education Curriculum (1984) *Profiles in Action*, London, HMSO.

Galloway, D. (1985) 'Pastoral Care and School Effectiveness' in Reynolds, D. (ed), *Studying School Effectiveness*, Lewes, Falmer Press.

Gleeson, D. (1975) 'Experiencing a curriculum project' in Whitty, G. and Young, M., *Explorations in the Politics of School Knowledge*, Driffield, Nafferton Books.

Gleeson, D. and Mardle, G. (1980) *Further Education or Training?* London, Routledge and Kegan Paul.

Goacher, B. (1983) *Recording Achievement at 16+*, York, Longman for Schools Council.

Goacher, B. (1984) *Selection post 16: the role of examination results*, York, Longman for Schools Council.

Goodson, I. (1983) *School Subjects and Curriculum Change*, London, Croom Helm.

Halpin, A. W. (1966) *Theory and Research in Administration*, New York, Macmillan.

Hamblin, D. (1978) *The Teacher and Pastoral Care*, Oxford, Basil Blackwell.

Hare, R. M. (1952) *The Language of Morals*, Oxford, Oxford University Press.

Hargreaves, A. (1977) 'Progressivism and Pupil Autonomy' *Sociological Review*, Vol. 25, No. 3.

Hargreaves, A. (1985) 'Motivation versus selection: some dilemmas for Records of Personal Achievement' in Lang, P. and Marland, M. (eds), *New Directions in Pastoral Care*, Oxford, Basil Blackwell.

Hargreaves, A. (1986a) 'Record B̊reakers?' in Broadfoot, P. (ed) *Profiles and Records of Achievement*, Eastbourne, Holt-Saunders.

Hargreaves, A. (1986b) *Two Cultures of Schooling*, Lewes, Falmer Press.

Hargreaves, A. (1988a) 'The Crisis of Motivation and Assessment' in Hargreaves, A. and Reynolds, D., *Educational Policy: controversies and critiques*, Lewes, Falmer Press.

Hargreaves, A. (1988b) 'Teaching Quality: a sociological analysis' *Journal of Curriculum Studies*.

Hargreaves, D. (1967) *Social Relations in a Secondary School*, London, Routledge and Kegan Paul.

Hargreaves, D. (1980) 'The occupational culture of teaching' in Woods, P. (ed) *Teacher Strategies*, London, Croom Helm.

Hargreaves, D. (1982) *The Challenge for the Comprehensive School*, London, Routledge and Kegan Paul.

Hemming, J. (1949) *The Teaching of Social Studies in Secondary Schools*, London, Longman.

Henderson, P. (1984) 'The Social and Personal Aspects of Outdoor and Residential Education', dissertation for the Special Diploma in Educational Studies, Department of Educational Studies, University of Oxford.

Her Majesty's Inspectorate (1977) *Curriculum 11–16*, London, HMSO.

Her Majesty's Inspectorate (1979) *Aspects of Secondary Education*, London, HMSO.

Her Majesty's Inspectorate (1983) *Learning Out of Doors*, London, HMSO.

Her Majesty's Inspectorate (1983) *Records of Achievement at 16: some examples of current practice*, London, HMSO.

Her Majesty's Inspectorate (1985a) *The Curriculum from 5 to 16*, London, HMSO.

Her Majesty's Inspectorate (1985b) *A Survey of Outdoor and Residential Education in South Tyneside*, Report by HM Inspectors, London, HMSO.

Her Majesty's Inspectorate (1986) *Health Education 5–16*, London, HMSO.

Hicks, D. (1983) *Studying Peace; the Educational Rationale*, Occasional paper No. 4, Centre for Peace Studies, St. Martin's College, University of Lancaster.

Hitchcock, G. (1986) *Profiles and Profiling*, Harlow, Longman.

Hodgkin, R. (1985) *Playing and Exploring*, London, Methuen Books.

Hodgkin, R. (1986) 'Civilising in the Wilds', *Times Educational Supplement*, 6th June.

Hogan, J. M. (1968) *Impelled into Experiences: The Story of the Outward Bound Schools*, Educational Productions Ltd.

Holmes, S. and Jamieson, I. (1986) 'Jobs and Careers; Class, Schools and the New Vocationalism' in Rogers, R. (ed), *Education and Social Class*, Lewes, Falmer Press.

Humberstone, B. (1986) 'Learning for a Change: a study of gender and schooling in outdoor education' in Evans, J. (ed), *Physical Education, Sport and Schooling*, Lewes, Falmer Press.

Hustler, D. and Ashman, I. (1985) 'Personal and Social Education for All: apart or together' in Hustler, D. and Payne, G., *Crisis in the Curriculum*, London, Croom Helm.

Inner London Education Authority (1984) *Improving Secondary Schools*, Report of the committee on the curriculum and organisation of secondary schools, London, ILEA.

Inner London Education Authority (1985) *Profiling in ILEA Secondary Schools*, London, ILEA.

Jackson, B. and Marsden, D. (1962) *Education and the Working Class*, Harmondsworth, Penguin.

James, D. (ed) (1957) *Outward Bound*, London, Routledge and Kegan Paul.

Jones, J. (1983) *The Use Employers Make of Examination Results and other tests for Selection and Employment: a Criterion Report for Employers*, School of Education, University of Reading.

Kohlberg, L. (1976) 'Moral Stages and Moralization: the cognitive developmental approach' in Lickona, T. (ed) *Moral Development and Behaviour, theory, research and social issues*, New York, Holt, Rinehart and Winston.

Lang, P. (1983) 'Review of Perspectives in Pastoral Care', *Pastoral Care in Education*, Vol. 1, No. 1.

Law, B. (1984) *The Uses and Abuses of Profiling*.

Lawton, D. and Dufour, B. (1973) *The New Social Studies*, London, Heinemann.

McBeath, J. (1986) 'The Organisation of Social Education', in Brown, C., Harber, C. and Strivens, J. *Social Education: Principles and Practice*, Lewes, Falmer Press.

McNaughton, J. (1982) Article in the *Times Educational Supplement*, April 23rd.

McNiff, J. (1985) *Personal and Social Education: a teacher's handbook*, Cambridge, Hobsons.

McPhail, P., Ungoed-Thomas, J. R. and Chapman, H. (1972) *Moral Education in the Secondary School*, Harlow, Longman.

Mansell, J. (1982) 'A Burst of Interest', in Further Education Curriculum Review and Development Unit (FEU), *Profiles: a review of issues and practice in the use and development of student profiles*, London, FEU.

Manpower Services Commission (1979) *Outdoor Education and Residential Elements within Youth Opportunities Programmes*, Conference Report, London, MSC.

Marcus, D. (1980) *The Bosworth Papers, No. 3 – reports and reporting*, Bosworth, Bosworth College.

Marks, J. (1985) *'Peace Studies' in our Schools; Propaganda for Defencelessness*, London, Women and Families for Defence.

Marland, M. (ed) (1974) *Pastoral Care*, London, Heinemann.

Marland, M. (1980) 'The Pastoral Curriculum', in Best, R., Jarvis, C. and Ribbins, P. (eds) *Perspectives in Pastoral Care*, London, Heinemann.

Marland, M. (1985) 'Our needs in schools', in Lang, P. and Marland, M., *New Directions in Pastoral Care*, Oxford, Basil Blackwell.

Measor, L. and Woods, P. (1984) *Changing Schools*, Milton Keynes, Open University Press.

Mortlock, C. (1973) *Adventure Education and Outdoor Pursuits*, Ambleside, F. Middleton & Son.

National Association for Outdoor Education (1984) *Adventure Education*, Vol. 1, No. 8.

National Union of Teachers (1984) *Education for Peace*, London, National Union of Teachers.

O'Connor, M. (1987) *Out and About: revised edition*, London, Methuen Books for the School Curriculum Development Committee.

O'Keefe, D. (ed) (1986) *The Wayward Curriculum*, Exeter, Short Run Press.

Olson, J. (1982) *Innovation in the Science Curriculum*, London, Croom Helm.

Oxford Certificate of Educational Achievement (OCEA) (1984) *The Personal Record Component: A Draft Handbook for Schools*, Oxford, OCEA.

Oxford Certificate of Educational Achievement (OCEA) (1987) *Student Reviewing and Recording*, Oxford, International Assessment Services.

Pearce, B. (1984) 'Developing the Profilers', in Further Education Unit (FEU), *Profiles in Action*, London, FEU.

Porter, A. (1979) 'The Programme for Political Education – a guide for beginners', *Social Science Teacher*, Vol. 8, No. 3.

Pratley, B. (1982) 'Profiles in practice' in Further Education Curriculum Review and Development Unit (FEU), *Profiles: a review of issues and practice in the use and development of student profiles*, London, FEU.

Prendergast, S. and Prout, A. (1985) 'The Natural and the Personal: reflections on birth films in schools', *British Journal of Sociology of Education*, Vol. 6, No. 2.

Pring, R. (1975) 'Socialization as an Aim in Education', in Elliot, J. and Pring, R. *Social Education and Social Understanding*, London, University of London Press.

Pring, R. (1984) *Personal and Social Education in the Curriculum*, London, Hodder and Stoughton.

Pupils' Personal Records Management Group (1984) *Pupils as Partners: Pupils' Personal Records Handbook*.

Pupils' Personal Records Management Group (1987) *Tutors' Handbook*, Plymouth, Southway School.

Quicke, J. (1986) 'Personal and Social Education: a triangulated evaluation of an innovation', *Educational Review*, Vol. 38, No. 3.

Radnor, H. (1987) *The Impact of the Introduction of GCSE at LEA and School Level*, Final Research Report, Windsor, NFER, March 1987.

Radnor, H., Ball, S. and Burrell, D. (1988) 'The Certificate of Prevocational Education: Analysis of curriculum conflict in policy and practice', in Hargreaves, A. and Reynolds D., *Educational Policy: controversies and critiques*, Lewes, Falmer Press.

Rennie, J., Lunzer, E. A. and Williams, W. T. (1974) *Social Education: an Experiment in Four Secondary Schools, Schools Council Working Paper 51*, London, Evans-Methuen.

Reynolds, D. (1982) 'The Search for Effective Schools' *School Organization*, Vol. 2, No. 3.

Reynolds, D. and Sullivan, M. (1987) *The Comprehensive Experiment*, Lewes, Falmer Press.

Ribbins, P. and Ribbins, P. (1986) 'Developing a Design for Living Course at 'Deanswater' Comprehensive School: an evaluation', *Pastoral Care in Education*, Vol. 4, No. 1.

Rose, A. (1986) 'Personal and Social Education and Religious Education; their status and interrelationship in secondary schools' M.A. Thesis, University of Warwick.

Rudduck, J. (1986) 'A strategy for Handling Controversial Issues in the Secondary School' in Wellington, J. J. (ed), *Controversial Issues in the Curriculum*, Oxford, Basil Blackwell.

Rutter, M., Maughan, B., Mortimore, P., Ouston, J. and Smith, A. (1979) *Fifteen Thousand Hours: secondary schools and their effects on children*, London, Open Books.

Salter, B. and Tapper, T. (1986) *Power and Policy in Education: the Case of Independent Schooling*, Lewes, Falmer Press.

Sandford Report (1974) *National Parks Policies Review Committee Report*, London, HMSO.

Scarth, J. (1987) 'Teaching to the Exam? – the case of the Schools Council History Project' in Horton, T. (ed) *GCSE: Examining the New System*, London, Harper and Row.

Schools Council (1980) *Outdoor Education in Secondary Schools*, a report from a working party of the Schools Council Geography Committee, London, Schools Council.

Schools Council (1983) *Outdoor Education: a pilot study*, report of a working party by the County of Avon Education Authority, London, Schools Council.

Schools Council Committee for Wales (1983) *Profile Reporting in Wales*, Cardiff, Schools Council Committee for Wales.

Scottish Council for Research in Education (SCRE) (1977) *Pupils in Profile*, Edinburgh, Hodder and Stoughton.

Scrimshaw, P. (1981) *Community Service, Social Education and the Curriculum*, London, Hodder and Stoughton.

Scruton, R. (1985) *World Studies; Education or Indoctrination?* Occasional Paper, No. 15, Institute for European Defence and Strategic Studies, London, Alliance Publishers.

Scruton, R., Ellis-Jones, A. and O'Keefe, D. (1985) *Education and Indoctrination*, London, Sherwood Press.

Sharp, R. and Green, A. (1975) *Education and Social Control*, London, Routledge and Kegan Paul.

Shipman, M. (1974) *Inside a Curriculum Project*, London, Methuen.

Simon, S. B. (1972) *Values Clarification: a Handbook*, New York, Hart.

Skidelsky, R. (1963) *English Progressive Schools*, Harmondsworth, Penguin.

Stansbury, D. (1980a) 'The Origins and Practice of Personally Compiled Records in Secondary Schools', Springline Trust, Devon.

Stansbury, D. (1980b) 'The Record of Personal Experience' in Burgess, T. and Adams, E., *Outcomes of Education*, London, Macmillan.

Stansbury, D. (1984) 'Principles of Personal Recording', Devon, Springline Trust.

Stewart, D. (1979) 'A critique of School Climate: what it is, how it can be improved, and some general recommendations' *The Journal of Educational Administration*, Vol. XVII, No. 2.

Stradling, R. (1986) 'Social Education: some questions of assessment and evaluation' in Brown, C., Harber, C. and Strivens, J. *Social Education: Principles and Practice*, Lewes, Falmer Press.

Stradling, R., Noctor, M. and Baines, B. (1984) *Teaching Controversial Issues*, London, Edward Arnold.

Stratton, N. (1986) 'Recording Achievement: the City and Guilds Experience' in Broadfoot, P. (ed); *Profiles and Records of Achievement*, Eastbourne, Holt, Rinehart and Winston.

Strivens, J. (1986) 'Moral Education in the Curriculum' in Brown, C., Harber, C. and Strivens, J. (eds), *Social Education: Principles and Practice*, Lewes, Falmer Press.

Sutton, R. with Bacon, R., Benton, R., Hodson, D. and Taylor, H. J. (1986) *Assessment in Secondary Schools; the Manchester experience*, York, Longman for SCDC.

Swales, T. (1980) *Records of Personal Achievement: an independent evaluation of the Swindon RPA Scheme*, London, Schools Council.

Tizard, B. (1984) 'Problematic Aspects of Nuclear Education' in Bishop of Salisbury; White, P., Andrews, R., Jacobsen, B. and Tizard, B., *Lessons Before Midnight: Educating for Reason in Nuclear Matters*, Bedford Way, Paper No. 19, Institute of Education, University of London.

Tomlinson, J. (1983) Foreword to David, K. *Personal and Social Education in Secondary Schools*, York, Longmans for Schools Council.

Tossell, T. (1984) 'An Examination of the Practice of Formative Self-Assessment in Secondary Schools with Particular Reference to Implementation Problems', Dissertation for the Special Diploma in Educational Studies, Oxford University, Department of Educational Studies.

Townsend, S. (1982) *The Secret Diary of Adrian Mole – aged 13¾*, London, Methuen.

Turner, J. (1986) *Profiling in Leicestershire TVEI: Report Number 1*, The Woodstock Centre, Leicester.

Wakeman, B. (1984) *Personal and Social and Moral Education: a Source Book*, Tring, Lion Publishing.

Walford, G. (1985) *Life in Public Schools*, London, Methuen.

Watkins, C. (1985) 'Does Pastoral Care = Personal and Social Education?' *Pastoral Care in Education*, Vol. 3, No. 3.

Wellington, J. (ed) (1986) *Controversial Issues in the Curriculum*, Oxford, Basil Blackwell.

Weston, P. (1979) *Negotiating the Curriculum*, Windsor, NFER.

Weston, P. and Harland, J. (1988) 'The Lower Attaining Pupils' Programme: myths and messages' in Hargreaves, A. and Reynolds, D., *Educational Policy – controversies and critiques*, Lewes, Falmer Press.

White, P. (1984) 'Facing the Nuclear Issues: a task for political education' in Bishop of Salisbury, Andrews, R., Jacobsen, B. and Tizard, B., *Lessons Before Midnight, Education for Reason in Nuclear Matters*, Bedford Way Papers No. 19, Institute of Education, University of London.

Whitty, G. (1985) *Sociology and School Knowledge: Curriculum Theory, research and policy*, London, Methuen.

Williamson, D. (1980) ' "Pastoral Care" or "Pastoralization"?' in Best, R. J., Jarvis, C. and Ribbins, P., *Perspectives in Pastoral Care*, London, Heinemann.

Willis, P. (1977) *Learning to Labour*, Farnborough, Saxon House.

Woods, P. (1979) *The Divided School*, London, Routledge and Kegan Paul.

Woods, P. (1983) *Sociology and the School*, London, Routledge and Kegan Paul.

Young, M. F. D. (ed) (1971) *Knowledge and Control*, London, Collier-Macmillan.

General index

Author index